I0793627

IMAGES
of America

MOUNT RAINIER

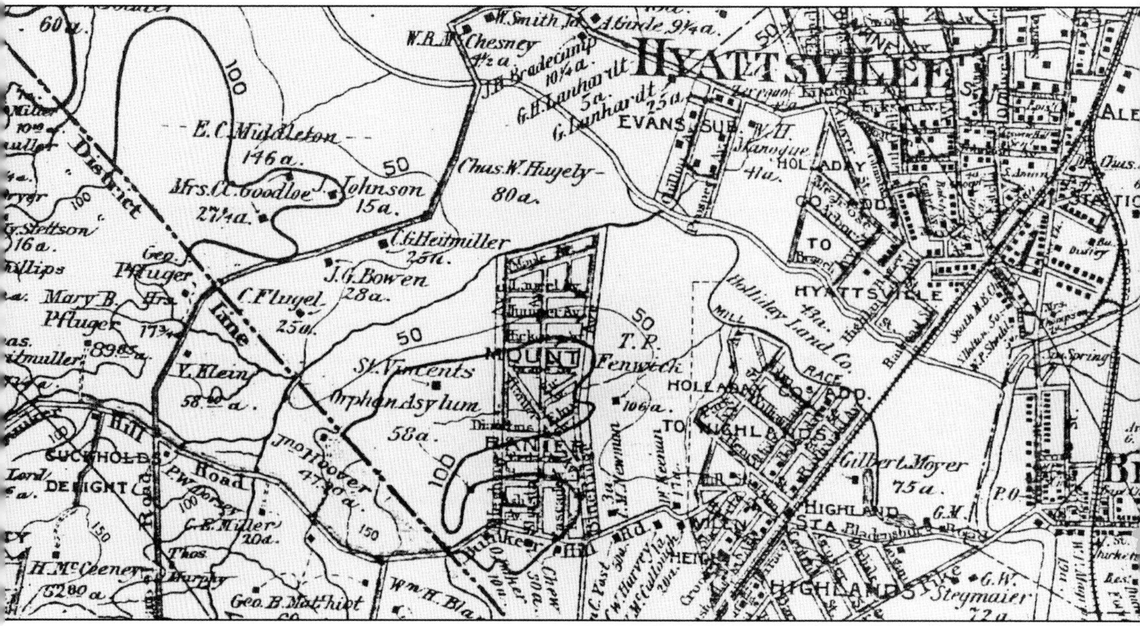

This 1894 Griffith M. Hopkins map documents that the name *Mount Rainier* was in use many years before the town's 1910 incorporation. The Mount Rainier subdivision was first attempted in 1891 when the former Clemson farm was sold to developers. This map is the only representation of the plat, which has been lost. (Courtesy of Prince George's County Historical Society.)

ON THE COVER: Children wave in front of a Mount Rainier landmark: the Cameo Theater on Thirty-fourth Street. On that day, the Cameo was screening the Joe Lewis–James J. Braddock boxing match that had occurred June 22, 1937, in which Lewis became the heavyweight champion of the world. The photograph is particularly rare, in that both black and white children are present in an image during a very segregated period. (Courtesy of Paul Sanchez.)

IMAGES
of America

MOUNT RAINIER

Bryan Knedler and Jimmy Tarlau

ARCADIA
PUBLISHING

ISBN 978-1-4671-1672-5

Published by Arcadia Publishing
Charleston, South Carolina

Printed in the United States of America

Library of Congress Control Number: 2016930980

For all general information, please contact Arcadia Publishing:
Telephone 843-853-2070
Fax 843-853-0044
E-mail sales@arcadiapublishing.com
For customer service and orders:
Toll-Free 1-888-313-2665

Visit us on the Internet at www.arcadiapublishing.com

Contents

ACKNOWLEDGMENTS

This book in large part rests on the work of several previous city-published history booklets produced for historic anniversaries, such as the 50th anniversary of incorporation in 1960, the 75th anniversary in 1985, and most recently, the centennial of Mount Rainier in 2010. We owe thanks to those individuals who helped with those projects.

With each prior history project, more material was uncovered, and we are indeed fortunate in the 21st century to have a wonderful invention—the Internet—that can provide new material as the result of a keyword search. Treasure troves of material have been discovered in various archives in the last few years. For the 2010 centennial history project, Patricia Pugsley spent many hours searching electronic databases for archival newspaper articles that provided valuable documentation used in creating this book.

Since the research done for Mount Rainier's 2010 centennial, dozens of additional historical photographs have been uncovered and are reproduced for the first time in this book. We were stunned every time one of these gems was uncovered; in some instances, just by plain luck, but in other cases, by leads provided to us by people interested in local history.

Many names appear on the following pages as the source of photographs. First and foremost, we thank our historian colleagues: George Denny, author of his own books on local history; Howard Berger, Historic Preservation Section, Maryland–National Capital Park and Planning Commission (M-NCPPC); Susan Perlman, Prince George's County Historical Society (PGCHS); and Daniel Ramirez, Hyattsville Branch of Prince George's County Memorial Library System (PGCMLS). Special thanks to John Mutchler of the Mount Rainier Volunteer Fire Department for providing us a cache of useful photographs, and Joseph Howell for his documentation of the 1970s (*Hard Living on Clay Street*). We also thank the staffs of the Maryland State Archives, Special Collections of the DC Public Library (the W.R. Ross postcard collection provided several new images), and the Historical Society of Washington, DC (HSWDC). The City Council of Mount Rainier provided permission to use the city's archival materials and, in particular, utilize the many photographs made over many years by city staff members Robert Page and Graciela Carbonell. Graciela's passing in 2014 was a great loss to the community, and her service to the city as photographer and videographer will long be remembered. Michael Paschal worked a miracle or two in bringing some faded photographs back to useful life.

Many thanks to local residents who opened their family scrapbooks and attic boxes, yielding valuable photographs—in particular, the late James R. Rice Jr. and his son Alan, Teresa Wilcox (whose family connections to the area go back more than a century), John Bowman, Lawrence Dungan, Jodi-Beth McCain, Marilyn Mowat, Fred Sissine, Becky Livingston, and Bruce Yarnall (for alerting us to the Cameo Theater photographs that resulted in the book's cover). Finally, we are thankful for Jodi Beder's copyediting, and the patient support of Vic Lemas in helping to transform our manuscript into a book.

We hope that this book will not only be informative, but will also inspire other local history sleuths to search for undiscovered gems and provide them in future publications.

Introduction

Mount Rainier is a city of roughly one square mile in Prince George's County, Maryland, sharing a border with the District of Columbia. Although a densely populated urban place, the city is known for its tree-lined streets and modest historic homes that create a small-town atmosphere.

One fascinating aspect of Mount Rainier is its evolution from segregated beginnings and an active Ku Klux Klan in the 1920s to a multicultural community that has in recent years elected a city council composed of renters as well as homeowners, and that is gay, straight, white, African American, Asian American, Latino, Christian, Muslim, Jewish, and atheist.

The Mount Rainier area maintained an agrarian character until the end of the 19th century. In 1835, the Washington Branch of the Baltimore & Ohio Railroad, one of the oldest rail lines in America, crossed Prince George's County; today, these rails form Mount Rainier's southern boundary. The coming of the railroad brought greater interest in the lands near it with access to Washington, DC; even in those early days, easy transit access to Washington was attractive to homebuyers. In 1853, Thomas and Anna Clemson purchased 100 acres of farmland abutting Bunker Hill Road, which was the main route between the ports of Georgetown and Bladensburg. After the Clemsons departed for South Carolina at the end of the Civil War, Estcourt Sawyer purchased their farm and recorded a subdivision plat of "Mt. Rainier" in 1891. According to local lore, the surveyors of the plat were from the Seattle area and named the subdivision after its famous mountain. Sawyer had no known connection to Seattle. However, in the 1890s, efforts were being made in Congress to establish Mount Rainier National Park, and the railroad companies were encouraging people to visit there. Could that have given someone the idea? Perhaps coincidentally, the Native American name of Mount Rainier is Tahoma or Tacoma, and the city's northerly neighbor of Takoma Park was incorporated in 1890.

About 15 houses stood in the vicinity in the 1890s, with a population of 50 people. With the arrival of the streetcar in 1898, the population grew to 1,242 in 1910, the year of incorporation. A small business district took shape around the intersection of the streetcar line (today's Rhode Island Avenue) and Thirty-fourth Street.

The original incorporation proposal called for inclusion of subdivisions over a wide area, from the District of Columbia border to Hyattsville. The 1909 committee that reviewed the proposal (the members of the group included men from the subdivisions of Mount Rainier, Holladay, Rhode Island Avenue, Wilen Heights, Brentwood, Cottage City, Edgemont, and the Colored Citizens Association of Brentwood) found that property owners in some of the subdivisions refused inclusion in the new Mount Rainier, but Edgemont, Rhode Island Avenue, and Wilen Heights joined with the subdivision of Mount Rainier to incorporate. The other subdivisions later became parts of Brentwood, Cottage City, North Brentwood, and Hyattsville.

In the 1940s, the expansion of the federal workforce and war-related jobs brought thousands of people to the area. The resulting housing shortage spurred the construction of new apartment complexes such as Kaywood Gardens, Queens Manor, and Queenstown. The addition of these large apartment complexes helped the population jump from 4,830 in 1940 to almost 11,000 in 1950. Yet the town remained racially segregated; the 1950 census found only 16 black residents and 23 persons of other races living in Mount Rainier.

A recurring theme throughout Mount Rainier's history has been the struggle over the town's image; in particular, a conflicted relationship with its main street of Rhode Island Avenue. Even though important and bustling today, the avenue did not exist until the 1920s. Mount Rainier was served by a trolley line beginning in 1898; it was the trolley connection to downtown Washington that spurred rapid development of the "streetcar suburbs," as they are known. But with the ascension of the automobile over the horse, a paved roadway became necessary. Paving began in downtown Washington and slowly moved outward to the suburbs. By 1918, the avenue was completed parallel to the trolley tracks to the Maryland line, and the Prince George's County Board of Commissioners was authorized to extend Rhode Island Avenue through Mount Rainier toward Hyattsville. The completed paved avenue received a grand opening in 1932.

By the 1950s, the avenue had become home to a number of loan agencies, acquiring the nickname of "Loan Shark Row." The city also had become known as a place to gamble. The seedy image was reinforced with pawn shops and liquor stores. By the 1980s, the city council had decided to move city hall away from the deteriorated downtown to the center of population near Queens Chapel Road. Yet, a dedicated group of activists strongly believed the city government should remain on Rhode Island Avenue and that a new city hall could be a catalyst for revitalization. That opinion prevailed, and one by one, the pawn shops and liquor stores closed; at the same time, various city-, county-, and state-funded revitalization projects, including the construction of a traffic circle, gave the city a sense of place, not just a busy highway leading in and out of Washington, DC.

Those civic activists of the 1980s sparked further transformations. A definite break with the old way of doing things occurred; progressive politics, focused economic redevelopment, and concern for environmental issues grew from roots in prior decades. Much of the city was listed in the National Register of Historic Places in 1990. Mount Rainier attracted artists and people living alternative lifestyles. Unlike many of its neighboring municipalities, during the 1980s, Mount Rainier elected black council members, and its city council embraced environmental issues and took stands on such matters as nuclear weapons. Without doubt, Mount Rainier became one of the most progressive places (if not the most) in Prince George's County. The decade of the 1980s continued the shift to a majority minority population, and by 1990, the tipping point occurred, with blacks and Hispanics in the majority.

An influx of new homebuyers in the 1990s reinforced the revitalization efforts begun in the 1980s, and by 1998, a *Prince George's Journal* writer described the city as a "multicultural Mayberry:" "There is a new energy in the city. . . . Streets are clean, crime is down, new businesses are moving in, and most noticeably, a new sense of community has penetrated the city." In the 21st century, with the creation of the Gateway Arts District, Mount Rainier along with neighboring municipalities embraced the arts as a revitalization tool.

As of the 2000 census, there were 8,498 people and 3,487 households in the city. The population density of 13,038.5 people per square mile makes the city the most densely populated incorporated area in the state (and 53rd in density among US incorporated places).

While Mount Rainier is not in the state of Washington, its proximity to Washington, DC, is again—as it was in 1910—an important factor for its economic vitality, attracting workers looking for a short commute to jobs and culture, but who also seek a suburb of tree-lined streets, modest homes, and the opportunity of civic involvement.

One

A Streetcar Suburb's Early Years

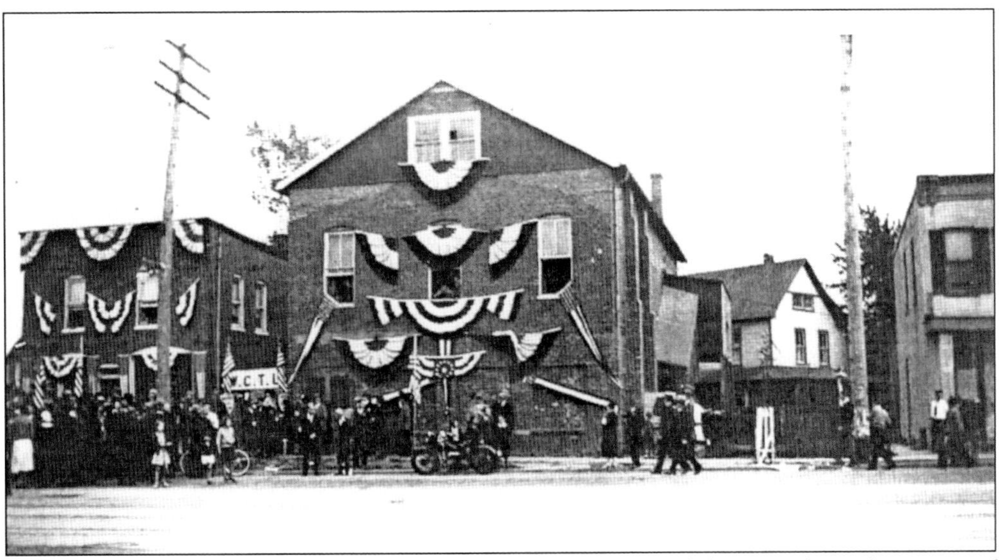

Potts Hall, built by Robert Potts in 1909, has been literally and figuratively at the center of Mount Rainier even before incorporation. The first town council meetings were held there, as were the initial services of several churches. In 1921, the Order of the Eastern Star purchased the building—making it Star-Potts Hall. This photograph was likely taken during the 1932 celebration for the opening of the newly paved Rhode Island Avenue. The building to the left served as town hall for several decades. (Courtesy of Adah Chapter 25 Order of the Eastern Star.)

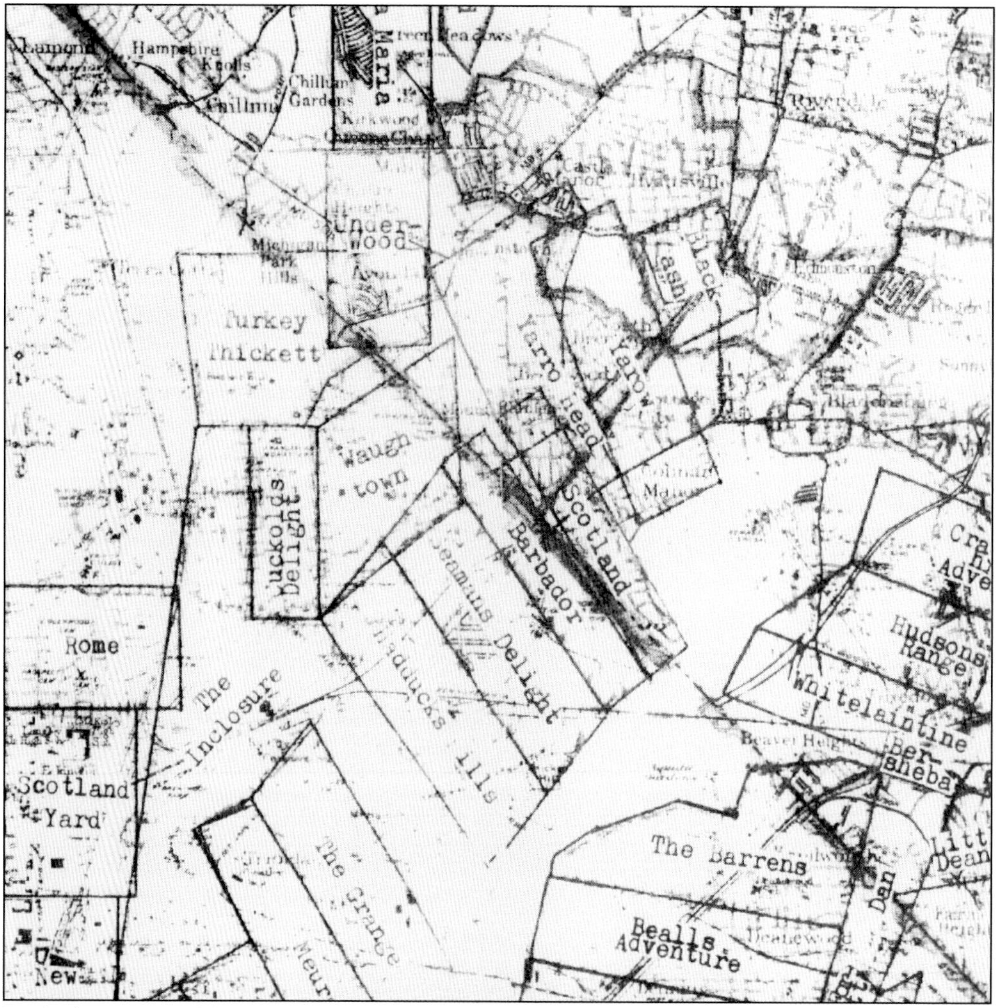

By the beginning of the 19th century, the area that would become Mount Rainier had been divided into large tracts of farmland, purchased out of the Yarrow Head, Scotland, and Barbador colonial land patents. This map shows the locations of those patents in relation to today's geography. By the 1850s, the land was divided into farms ranging in size from 7 to 120 acres, some of which included acreage in both Prince George's County and the adjoining area of the District of Columbia, which had been part of Maryland until 1790. The specific configuration of those farms would later directly affect the boundaries of the future Mount Rainier and its street grid. Through the 19th century, the area was sparsely populated. Until the founding of Hyattsville in the 1870s, the entire area was considered the western part of Bladensburg. (Courtesy of M-NCPPC.)

In 1792, the District of Columbia border was marked with stones made of Aquia Creek sandstone set at one-mile intervals. The stones, each of which has an identifying number, are the oldest federal monuments. Stone NE6 is located at the corner of Eastern Avenue and Thirty-fourth Street (right). Eastern Avenue did not, of course, exist in 1792, but when built, it was placed several feet inside the District boundary, meaning that the front yards of Eastern Avenue homes are partially in the District. On each stone, the side facing the District displays the inscription "Jurisdiction of the United States" and a mile number. Stone NE5 is located just north of Varnum Street on Eastern Avenue. The Daughters of the American Revolution installed protective iron fences around the stones in 1915. In 2012 (below), the National Park Service initiated a restoration effort. (Courtesy of Jimmy Tarlau.)

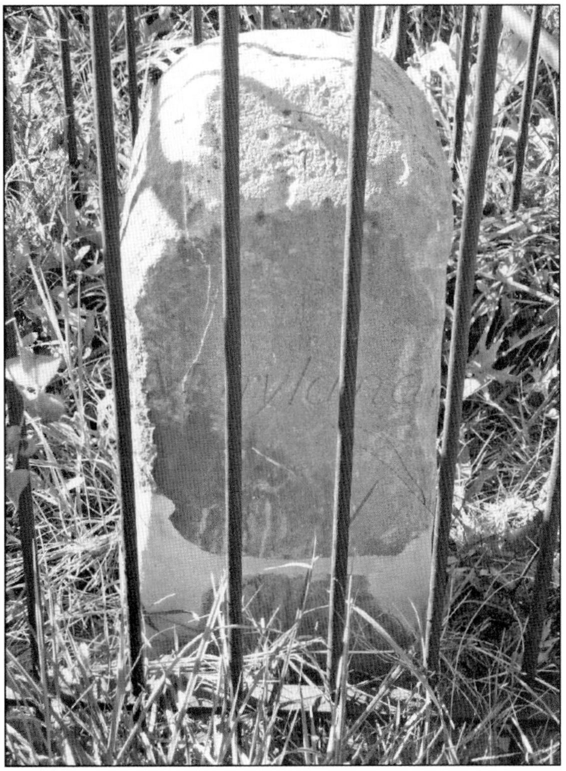

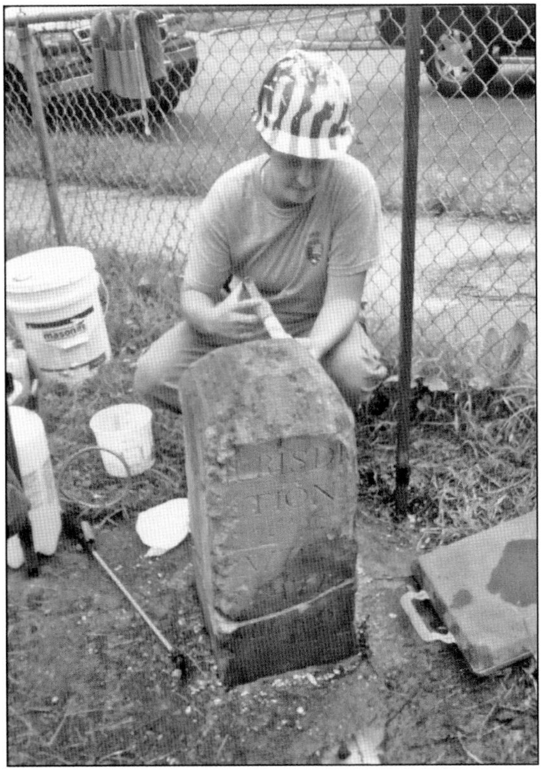

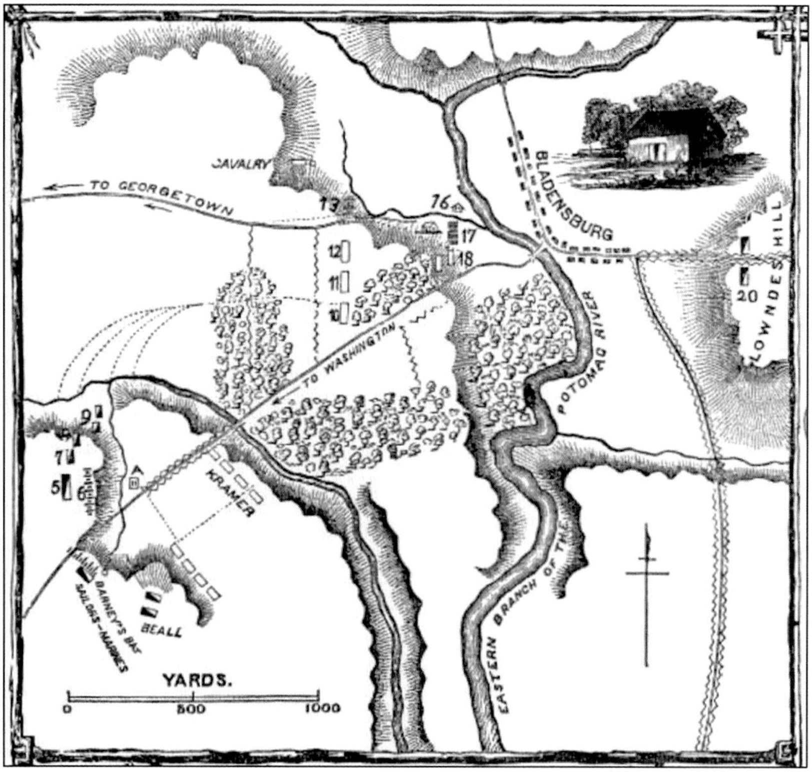

The Battle of Bladensburg took place August 24, 1814. Some American troops (numbers 5, 6, 7, 8, and 9 on the left edge of the map above, drawn in 1869 by Benson Lossing for his *Pictorial Field-book of the War of 1812*) were stationed along what today is Mount Rainier's Newton Street, which runs along a defensible ridge above the headwaters of Dueling Creek (now diverted into a storm drain alongside Otis Street). Adm. Joshua Barney positioned his men in the middle of Bladensburg Road at the District of Columbia border. He was wounded, fell from his horse, and was taken to a nearby spring that became known as Barney's Spring (seen below in a 1909 W.R. Ross photograph). Archeological research determined that the lost spring was south of Bladensburg Road just inside the District of Columbia. (Above, courtesy of Brian Knedler; below, courtesy of DC Public Library Special Collections.)

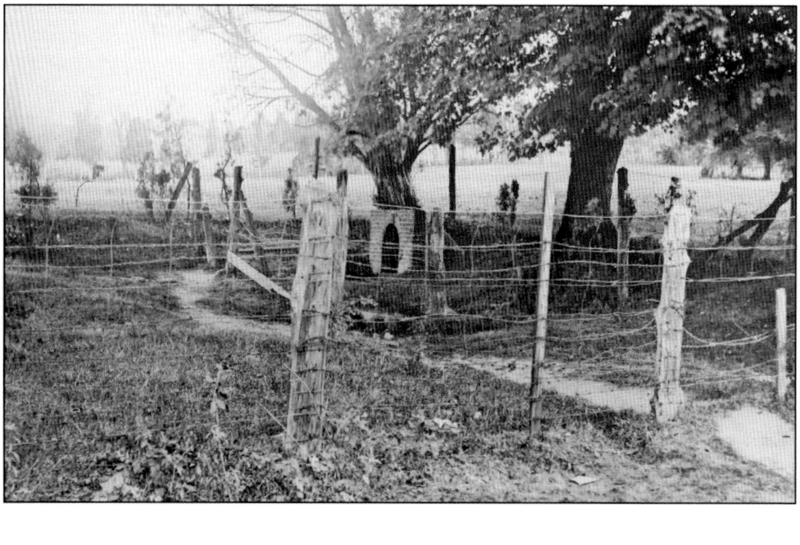

The 1853 survey of "Granby" places it both in the District of Columbia and in Maryland south of Bunker Hill Road. In 1927, St. Joseph's Orphanage (below) was built on the hill just to the west of today's Eastern Avenue, within what was the Granby tract. The Dodge Farm, south of Granby, belonged to Francis Dodge, a wealthy Georgetown resident engaged in shipping in the West Indies, who was an early land speculator in the area. Ten acres of his vast holdings were located in the southern part of present-day Mount Rainier. Originally, as on this survey, Bunker Hill Road was known as the "North Bladensburg Road" (later renamed after the Civil War–era fort in the District) to distinguish it from the Bladensburg Road that still exists today. (right, courtesy of M-NCPPC; below, courtesy of Bryan Knedler.)

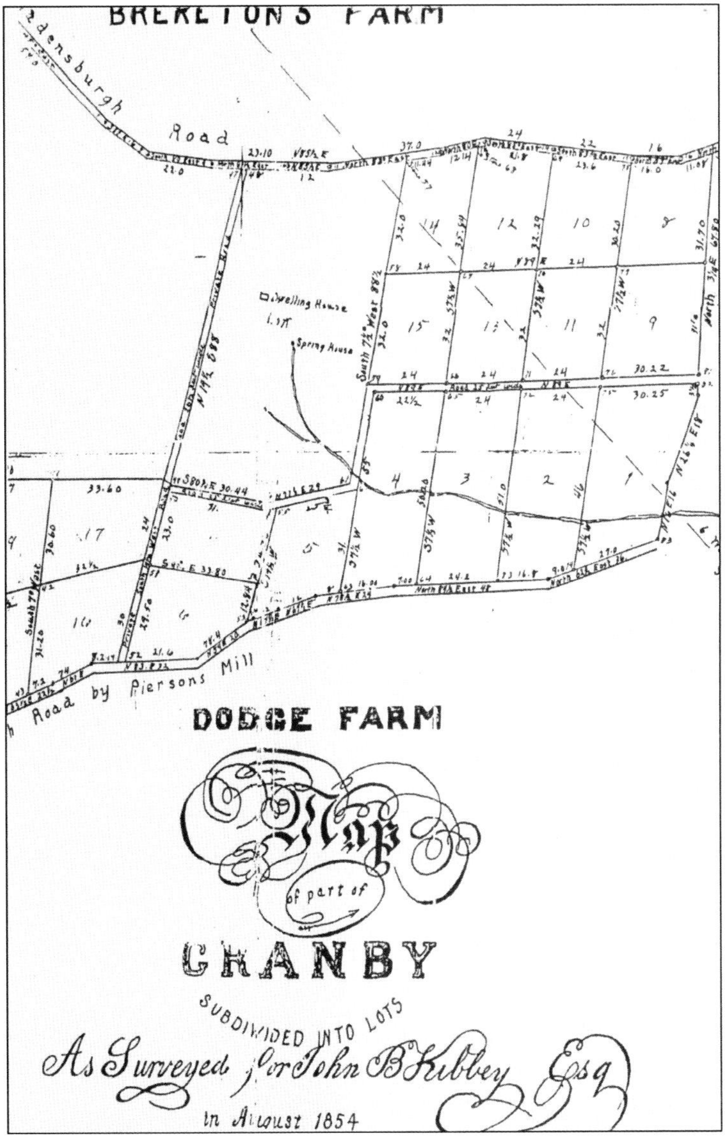

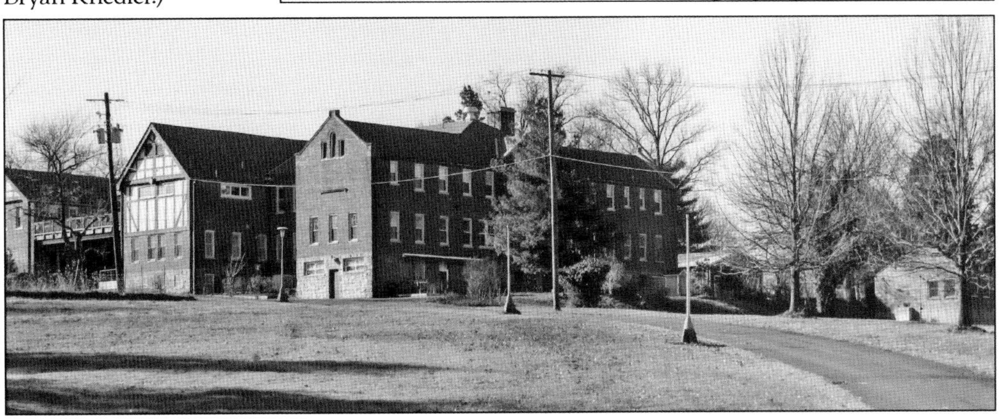

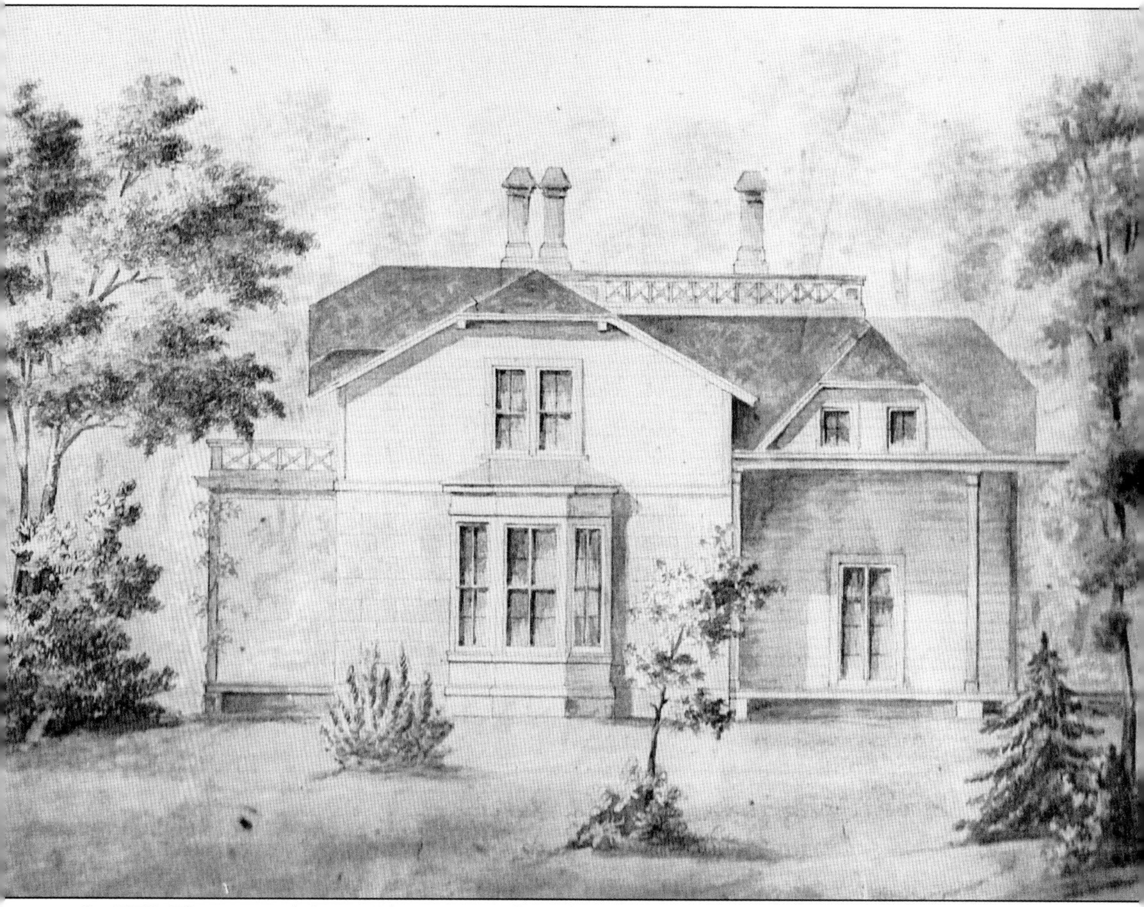

In 1853, Thomas and Anna Clemson purchased 100 acres fronting on Bunker Hill Road. Anna's father was Sen. John C. Calhoun. Their residence, "The Home," seen in this c. 1856 watercolor, stood at the area's highest point near Thirty-first and Shepherd Streets. Their farm was sold to developers in the 1890s and became the subdivision of Mount Rainier. Published correspondence between Anna and daughter Floride provides a glimpse of antebellum life, including accounts of their slaves, neighbors, and politics. They socialized with the Calverts at Riversdale and the Brookes in the District of Columbia (whose mansion still stands in the Brookland neighborhood). After the Civil War, the Clemsons returned to the South Carolina family estate that later became Clemson University. The *Washington Post* in 1890 described the long-abandoned farm: "The house is on a high hill and is surrounded by several acres of the largest forest trees in this section and was, and is today, one of the most beautiful places around Washington despite the rack and ruin the place is in." (Courtesy of Fort Hill: Home of John C. Calhoun & Thomas G. Clemson, Clemson University.)

Homes clustered around the old spring at Shepherd and Thirty-third Streets used it to supply a small water system, but most homes at first depended on individual wells and outhouses. The origin of the brick and stone structure is lost to history, but the spring likely supplied the Clemson home in the 1850s and may have been the site of their bathhouse mentioned in letters. In 1917, bonds were issued and construction began on a town water system, but litigation slowed completion. In 1922, the system, including the springs and pumping station on Columbia Avenue (now Hamilton Street), was sold to the Washington Suburban Sanitary Commission. The Clemson spring was diverted into an underground storm drain system in 1947. The boys in the early photograph to the right are, from left to right, Norman Gill, Norman Venning, and Walter Pryor. (Right, courtesy of James R. Rice Jr.; below, courtesy of Jimmy Tarlau.)

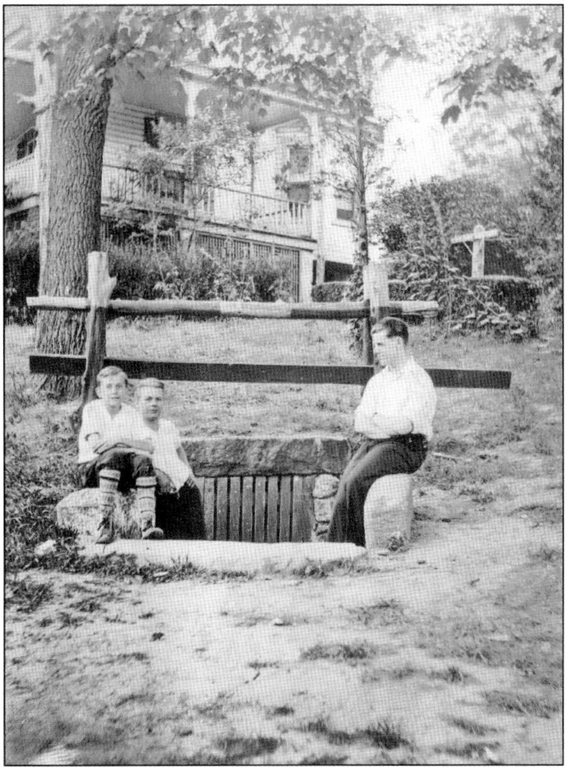

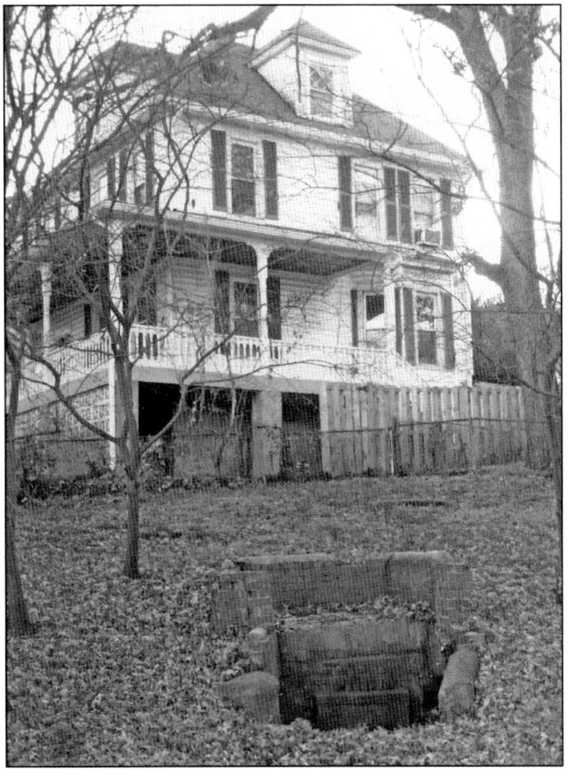

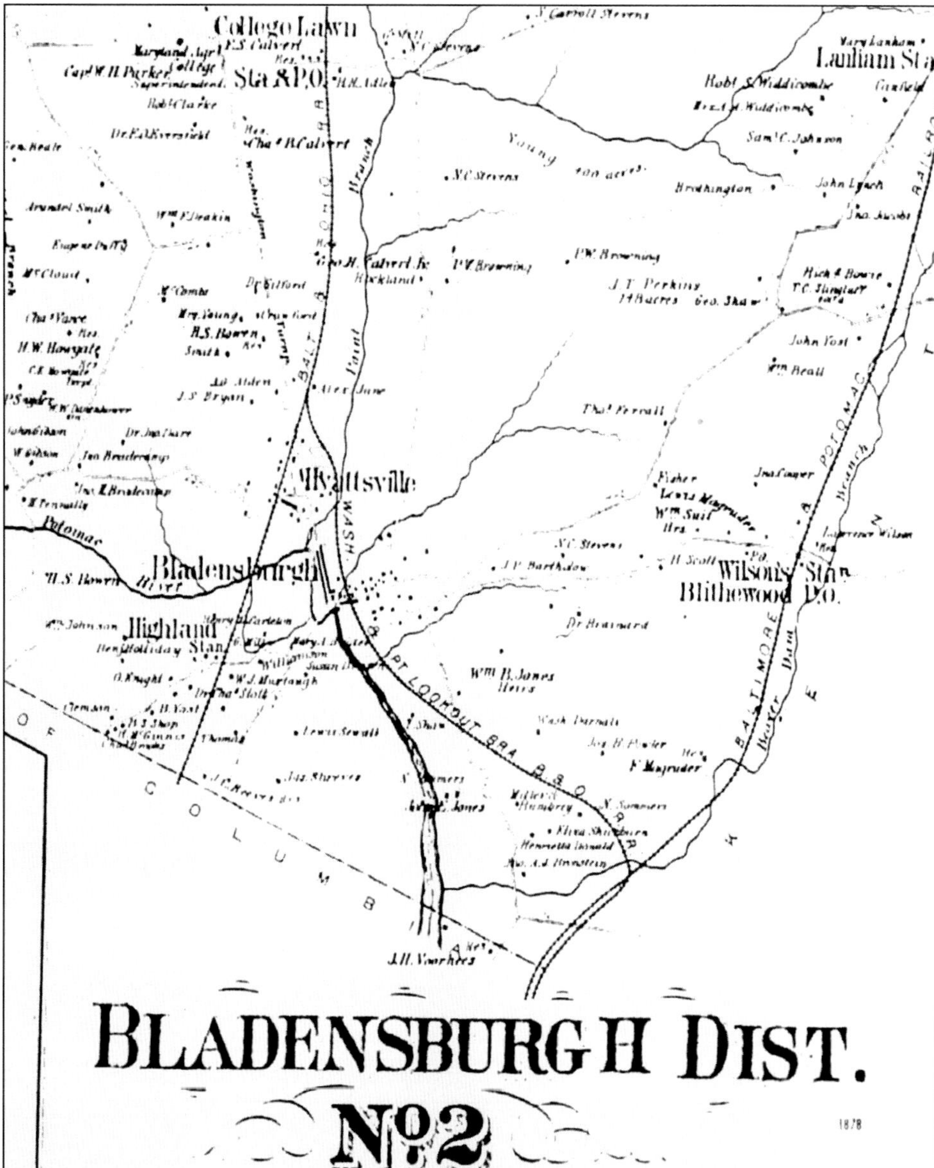

In the mid-19th century, the Mount Rainier area was included in the Bladensburg District. In this 1878 Griffith M. Hopkins map, the Baltimore & Ohio (B&O) Railroad slices through the middle of the map from College Lawn (now College Park) at the top to the bottom where it enters the District of Columbia. Present-day Mount Rainier is to the left of where the rail line enters the District to the left edge where Queens Chapel Road is visible. The B&O Railroad opened in 1835, and that section of the line is one of the oldest railways in the United States. In 1844, Benedict Yost bought 120 acres north of the railway and built his home near what is now the corner of Thirty-fifth Street and Bunker Hill Road. On the map, the Yost and Clemson properties are noted along Bunker Hill Road, which crosses into Maryland to the left of the rail line. Bunker Hill Road (also called the North Bladensburg Road) connected Bladensburg with Georgetown. (Courtesy of M-NCPPC.)

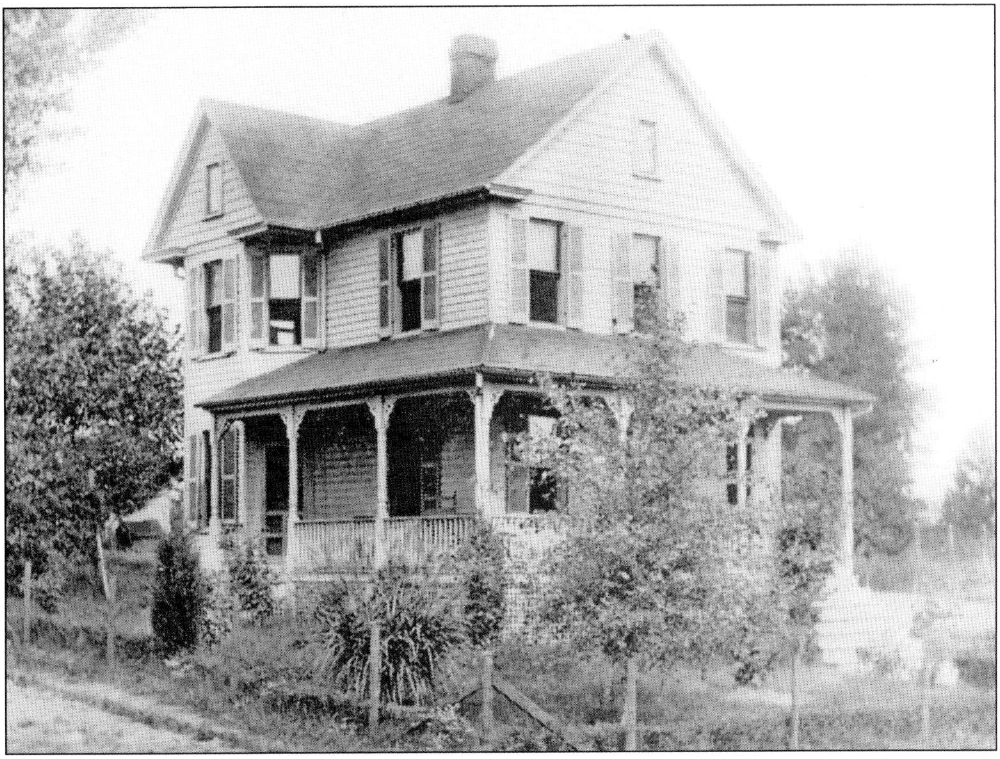

Mount Rainier was an area of farms in the late 19th century. The gable-and-wing house style was one of the most popular, as epitomized by the Cleaves home at 3200 Upshur Street (above) and the nearly identical Smith Farmhouse at 3426 Newton Street (below). The Smith home was built around 1900 for prominent businessman Thomas W. Smith, who used it as a country residence. It was originally the center of a 10-acre farm and remained in the Smith family until 1923. The house is a Prince George's County historic site. (Above, courtesy of Teresa Wilcox; below, courtesy of Jimmy Tarlau.)

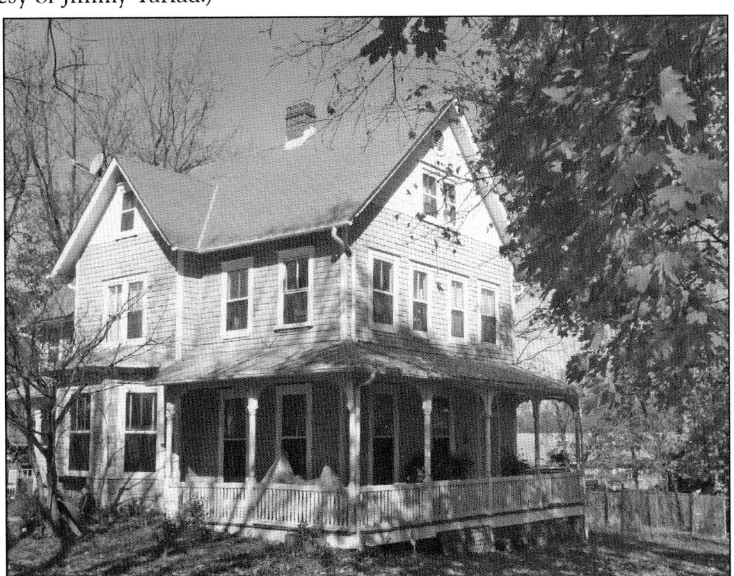

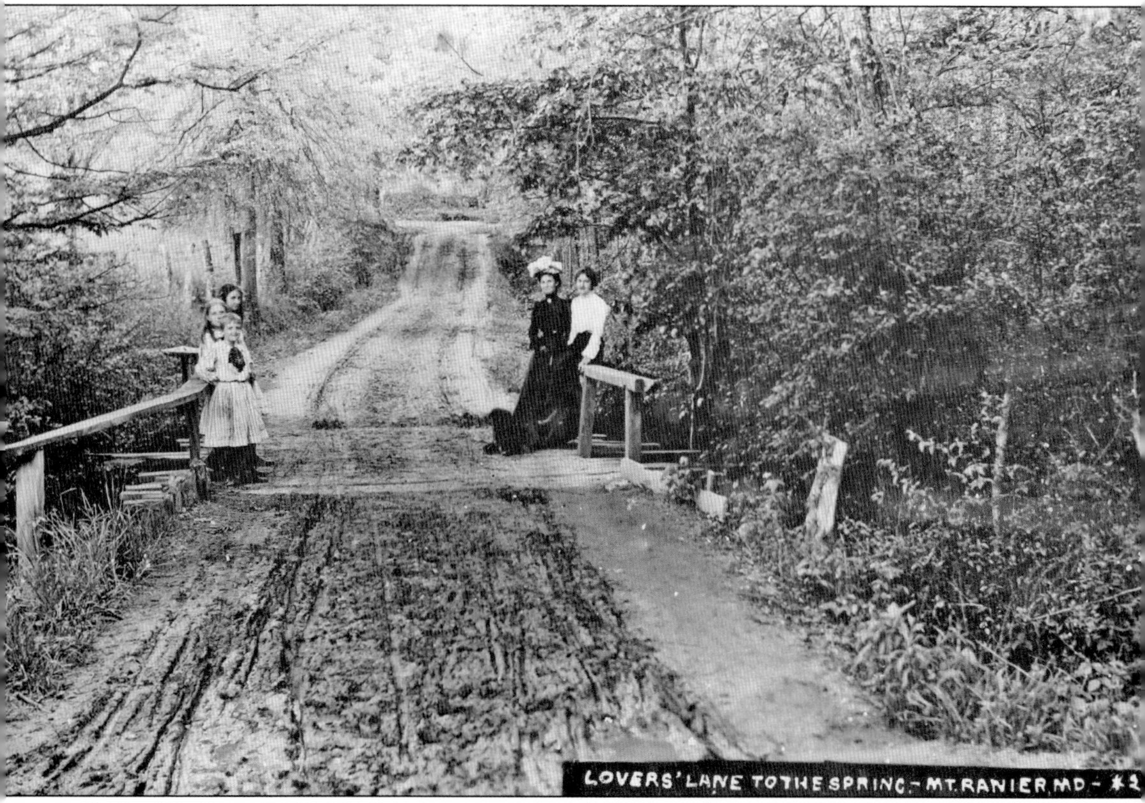

Willard R. Ross (1860–1948) became a postcard photographer around 1910. He specialized in hometown images of houses, streetscapes, churches, and natural settings, such as this view of "Lover's Lane to the Spring." Unfortunately, the photograph provides no clues as to the lane's exact location. The spring could be one of many, including the Clemson spring at Thirty-third and Shepherd Streets; Czarra Springs in Hyattsville, which provided water to Mount Rainier; or perhaps Barney's Spring, which existed at that time on Bladensburg Road just west of the District of Columbia boundary and was the subject of another Ross postcard (see page 12). Fortunately, Ross also used a number of more identifiable Mount Rainier area images for his postcards. Longtime resident Norman Venning recalled that the postcards were sold at Mikules's drugstore at the corner of Thirty-fourth Street and Rhode Island Avenue (see facing page). Another Ross photograph of the 1912 Mount Rainier Carnival includes a booth that advertises postcards for sale (see page 30). The District of Columbia Public Library owns a large collection of Ross postcards. (Courtesy of DC Public Library Special Collections.)

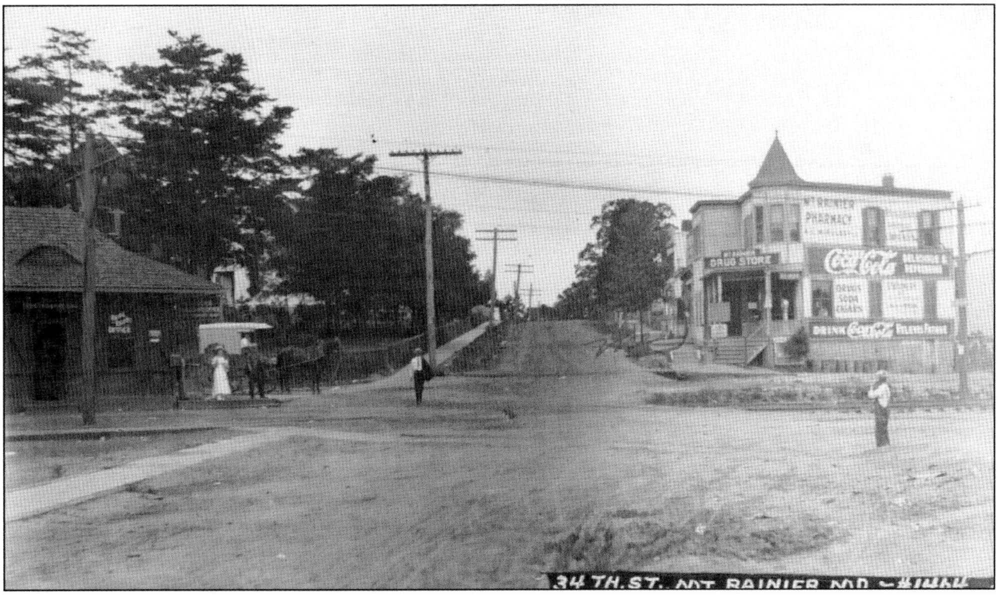

Above, Roger's real estate office was located in the District Line station, which was also called Plumer's Station because of the nearby Plumer's newsstand. Even in the early days, there were street trees. Below, a buggy struggles with the mud at Thirty-fourth Street and what is today Rhode Island Avenue, which was dominated by Mr. Mikules's Mount Rainier Pharmacy. By 1920, the citizens were tired of the mud, and the state approved bonds of $10,000 to lay cinders on Bunker Hill Road and Thirtieth Street and another $10,000 for paving Perry Street (then called Newton) from Thirty-fourth to Thirty-seventh Streets. Such legislative acts had to be approved in a referendum vote. Prior to the vote, the town issued a statement: "It requires no argument to demonstrate to the people of Mount Rainier that they cannot enjoy the ordinary conveniences of proper living, to say nothing of the improvement of property values and the growth of the town, without making immediate effort to improve the present condition of the roads and sidewalks in the town." (Above, courtesy of Teresa Wilcox; below, courtesy of Jimmy Tarlau)

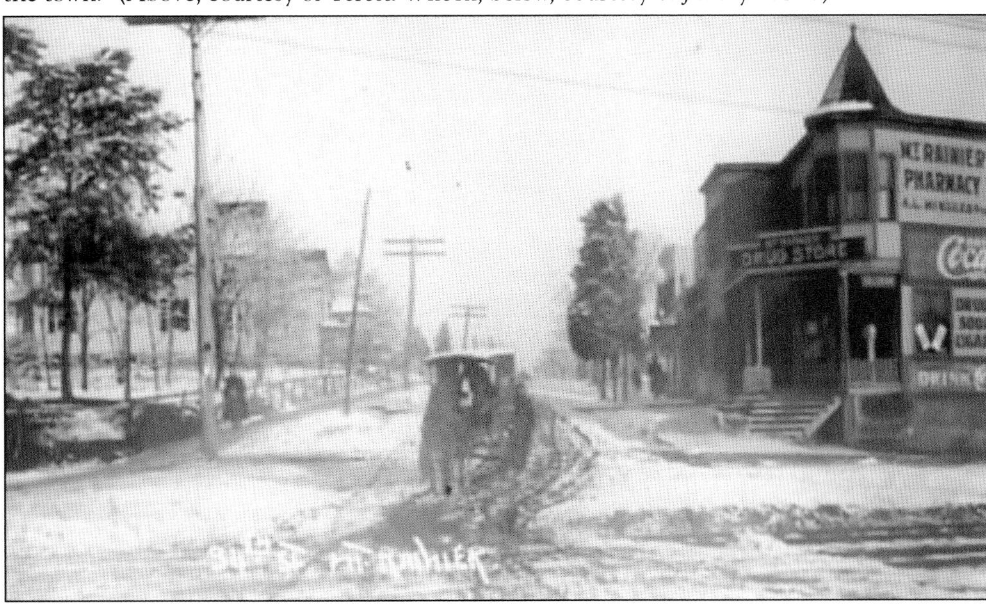

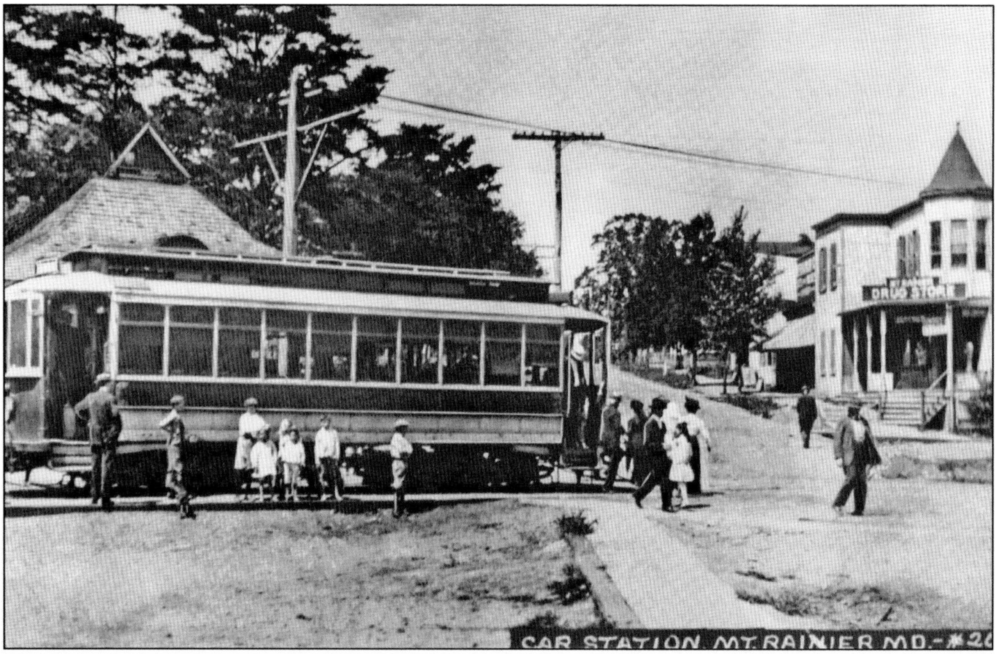

The City and Suburban Railway of Washington began service to Mount Rainier in 1898 along the path that later became Rhode Island Avenue. The line ran from the treasury department in the District of Columbia to Hyattsville by 1899, and to Laurel by 1902. Rhode Island Avenue was paved beginning in 1904 at Fourth Street in the District. Pavement reached South Dakota Avenue in 1910. From that point, however, the tracks of the railway were on fill, and no roadway existed until 1918, when the county was authorized to build an extension of Rhode Island Avenue along the south side of the streetcar tracks. The Prince George's Bank (below) was built next to the station in 1922. (Both, courtesy of City of Mount Rainier.)

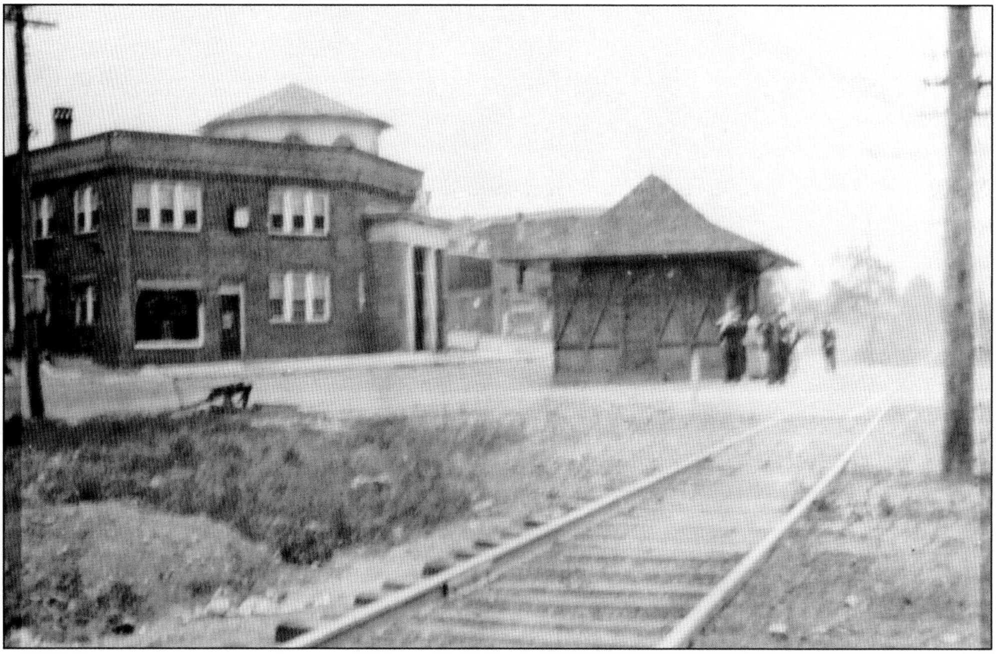

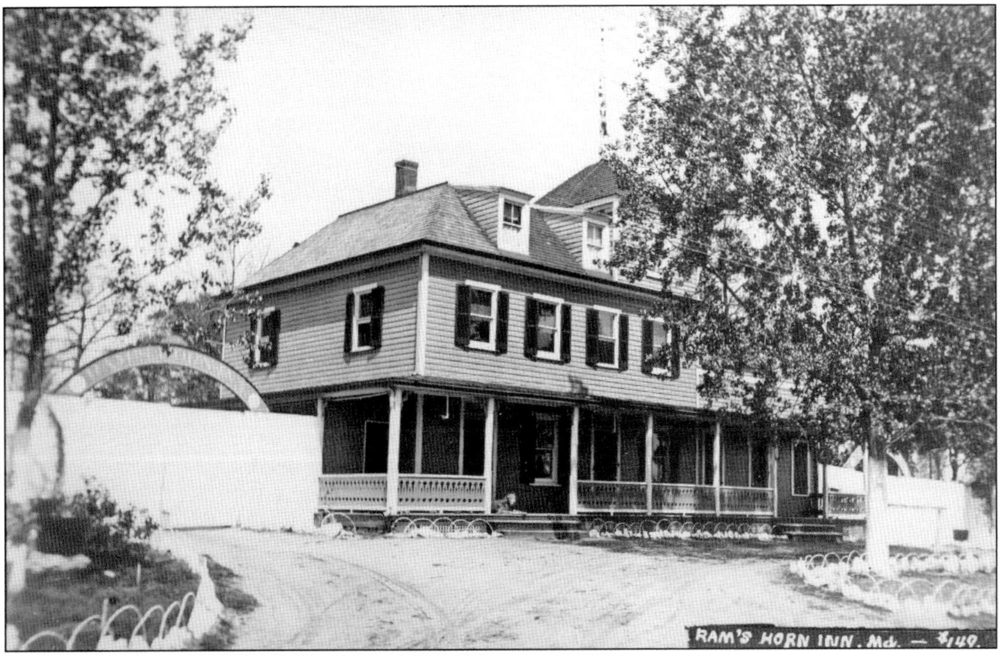

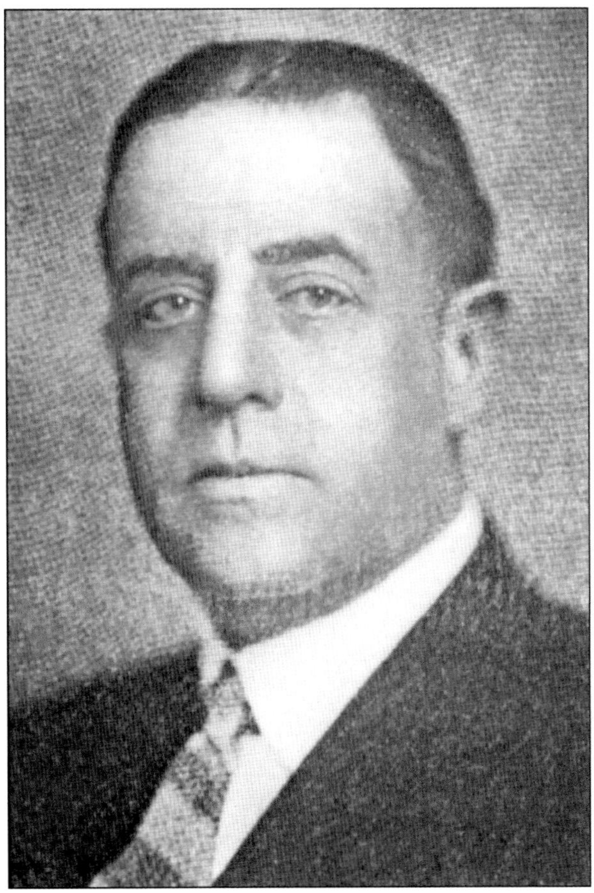

The Ram's Horn Inn stood northwest of today's intersection of Queens Chapel and Chillum Roads (now the Queens-Chillum Shopping Center). In 1910, the inn's manager, Robert Laupp, was found dead with a gunshot to his head. At first, the incident appeared a suicide, but the insurance company insisted on further investigation that determined the revolver at the scene had not been recently fired. Judge Robert E. Joyce (right), expecting a large crowd for the inquest, utilized Potts Hall, the largest space available at that time. Joyce not only served as a justice of the peace, but he also became Mount Rainier's first mayor. His rivals called him a "political boss." In 1934, the American Automobile Association won a suit against Joyce by challenging the system that awarded a fee to a justice only if the defendant was found guilty. (Above, courtesy of DC Public Library, Special Collections; right, courtesy of City of Mount Rainier.)

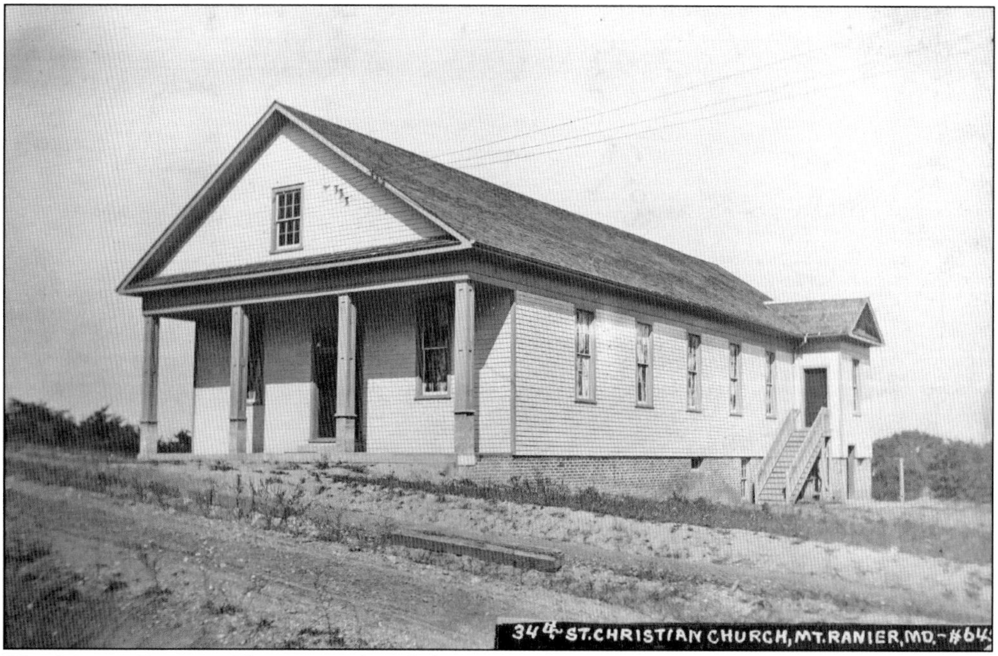

The Mount Rainier Christian Church began in 1902, with 20 members, as the Edgemont Christian Mission, in the home of Edgar and William BonDurant. A year later, Edgar donated the lot on Thirty-fourth Street where a chapel was built and appropriately called the Thirty-fourth Street Christian Church. The congregation grew, necessitating more space, so in 1909, a new larger wooden church (above) was built on Thirty-third Street just above Bunker Hill Road. The congregation changed the name to the Mount Rainier Christian Church. The current large brick edifice facing Bunker Hill Road (below) was built in 1923. (Above, courtesy of DC Public Library Special Collections; below, courtesy of Bryan Knedler.)

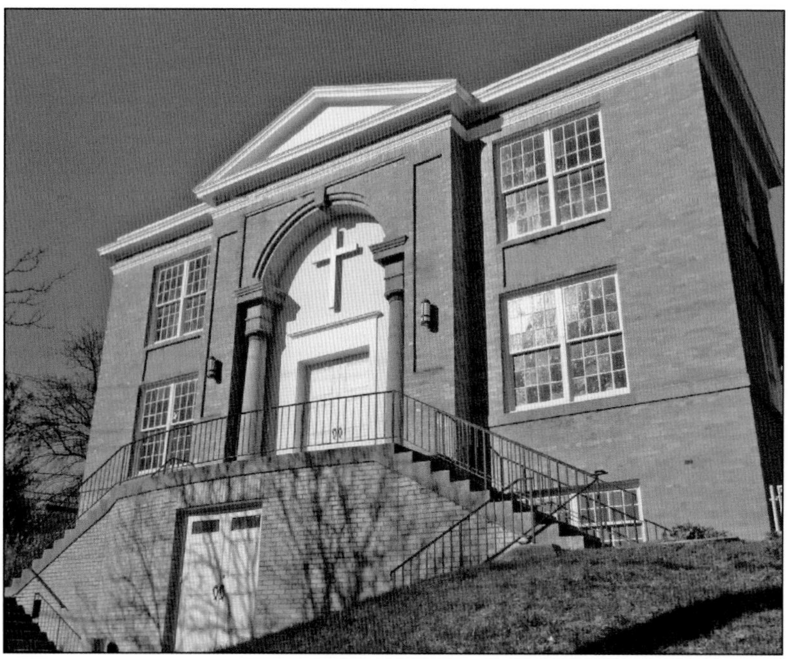

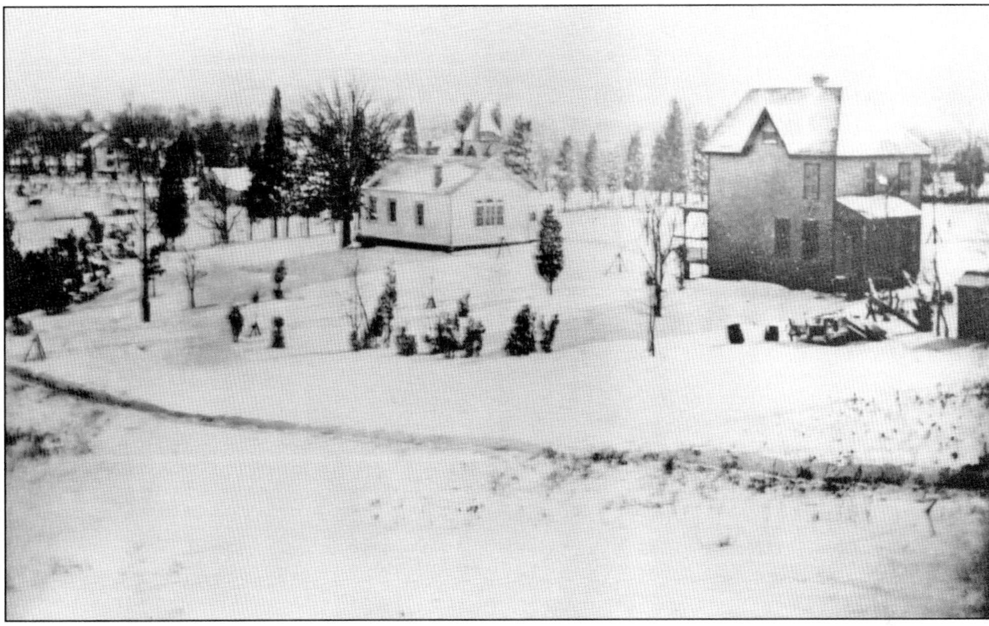

The committee that planned the town's incorporation met at the Thirty-fourth Street Christian Church (at center above, now the home at 4029 Thirty-fourth Street, below). Once agreement was reached on which subdivisions would be included, the state legislature enacted the charter on April 11, 1910. The citizens ratified the charter in a special vote on April 14, 1910. That year's federal census found 1,242 persons residing within the new town, which was as large as nearby Takoma Park and larger than most other Maryland suburbs (neighboring Hyattsville was a bit larger, with 1,917). The population increased to 2,400 over the next decade. In 1910, a quarter of the population was employed in the building trades, with the next largest employer the federal government, especially the Government Printing Office and Navy Yard. Mount Rainier was a blue-collar suburb from the start. (Above, courtesy of James R. Rice; below, courtesy of Jimmy Tarlau.)

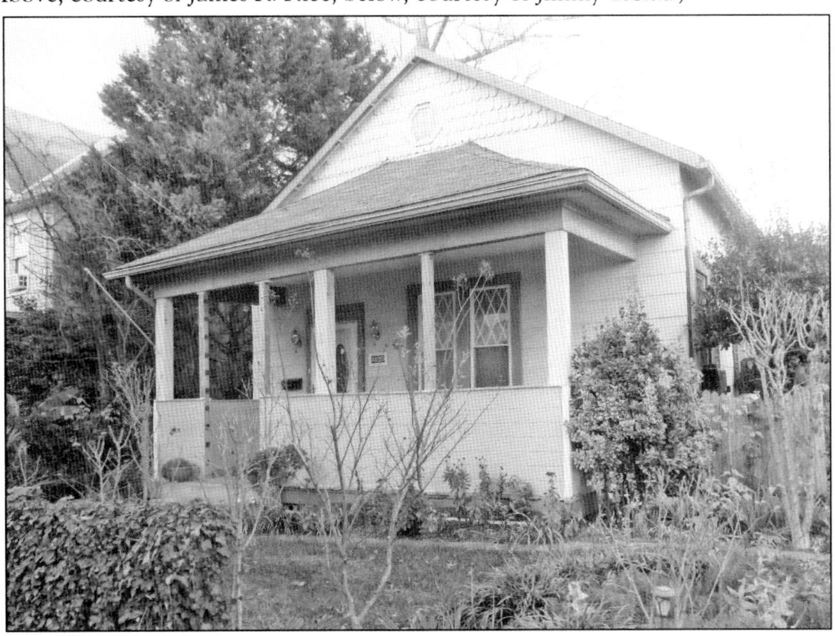

Each ward to be represented by a councilman resident of said ward who shall be voted for only by the voters residing in the ward he is to represent.

SEC. 3. *And be it enacted,* That all male citizens of the said town of twenty-one years of age or over, who have actually resided in said town for a space of 365 days next preceding the next Monday in May, 1910, and who have never been convicted of any infamous crime under the laws of the State of Maryland, and who shall come within any one of the three following classes of male citizens: (1) All duly authorized citizens (2) and male children of naturalized citizens who have reached the age of 21 years (3) all citizens who prior to January 1st, 1868, were entitled to vote in the State of Maryland or any other State of the United States at a State election, and the lawful male descedants of any person who prior to January 1st, 1868, was entitled to vote in this State or in any other State of the United States at a State election, and no person not coming within one of the three enumerated classes shall be registered as a legal voter and entitled to vote at any municipal election held in said town of Mount Rainier, Maryland, shall elect on the first Monday in May, 1910, at such place as shall be selected for the holding of elections, one person, a legal voter of said town, who has resided therein for two years at least next preceding the election to be Mayor of said town, and four persons who possess the same qualification one from each ward who shall be voted for only by the voters residing in the ward he is to represent, to be Common Councilmen of said town, and thereafter annually, on the first Monday in May, such citizens, with the above qualifications, shall elect one person having the qualifications above described to be Mayor, provided, that two of said Councilmen shall at the first election held under the provisions of this section, be elected to serve one year and two to serve two years, terms of office to be decided by casting of lots and thereafter two Councilmen to be elected each year who shall serve two years. If any vacancy occurs in the office of Councilman the Mayor, with the advice and consent of the remaining members of said Council, shall appoint a person to fill such vacancy during the balance of the unexpired term. In case of a vacancy in the office of Mayor a special election shall be ordered by the Common Council to be held within thirty days after publication of such order, for the purpose of electing a person to fill such vacancy. No person shall be eligible as Mayor or Councilman of said town unless he be the owner of real estate in said town, in his own name, to the amount of $\$500$, and shall so remain during his term of office, and his term of office shall terminate upon his removal of residence from the town limits. Neither the Mayor nor any of the Coun-

Section 3 of the 1910 charter prevented African Americans from voting, since it prohibited registration of any man who did not have a relative entitled to vote prior to Jan. 1, 1868. Previously naturalized citizens had been provided a loophole so that they could register. Such grandfather clauses were not uncommon in the Southern states after Reconstruction. After the US Supreme Court found a similar grandfather clause in the Oklahoma Constitution to be invalid, the Maryland legislature removed this clause from the town's charter in 1916. But the town continued to keep its own voter registration rolls and thereby control who was added to the list. The 19th Amendment to the US Constitution, ratified in 1920, gave women the right to vote (overriding the town's charter language, which provided only men with the right to register). (Courtesy of Maryland State Archives.)

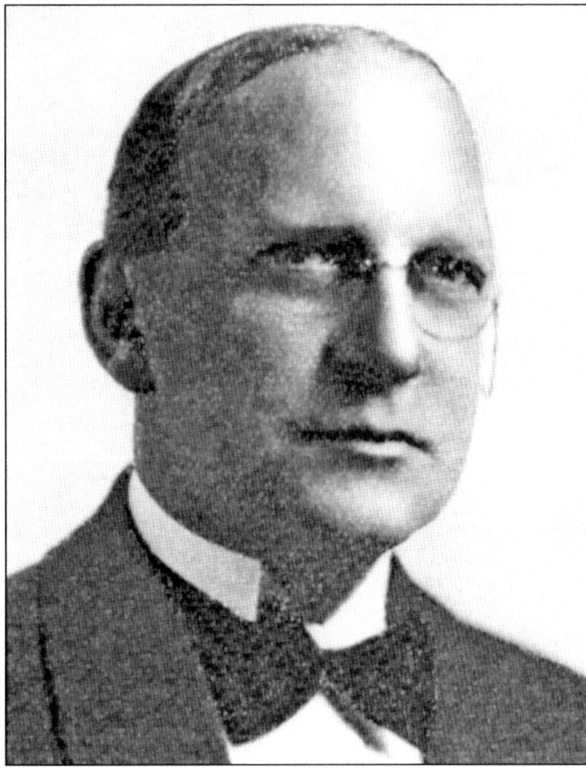

Joseph T.K. Plant (pictured) defeated Robert Joyce in the second town election. His rivals made a failed attempt to recall him. The right of citizens to recall an elected official was included in the town charter. While recalls were more common in the western United States, it is believed this attempt in 1911 was the first time such a recall process was tried in the East. (Courtesy of City of Mount Rainier.)

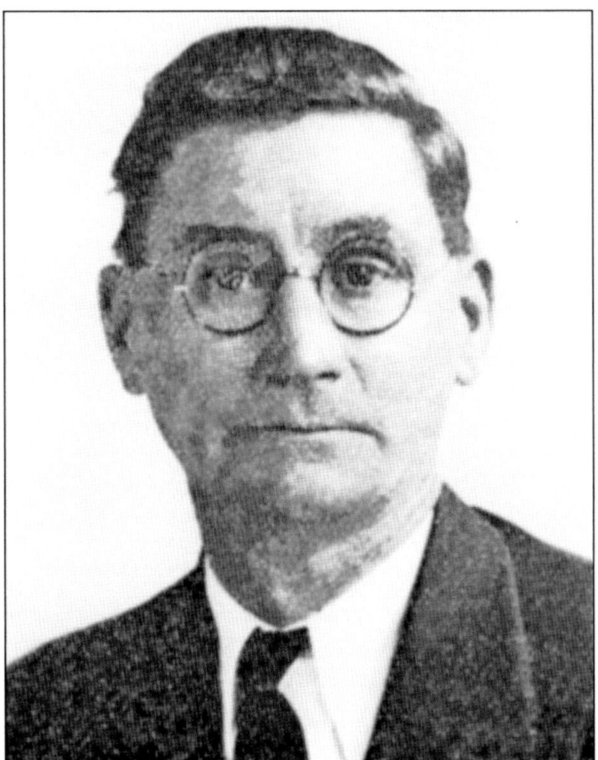

William H. Vanneman served first as town clerk, then councilman, and finally as mayor in 1913. He was active in organizing the volunteer fire department and served as the chairman of the trustees for the local public schools. His efforts resulted in funding for Mount Rainier Elementary School. (Courtesy of City of Mount Rainier.)

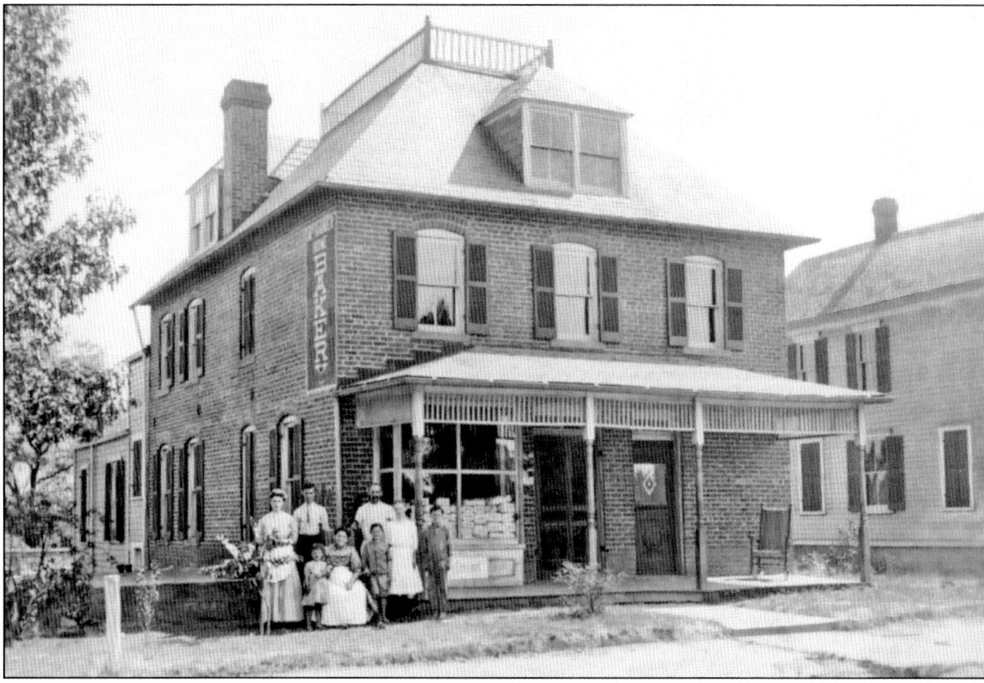

Klein's Bakery (seen in 1905) is closely tied to the volunteer fire department, which was founded in its kitchen in 1911. In 1922, John Klein hosted members of four departments—Hyattsville, Cottage City, Mount Rainier, and Brentwood—in his dining room to organize the Prince George's County Firemen's Association. The bakery still stands at Thirty-fourth Street and Bunker Hill Road, albeit behind a later brick commercial storefront. (Courtesy of City of Mount Rainier.)

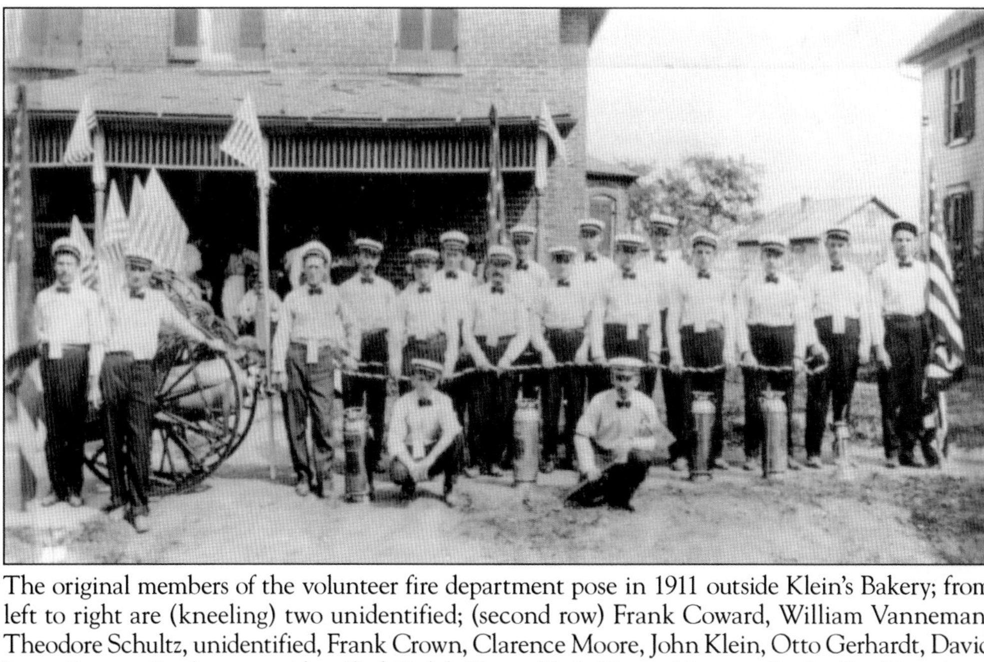

The original members of the volunteer fire department pose in 1911 outside Klein's Bakery; from left to right are (kneeling) two unidentified; (second row) Frank Coward, William Vanneman, Theodore Schultz, unidentified, Frank Crown, Clarence Moore, John Klein, Otto Gerhardt, David Lang, Earnest Bankman, unidentified, Ralph Keyes, Herb Green, Norman Pruitt, Jim Dunnigan, and Charles Miller. Vanneman and Pruitt later served as mayor. (Courtesy of Vernie Vanneman.)

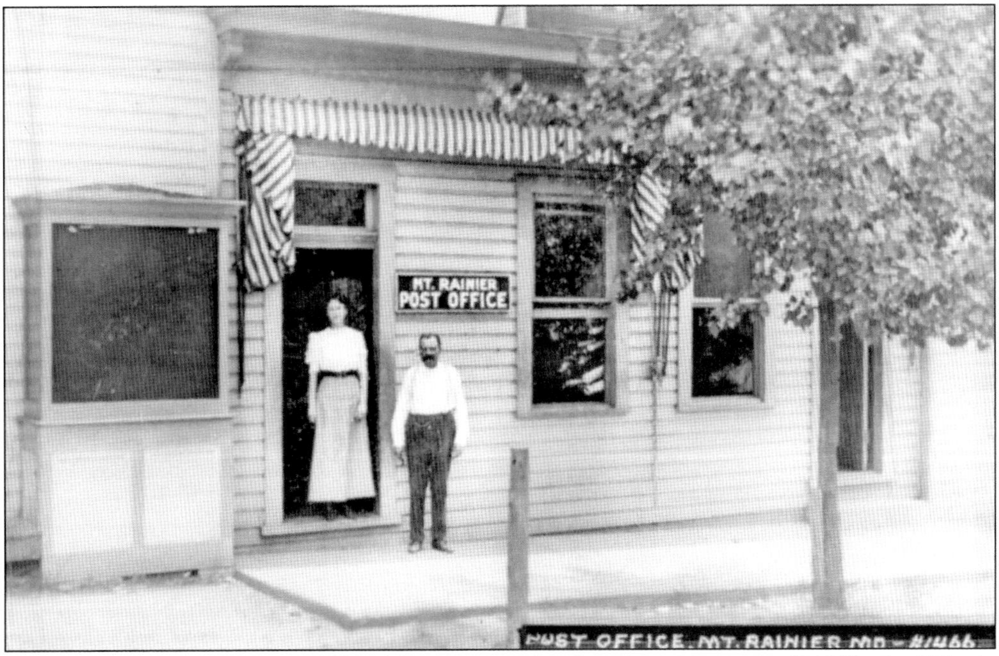

The first Mount Rainier Post Office (above) opened in October 1904 in the 3300 block of Rhode Island Avenue where the Artspace Building now stands. Mail was retrieved from the B&O Railroad's Rives Station, which was near today's Eastern Avenue bridge. The first postmaster was Rachel R. Bengel. Village delivery began in 1923 and city delivery in 1929. The location later moved to 3822 Thirty-fourth Street—adjacent to the Cameo Theater—and then, in 1953, to 3709 Rhode Island Avenue, where it remains today in the Blair Building. The photograph below shows Alice Cleaves at the post office. (Above, courtesy of City of Mount Rainier; below, courtesy of Teresa Wilcox.)

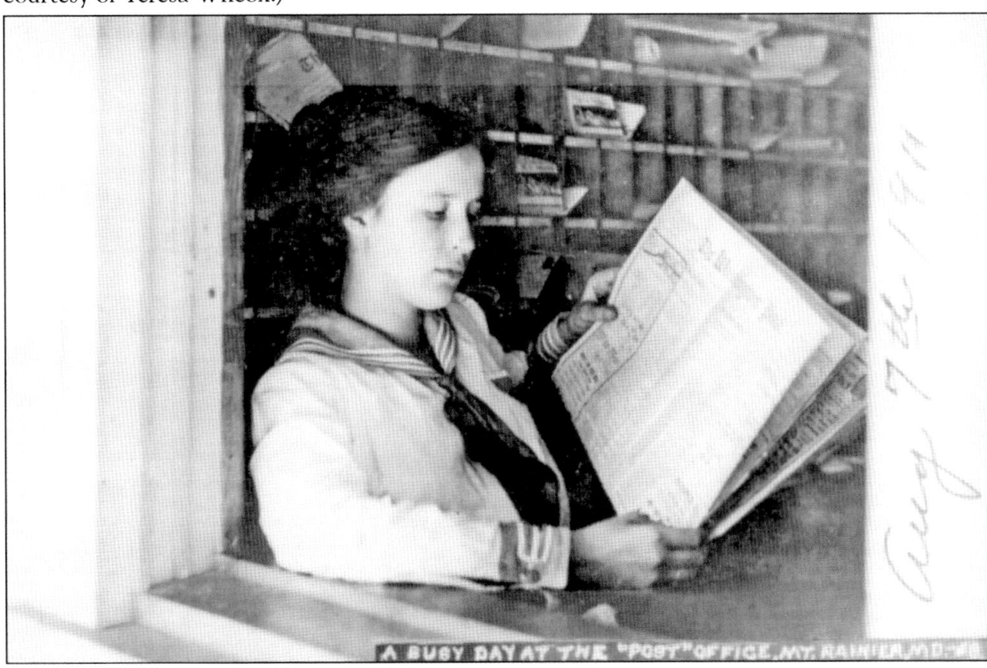

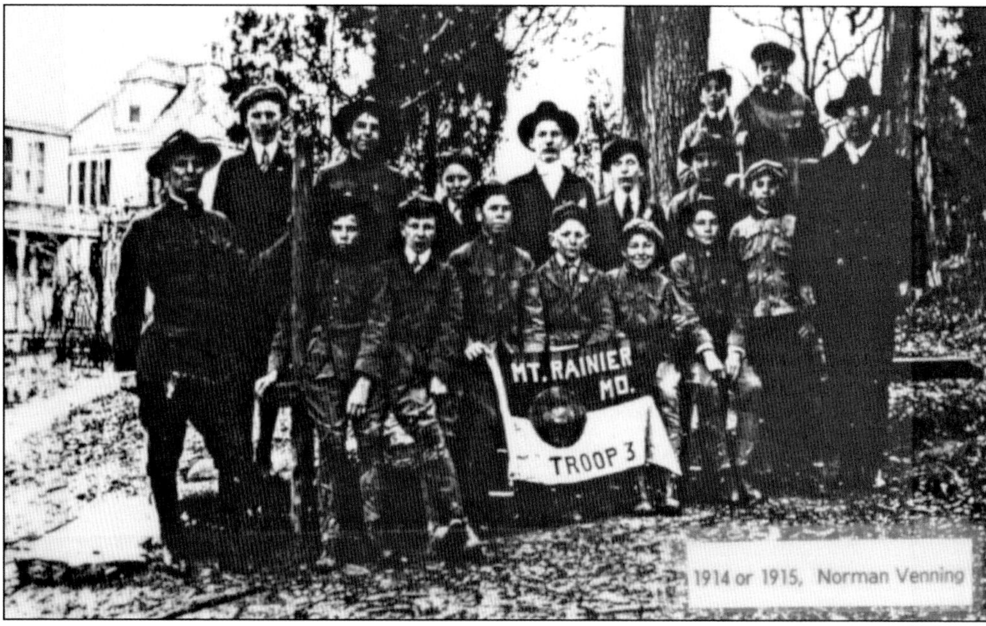

In 1909, neighborhood boys contacted Daniel Carter Beard, who was organizing a national Boy Pioneers or Sons of Daniel Boone, which became the Boy Scouts of America in 1910. The local boys became their own "stockade" of the Boy Pioneers of America. Boy Scout Troop No. 3 (above, at Spring Park), officially recognized in 1912, was sponsored by the Mount Rainier Christian Church. The troop marched in the 1912 carnival parade (below). A reorganization of the Washington Area Scouts in 1918 resulted in the local troop becoming Troop 203. The scouts later met in St. John's Episcopal Church. Today's Mount Rainier Boy Scouts belong to Troop 224 in Hyattsville. Several Girl Scout troops also existed in Mount Rainier, with the first organized around 1930. The local area's council headquarters was housed in the city at one time. (Above, courtesy of Norman Venning; below, courtesy of DC Public Library Special Collections.)

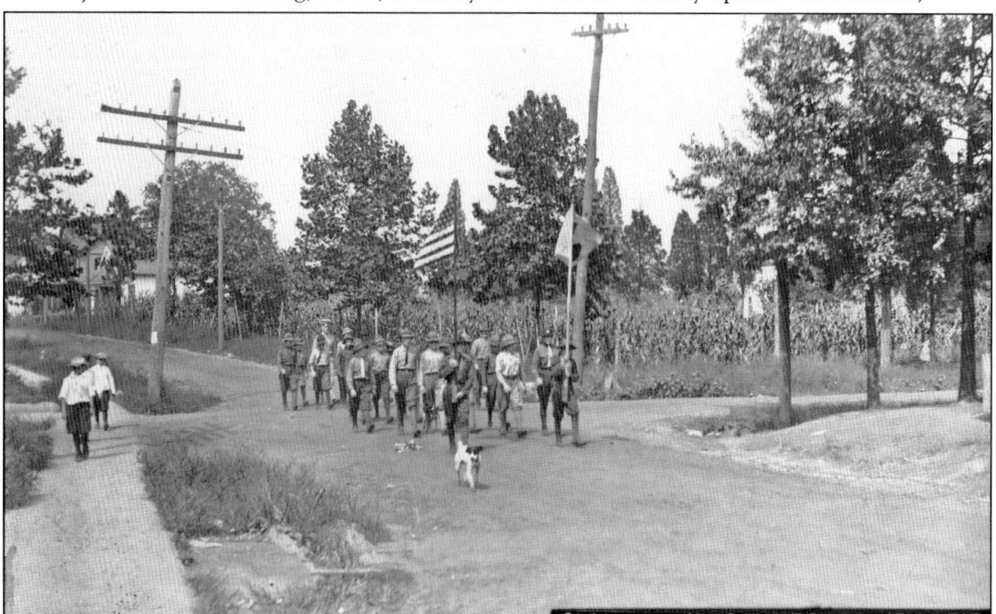

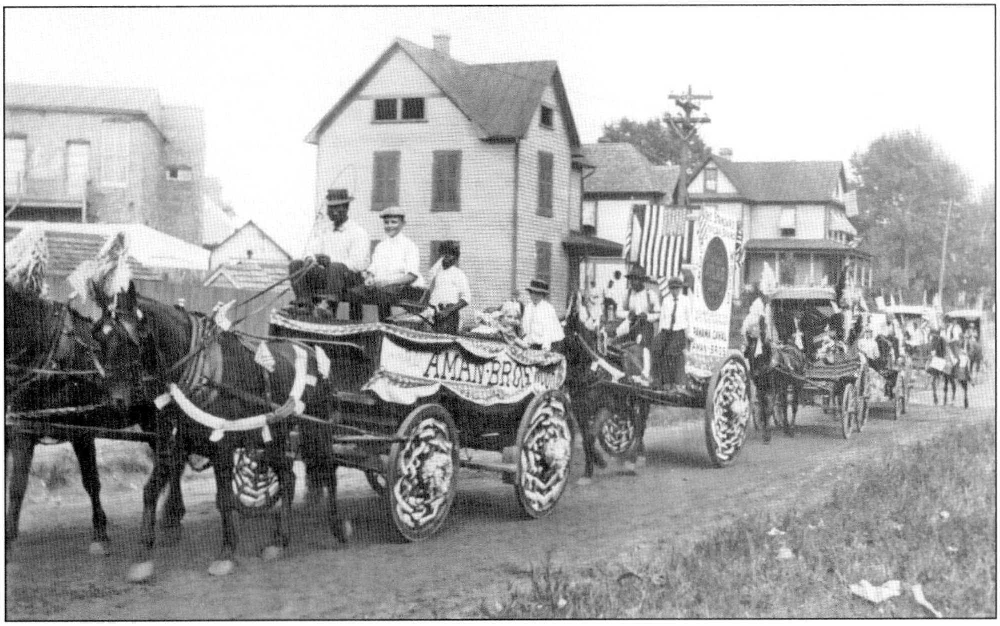

The 1912 carnival parade marches westward along today's Perry Street (then known as Newton Street). The brick building on the left edge of both postcards is the rear of Star-Potts Hall. The home (3500 Perry Street) in the middle of the photographs is arguably the most photographed structure in the city, appearing in many images through the decades. Mount Rainier City Hall now occupies the site. Carnivals raised funds for civic purposes, including the purchase in 1920 of the building at 3409 Rhode Island Avenue as town hall. Perry Boswell had operated a grocery in the building prior to its purchase. The photograph above is the first known showing African Americans participating in town events. (Both, courtesy of City of Mount Rainier.)

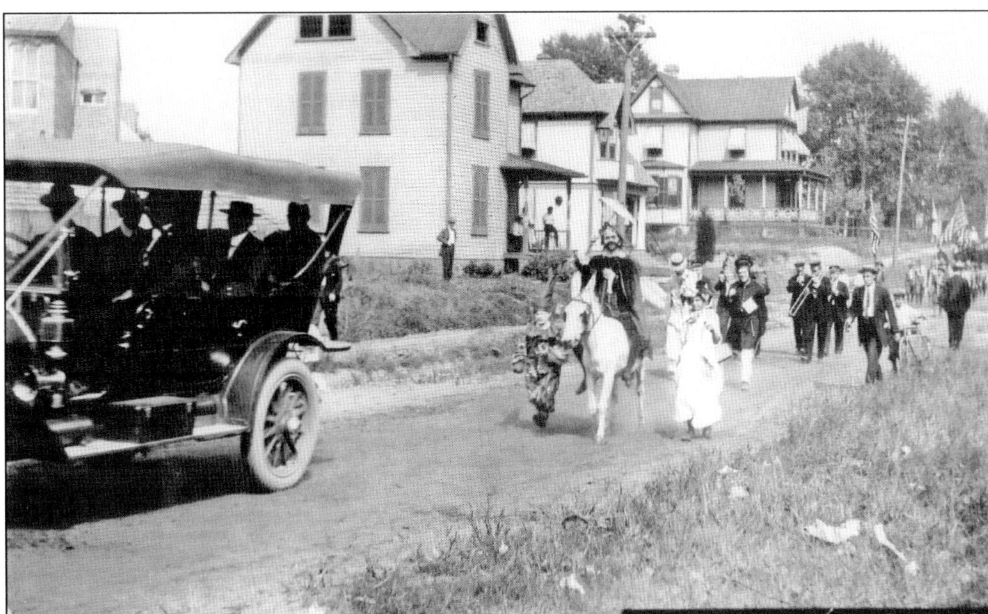

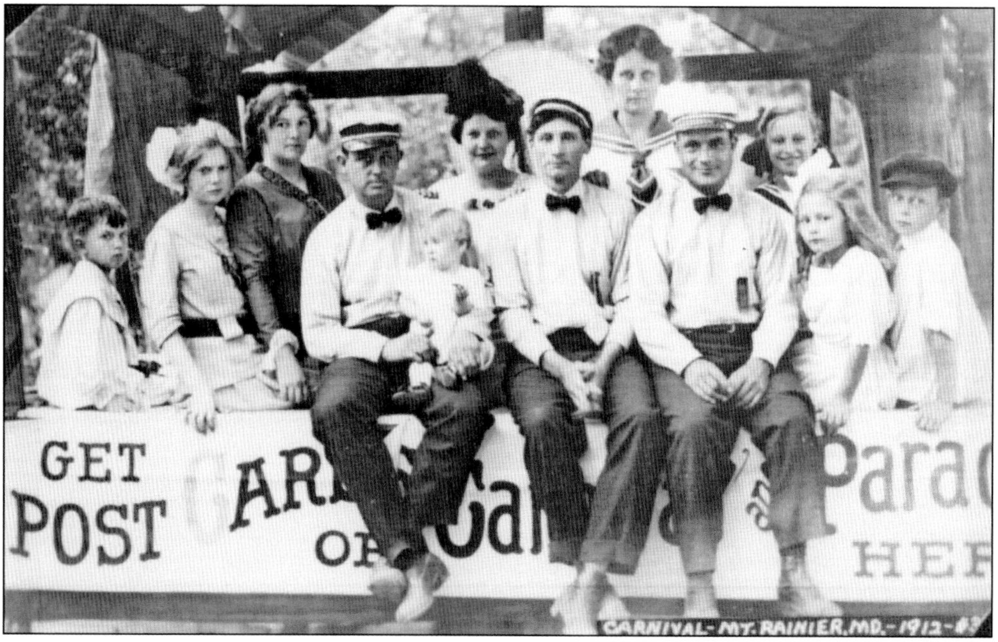

The annual carnival parades ended at the carnival grounds, which at that time was a partly wooded area between Thirty-first and Thirty-second Streets—the area where the Clemson home had stood. Longtime resident Norman Venning recalled in a 1988 interview that the grounds included an open-air dance pavilion with bandstand. Note that postcards are offered for sale in the upper photograph. Below, the newly organized volunteer fire department poses in front of its carnival booth. (Both, courtesy of City of Mount Rainier.)

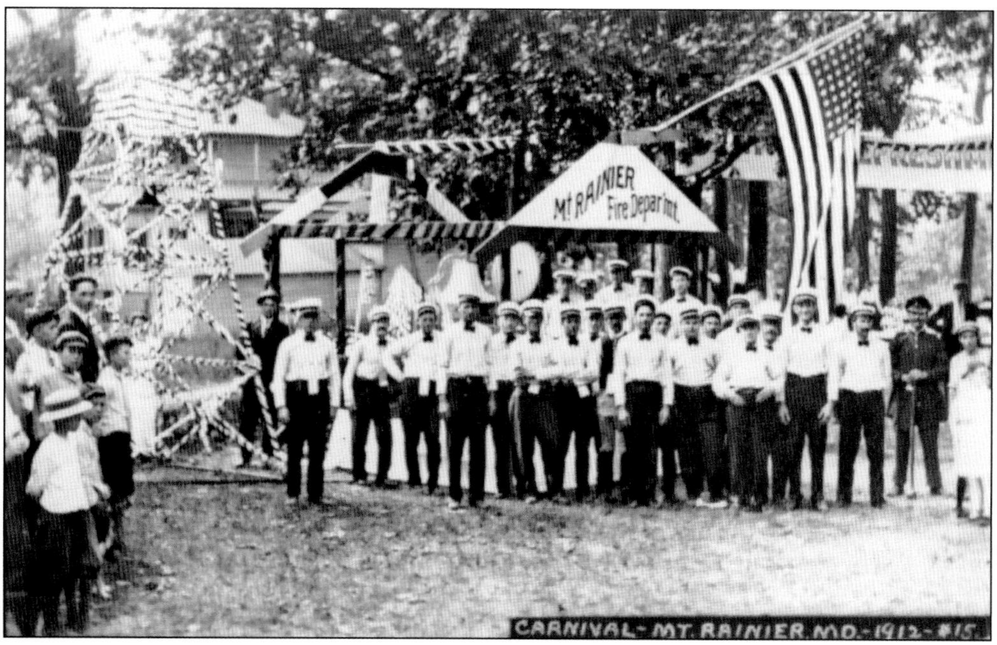

Fred E. Weber was elected mayor in 1914. During his time in office, the water and sewer system was authorized and planned. He was responsible for the town's purchase of the Czarra Springs, located near today's Magruder Park in Hyattsville, as the source of water for the system. (Courtesy of City of Mount Rainier.)

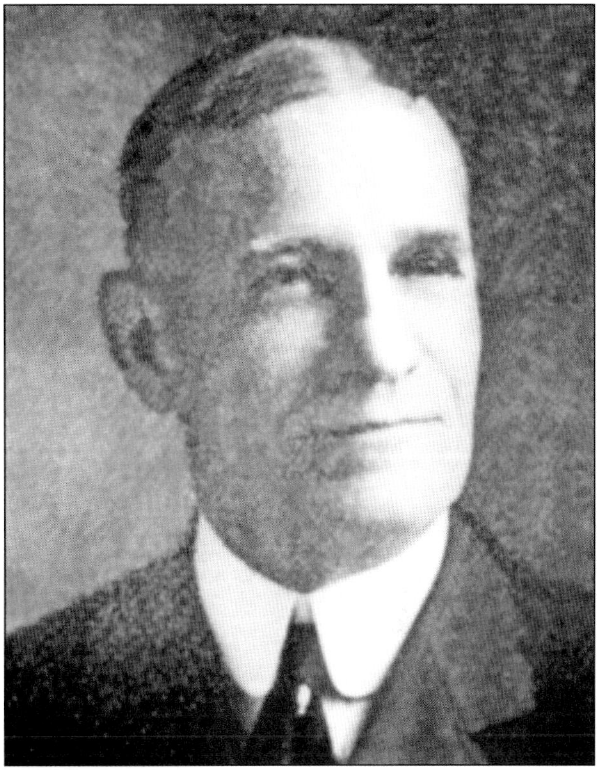

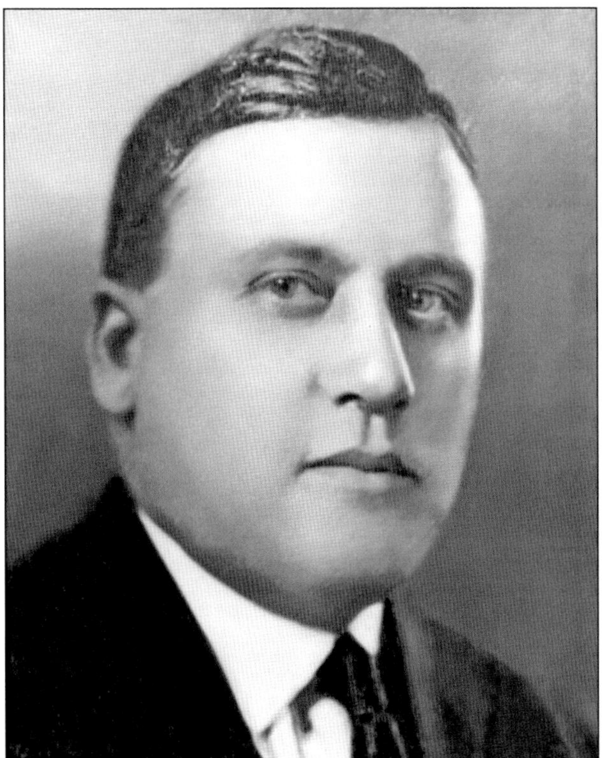

Perry Boswell became mayor in 1917. The water and sewer system was completed during his time in office. He was president of the county's board of education and a director of the Prince George's Bank and Trust Co. Boswell later served as president of the Prince George's County Board of Commissioners. (Courtesy of City of Mount Rainier.)

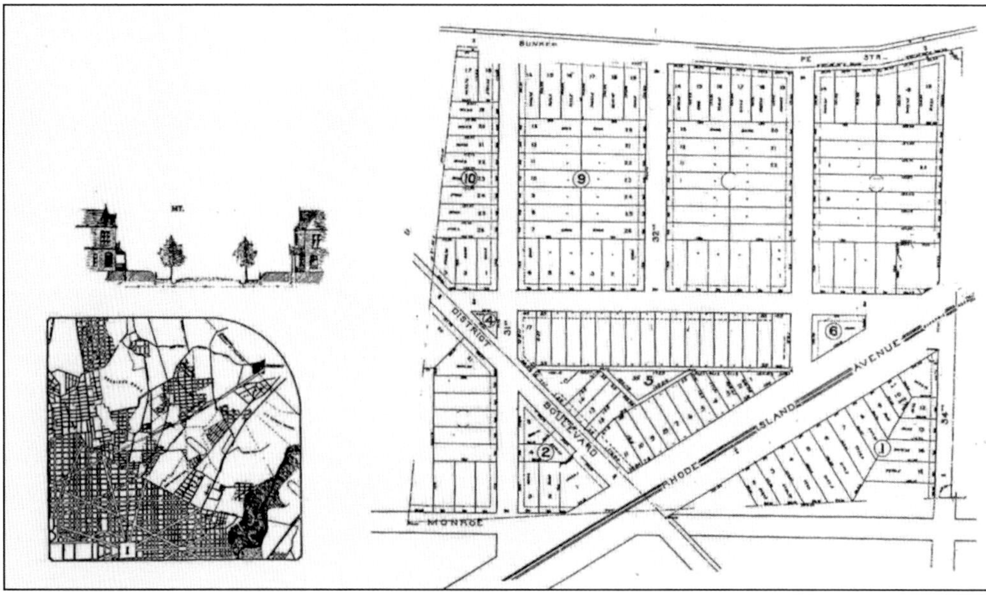

Rogers Addition to Mount Rainier and Rogers Second Addition (the 1907 plat seen above) are subdivisions adjacent to the original Mount Rainier subdivision. The Rogers brothers—James Harris, James C., and William Sheppard—were among the most active real estate developers in Prince George's County in the early 20th century. They also developed parts of Hyattsville, Cottage City, Edmonston, Riverdale, and Rogers Heights. Pictured below from left to right are James C., wife Blanche Mattingly, sister Anna Mae, and brother Dr. James Harris. James C. graduated from Georgetown Law School and was the most active of the brothers in real estate ventures. Dr. James Harris Rogers was chief electrician of the Capitol and held dozens of patents, most of which concerned the development and refinement of communications equipment. His most important invention was an underground and underwater antenna used by the Army during World War I to intercept German messages. (Above, courtesy of M-NCPPC; below, courtesy of HSWDC.)

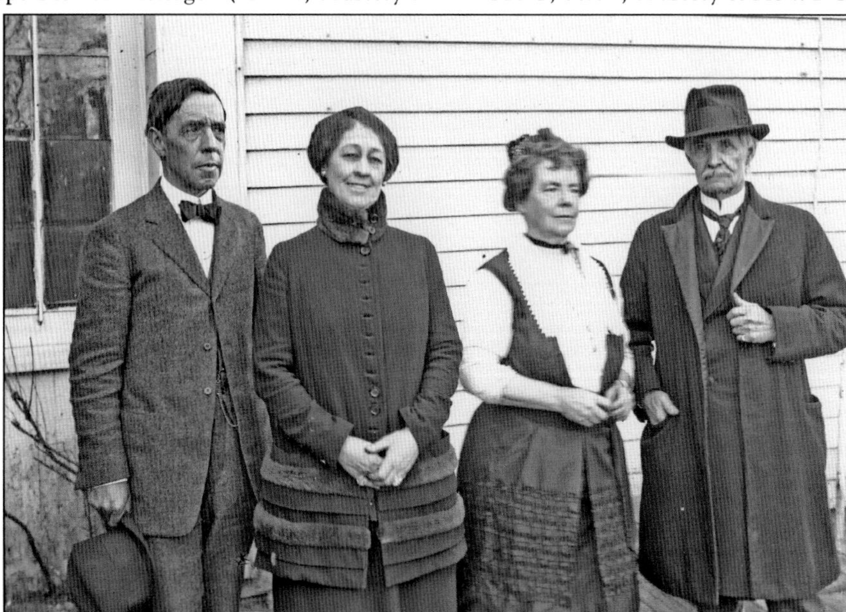

Edgar and Mary Bean pose at 4213 Thirty-fourth Street (with their neighbor's house in the background) in 1920. Real estate advertisements stressed that homes were "charmingly located" on "very large (rich) grounds" that were "high and healthy." An ad for one house described it as having a barn and outbuildings, fences, shade and fruit trees, and a wide porch. (Courtesy of Judy Rice.)

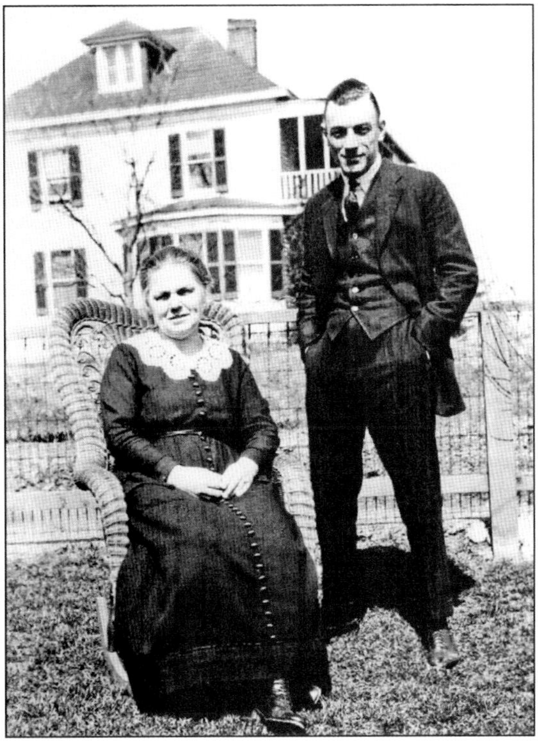

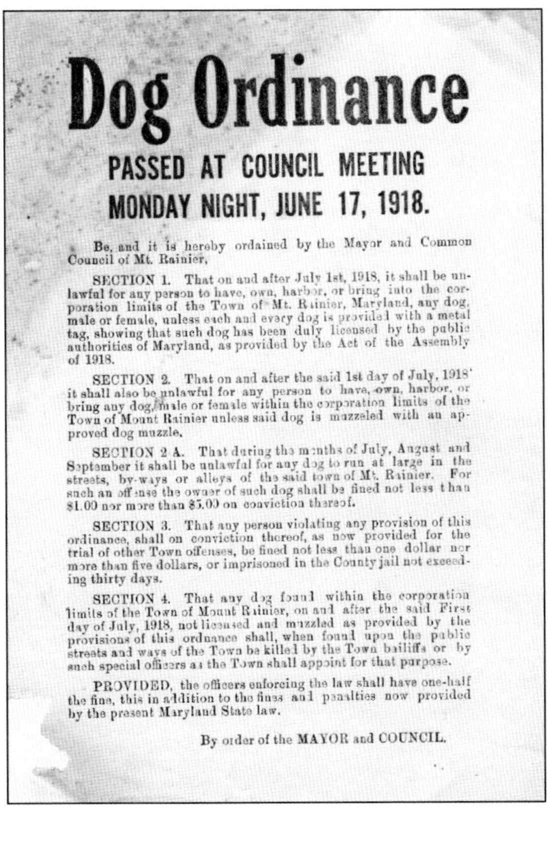

Dog Ordinance

PASSED AT COUNCIL MEETING MONDAY NIGHT, JUNE 17, 1918.

Be, and it is hereby ordained by the Mayor and Common Council of Mt. Rainier,

SECTION 1. That on and after July 1st, 1918, it shall be unlawful for any person to have, own, harbor, or bring into the corporation limits of the Town of Mt. Rainier, Maryland, any dog, male or female, unless each and every dog is provided with a metal tag, showing that such dog has been duly licensed by the public authorities of Maryland, as provided by the Act of the Assembly of 1918.

SECTION 2. That on and after the said 1st day of July, 1918 it shall also be unlawful for any person to have, own, harbor, or bring any dog, male or female within the corporation limits of the Town of Mount Rainier unless said dog is muzzeled with an approved dog muzzle.

SECTION 2 A. That during the months of July, August and September it shall be unlawful for any dog to run at large in the streets, by-ways or alleys of the said town of Mt. Rainier. For such an offense the owner of such dog shall be fined not less than $1.00 nor more than $5.00 on conviction thereof.

SECTION 3. That any person violating any provision of this ordinance, shall on conviction thereof, as now provided for the trial of other Town offenses, be fined not less than one dollar nor more than five dollars, or imprisoned in the County jail not exceeding thirty days.

SECTION 4. That any dog found within the corporation limits of the Town of Mount Rainier, on and after the said First day of July, 1918, not licensed and muzzled as provided by the provisions of this ordnance shall, when found upon the public streets and ways of the Town be killed by the Town bailiffs or by such special officers as the Town shall appoint for that purpose.

PROVIDED, the officers enforcing the law shall have one-half the fine, this in addition to the fines and penalties now provided by the present Maryland State law.

By order of the MAYOR and COUNCIL.

In 1918, the town charter was amended to give the council more zoning and code enforcement powers. The legislation was the first emergency law (one that became effective immediately) ever adopted in the Maryland assembly. The dog ordinance permitted bailiffs to kill dogs without tags found on the streets. The bailiffs were awarded half of any levied fine. (Courtesy of City of Mount Rainier.)

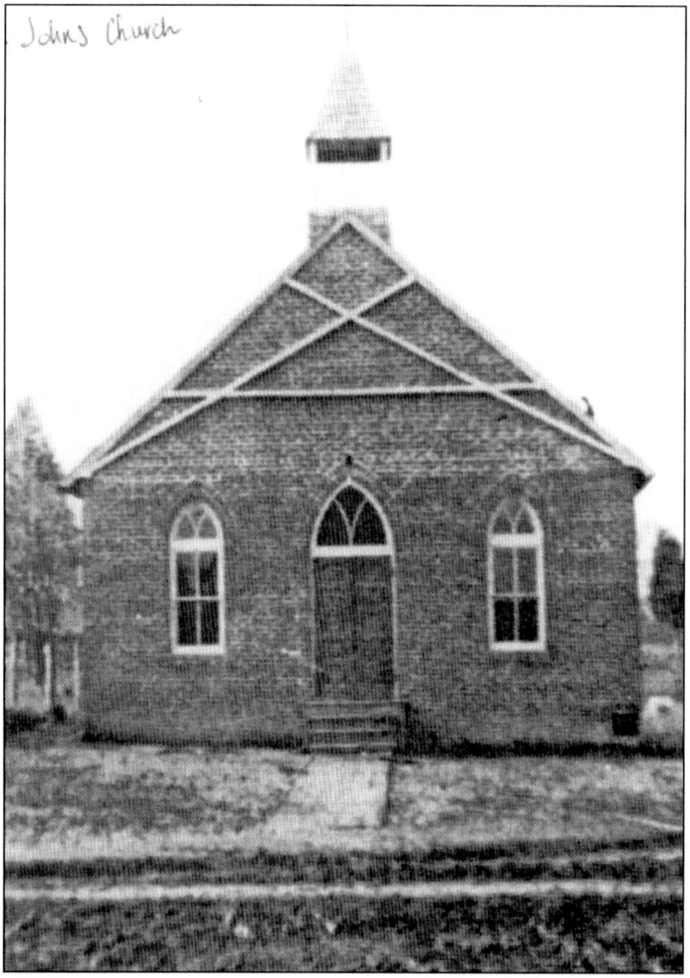

On October 17, 1909, a group of Episcopalians met in Potts Hall to form St. John's Chapel. The officiant was the Rev. Henry Thomas of St. Matthew's Parish in Hyattsville. On Easter Sunday, April 7, 1912, the first church was dedicated at the corner of Thirty-fourth Street and Rainier Avenue (left). By 1913, the church had a membership of 50 families and 40 confirmed persons. The original brick chapel was later modified with a board-and-batten Gothic style frame facade (below). A parish hall, seen to the left of the church, was built in 1930, designed by Washington, DC, architect Howard W. Cutler. In 1932, Rev. Walter Plumley Jr. became rector; during his six years, the membership grew to 375. (Both, courtesy of St. John's Episcopal Church.)

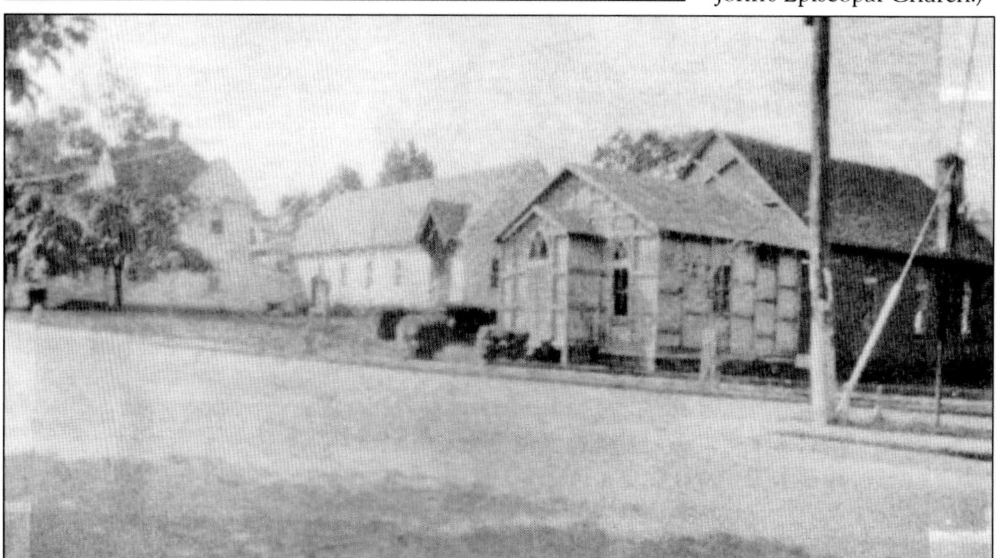

The segment of Queens Chapel Road from the District of Columbia boundary to just south of Ager Road was paved by Prince George's County with state aid by 1915. Queens Chapel Road is named for the Queen's Chapel, a Catholic church founded on the estate of the Queen family in 1722 in what is now the Langdon neighborhood of Washington near Twentieth and Evarts Streets. The 1914 topographical map below shows the original route of Queens Chapel Road moving northward from the Langdon neighborhood, crossing Bunker Hill Road, and entering Maryland (as it does to this day); at right, the Heitmuller sisters pose in 1915 at this border. (Right, courtesy of Teresa Wilcox; below, courtesy of M-NCPPC.)

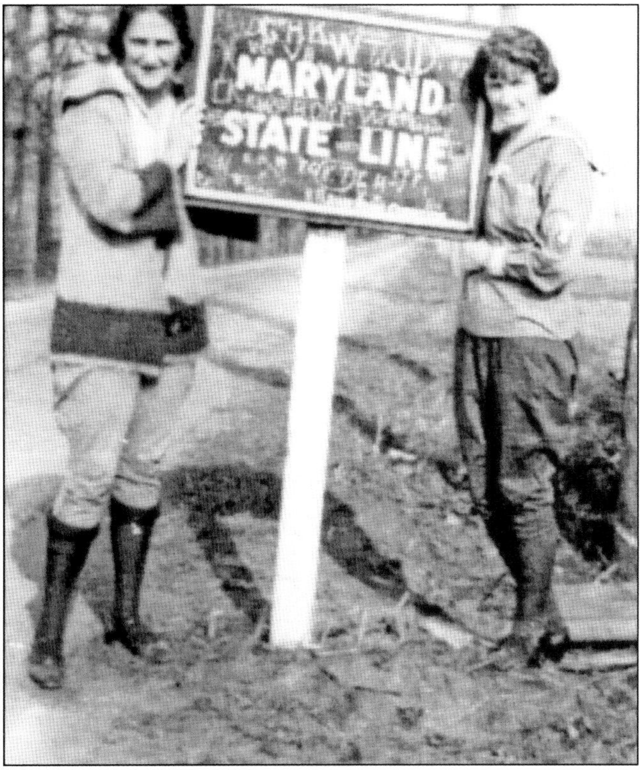

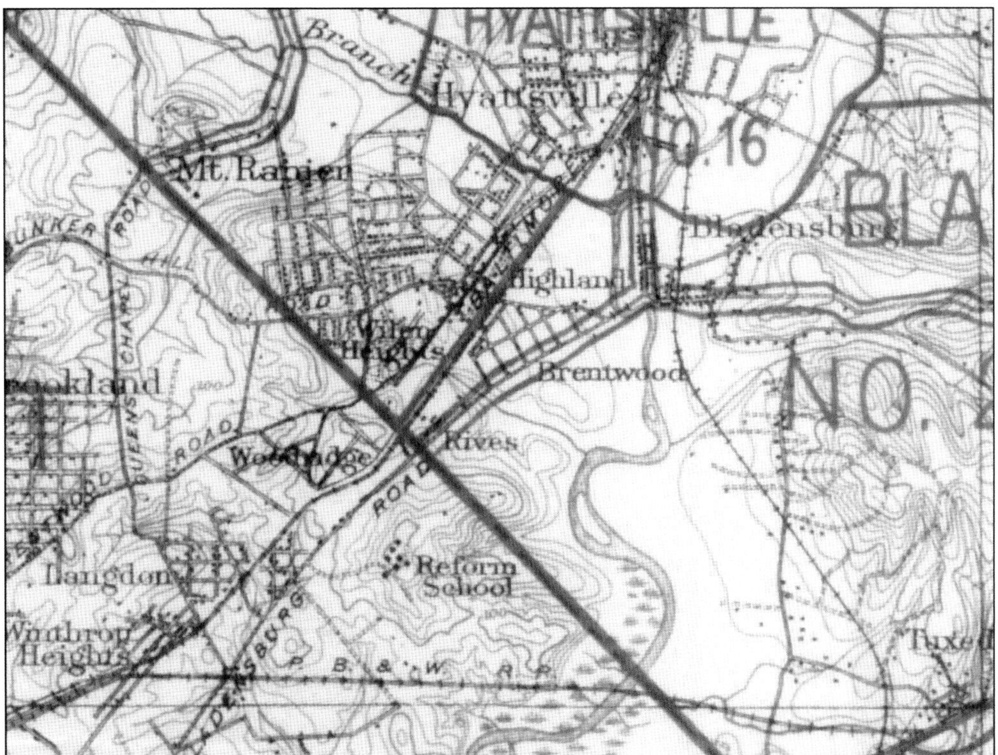

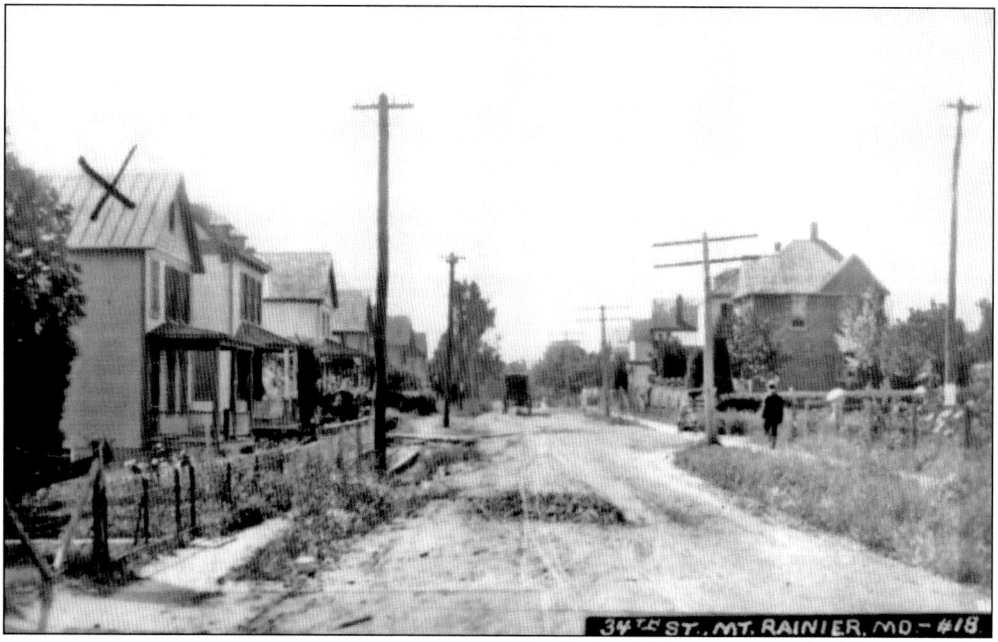

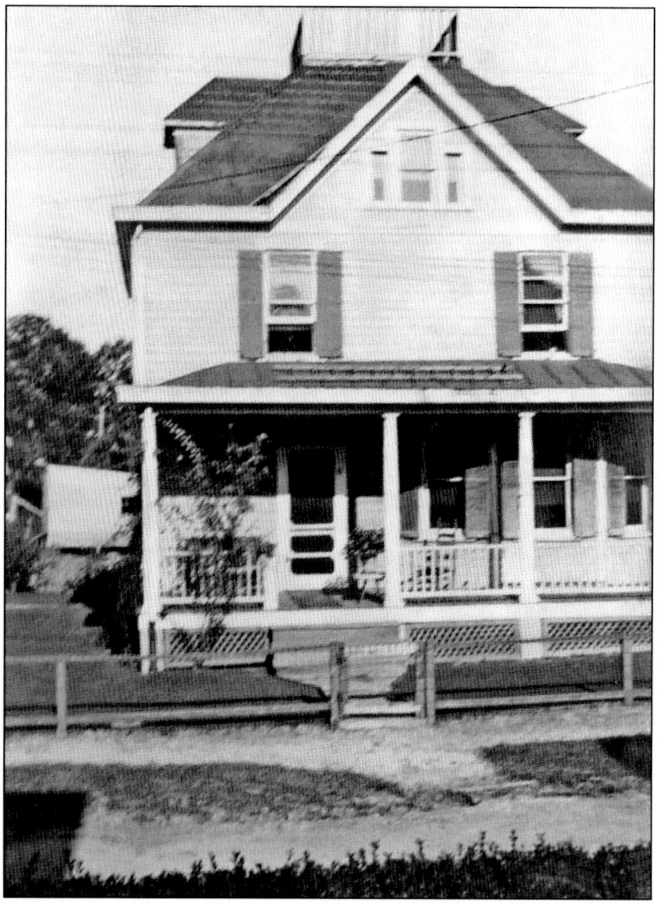

The town was known as "Mud Rainier" for good reason. Above is a 1912 view of unpaved Thirty-fourth Street looking toward Bunker Hill Road. The act of April 9, 1920, known as the $50,000 Road Improvement Act, provided for the issuance and sale of bonds, not to exceed $50,000 at any one time, for construction of sidewalks, streets, and gutters. One half of the cost of the improvements was assessed against the abutting front footage and the other half paid by the town on the valuation basis. The widow's walk on the roof of 4213 Thirty-fourth Street (left) must have provided a view of the Anacostia River valley to the east. (Above, courtesy of Teresa Wilcox; left, courtesy of Judy Rice.)

Two

The Roaring Twenties and the Great Depression

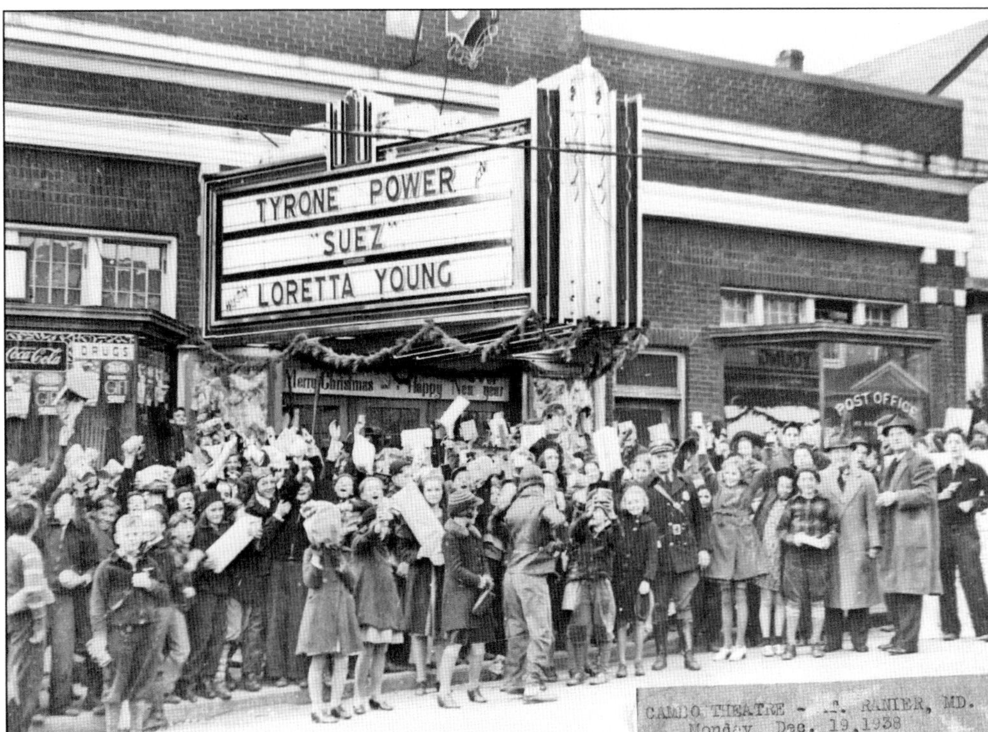

Children wave their Christmas presents in the air after a benefit for the poor was held in the Cameo Theater, 3822 Thirty-fourth Street, in December 1938. The Cameo was built in 1927, but the first movie theater in Mount Rainier, the Tu-Max, operated by J.P. McKallor and E.M. McClees (the two "Macs"), screened silent films in Potts Hall beginning in 1914. (Courtesy of Paul Sanchez.)

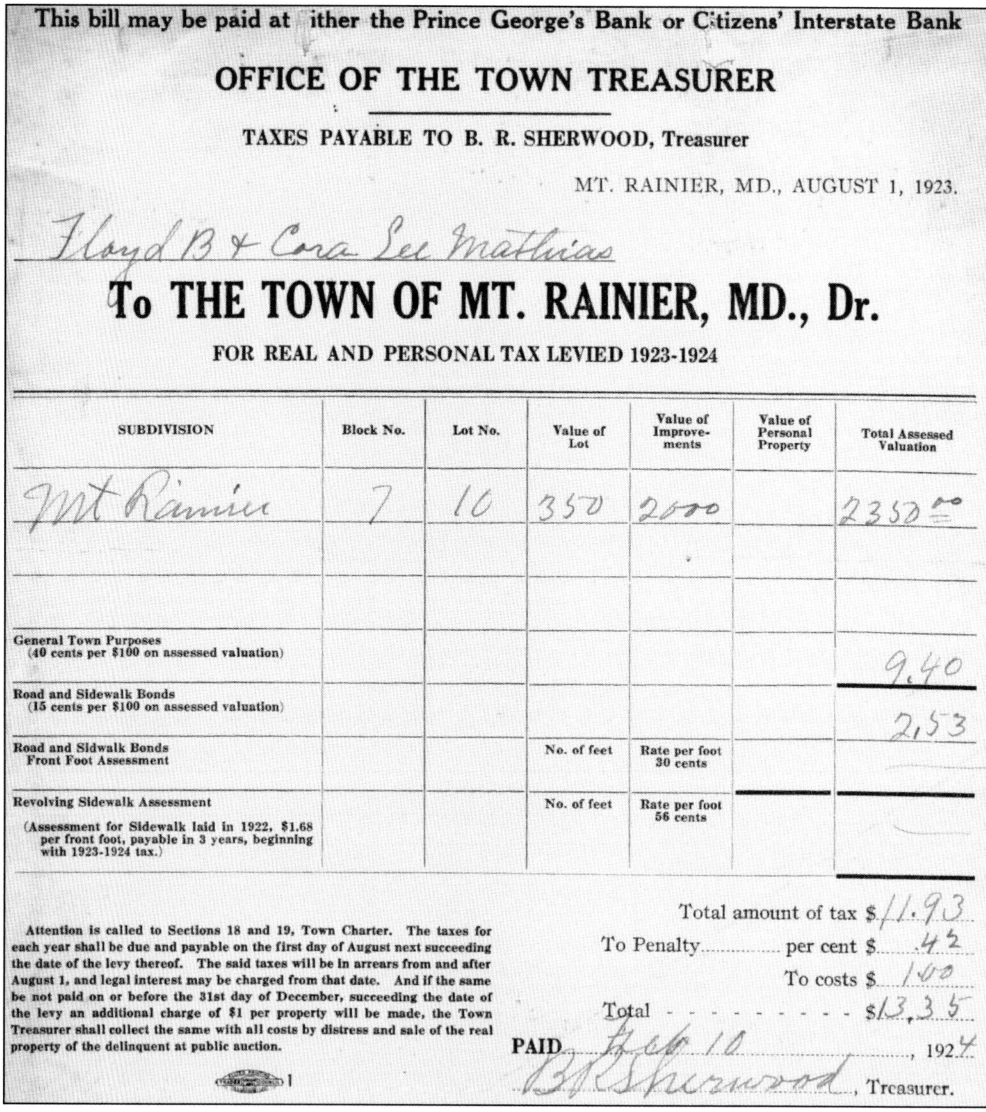

This bill may be paid at ither the Prince George's Bank or Citizens' Interstate Bank

OFFICE OF THE TOWN TREASURER

TAXES PAYABLE TO B. R. SHERWOOD, Treasurer

MT. RAINIER, MD., AUGUST 1, 1923.

Floyd B & Cora Lee Mathias

To THE TOWN OF MT. RAINIER, MD., Dr.

FOR REAL AND PERSONAL TAX LEVIED 1923-1924

SUBDIVISION	Block No.	Lot No.	Value of Lot	Value of Improve-ments	Value of Personal Property	Total Assessed Valuation
Mt Rainier	7	10	350	2000		2350.00
General Town Purposes (40 cents per $100 on assessed valuation)						9.40
Road and Sidewalk Bonds (15 cents per $100 on assessed valuation)						2.53
Road and Sidwalk Bonds Front Foot Assessment			No. of feet	Rate per foot 30 cents		
Revolving Sidewalk Assessment (Assessment for Sidewalk laid in 1922, $1.68 per front foot, payable in 3 years, beginning with 1923-1924 tax.)			No. of feet	Rate per foot 56 cents		

Attention is called to Sections 18 and 19, Town Charter. The taxes for each year shall be due and payable on the first day of August next succeeding the date of the levy thereof. The said taxes will be in arrears from and after August 1, and legal interest may be charged from that date. And if the same be not paid on or before the 31st day of December, succeeding the date of the levy an additional charge of $1 per property will be made, the Town Treasurer shall collect the same with all costs by distress and sale of the real property of the delinquent at public auction.

Total amount of tax $11.93
To Penalty........ per cent $ .42
To costs $ 1.00
Total - - - - - - - - - $13.35
PAID Feb 10, 1924
B R Sherwood, Treasurer.

In 1920, Mount Rainier's tax rate was 20¢ per $100 of assessed value, which raised $1,850 annually. The town informed the citizens that this was inadequate to pay the town's ordinary expenses, let alone pave sidewalks and streets. For comparison, the town council publicized that Hyattsville's tax rate was 65¢ per $100 of assessed value of the land, plus 60¢ for each $100 of improvements, together with a special sewer tax of 20¢ on each $100 of total valuation. In addition, the Hyattsville council required the abutting property owners to pay for street work without any contribution from the town. Mount Rainier's arrangement included that the town pay for half the cost, while the abutting property owners on each side paid one-fourth each. The act of March 27, 1922, amended the Mount Rainier town charter relating to assessments and taxes, allowing for the borrowing of money for sidewalk construction. This 1923 tax bill includes the fee for the sidewalk program. (Courtesy of City of Mount Rainier.)

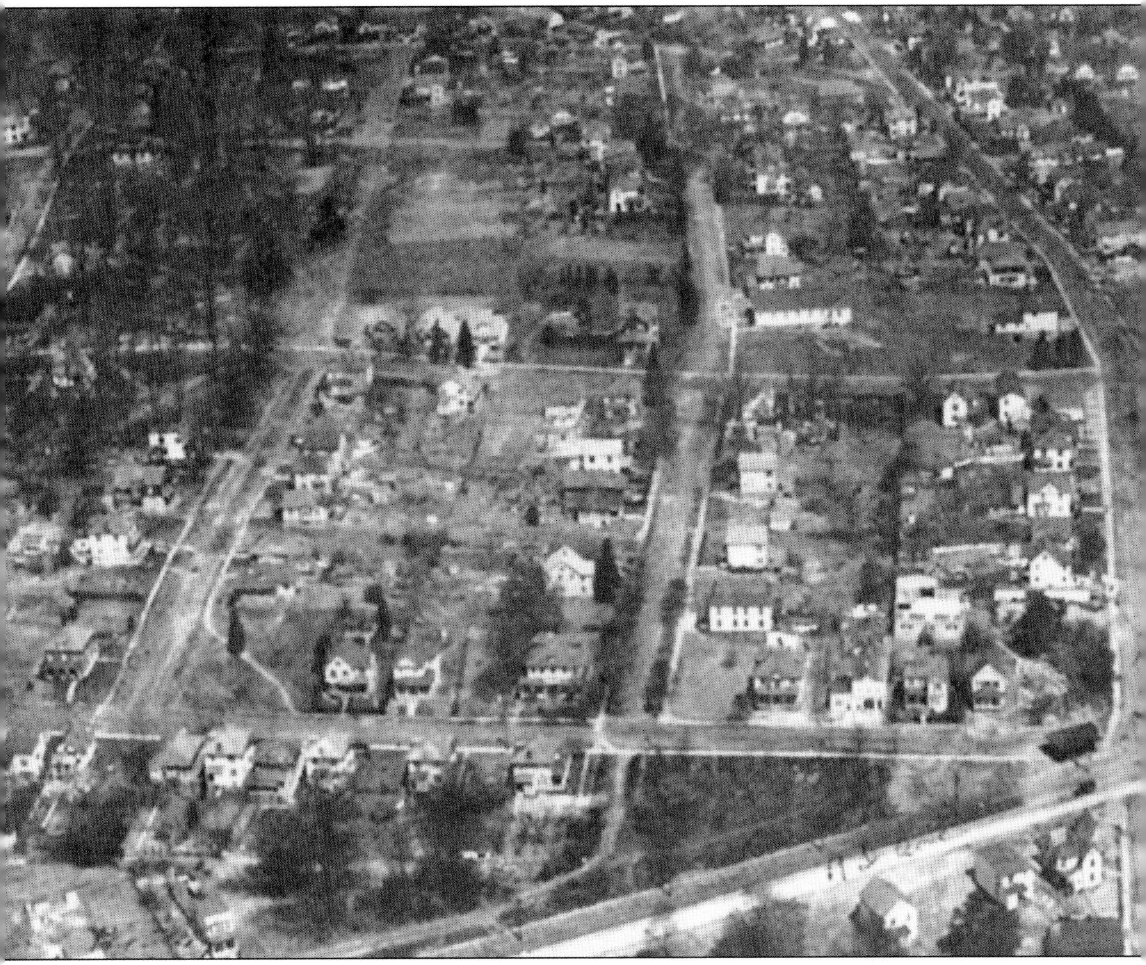

In this 1920 aerial view, Rhode Island Avenue runs diagonally along the bottom and intersects Thirty-fourth Street, which runs along the right side. The District Line Station is the black rectangular roof at the northwest corner of the intersection (at lower right). Bunker Hill Road runs horizontally across the center. The open field in the upper middle is now the location of Mount Rainier Elementary School. The wooded area at top left (at Shepherd and Thirty-second Streets) is the remnant of the grove that had surrounded the Clemsons' house (see page 14) and served as the town's carnival grounds. Most of the streets were still muddy lanes at this time, but in 1920, the state authorized the sale of bonds to finance paving of streets and sidewalks. By 1931, nearly every street was paved in what was once called Mud Rainier. (Courtesy of City of Mount Rainier.)

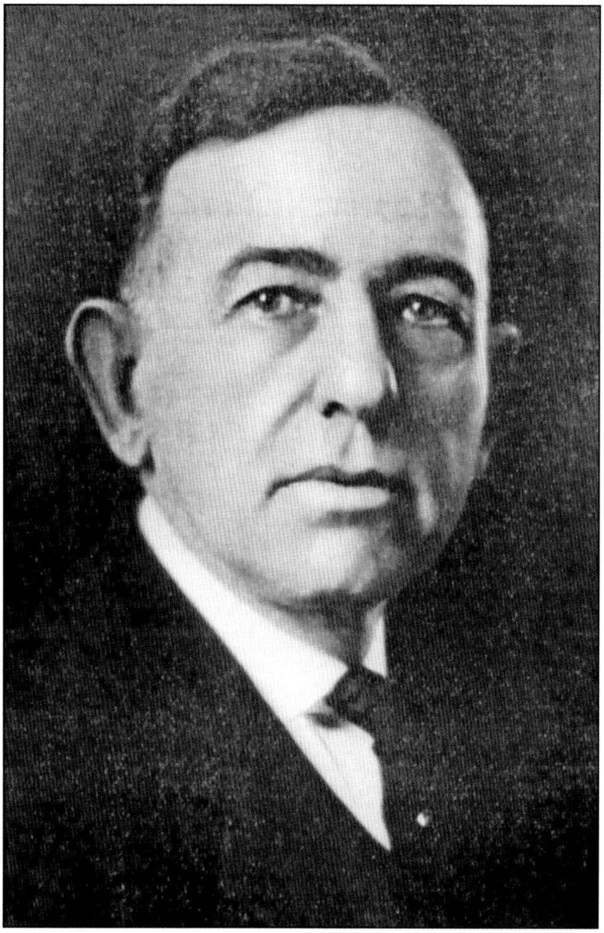

The Prince George's Bank, founded in 1915 in Hyattsville, built its Mount Rainier Branch in 1922 at the prominent location on Thirty-fourth Street adjacent to the streetcar line. J. Enos Ray (left), the bank's president, was involved in numerous civic projects and served as speaker of the House of Delegates in 1909. The Prince George's Trust Company was created in 1930 with the merger of the bank and the First National Bank of Hyattsville. In 1949, the bank's successor, the Suburban Trust Company, moved to a larger building at 3716 Rhode Island Avenue (razed in 1999 for construction of the Bunker Hill Fire Station). Perry Boswell purchased the original edifice to house his real estate business. The former bank's building remains a landmark facing the traffic circle at the center of Mount Rainier's business district and is a county historic site. (Left, courtesy of City of Mount Rainier; below, courtesy of M-NCPPC.)

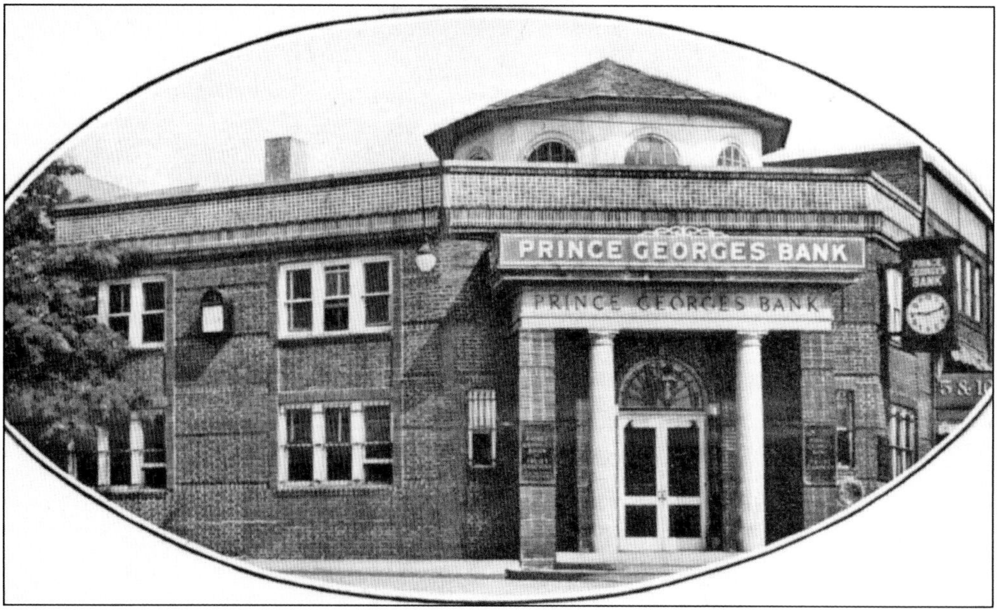

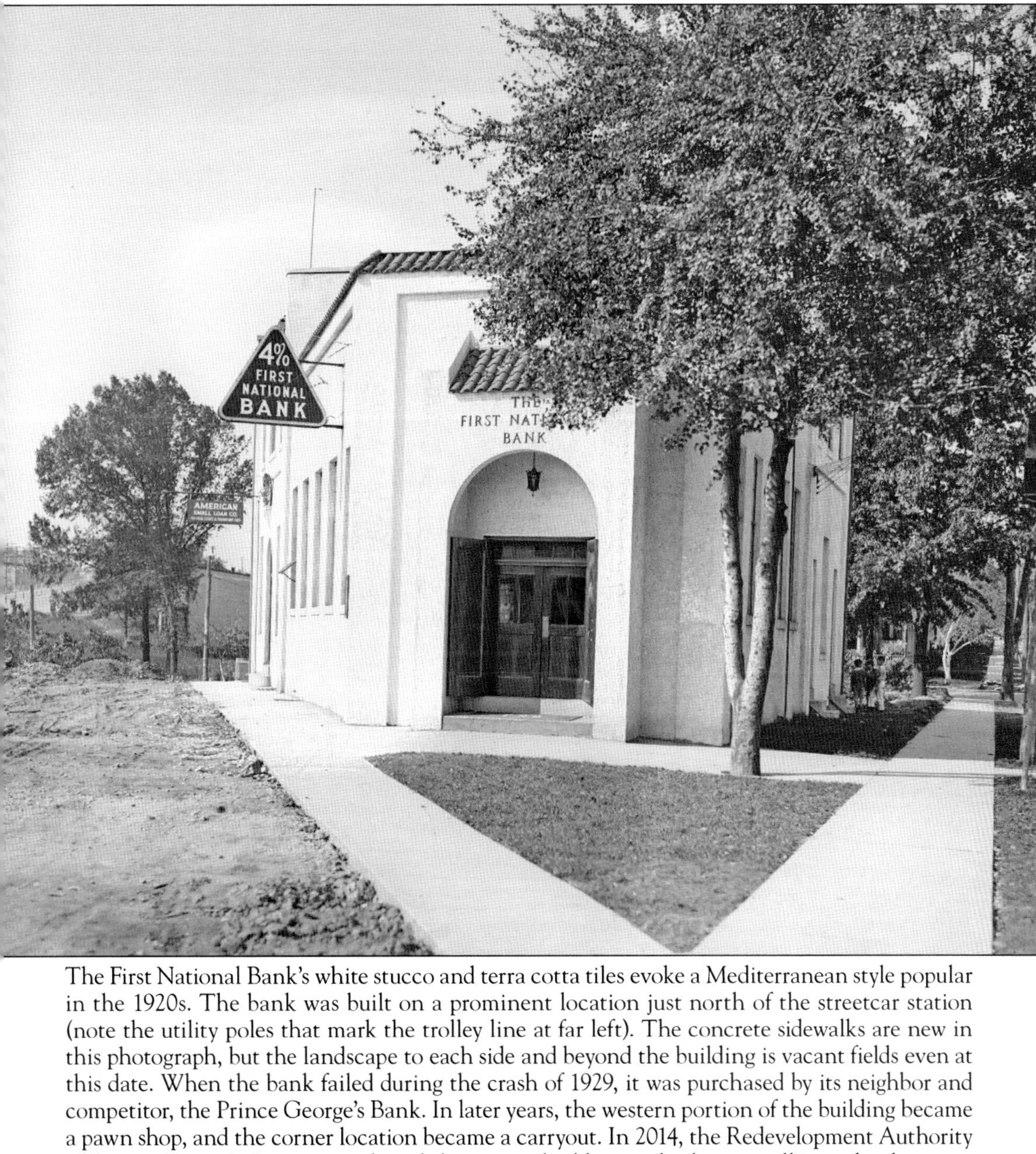

The First National Bank's white stucco and terra cotta tiles evoke a Mediterranean style popular in the 1920s. The bank was built on a prominent location just north of the streetcar station (note the utility poles that mark the trolley line at far left). The concrete sidewalks are new in this photograph, but the landscape to each side and beyond the building is vacant fields even at this date. When the bank failed during the crash of 1929, it was purchased by its neighbor and competitor, the Prince George's Bank. In later years, the western portion of the building became a pawn shop, and the corner location became a carryout. In 2014, the Redevelopment Authority of Prince George's County purchased the vacant building with plans to sell it to developers to restore and repurpose. (Courtesy of Library of Congress.)

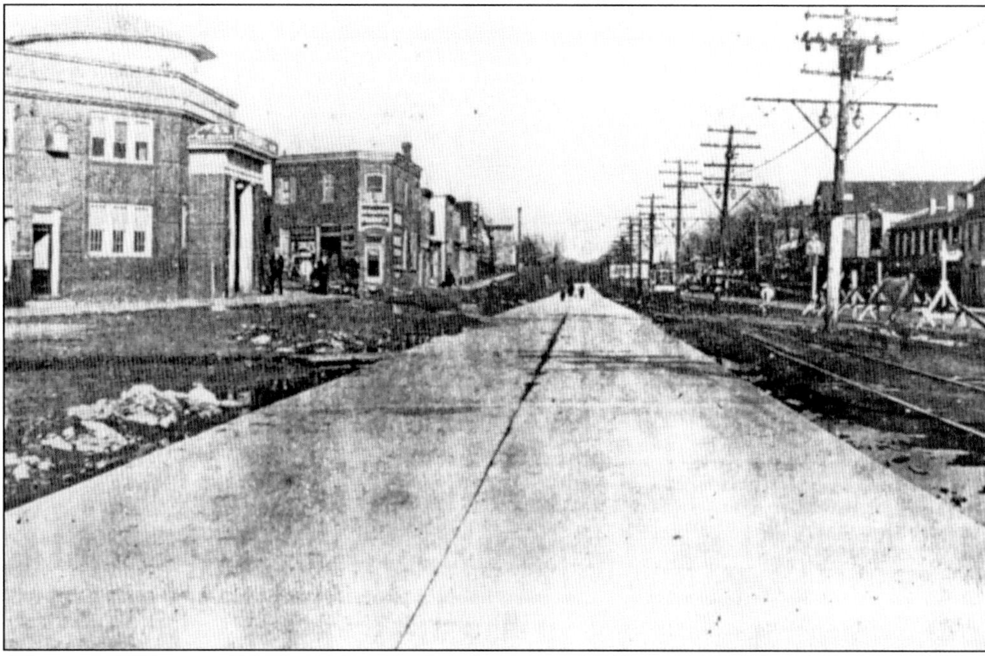

In June 1929, the streetcar company gave the State Roads Commission the right to pave on the north side of its tracks (as seen here looking east, with the bank on the corner of Thirty-fourth Street) in connection with construction of the highway to Hyattsville. The District Line Station was razed to make way for the road. (Courtesy of PGCHS.)

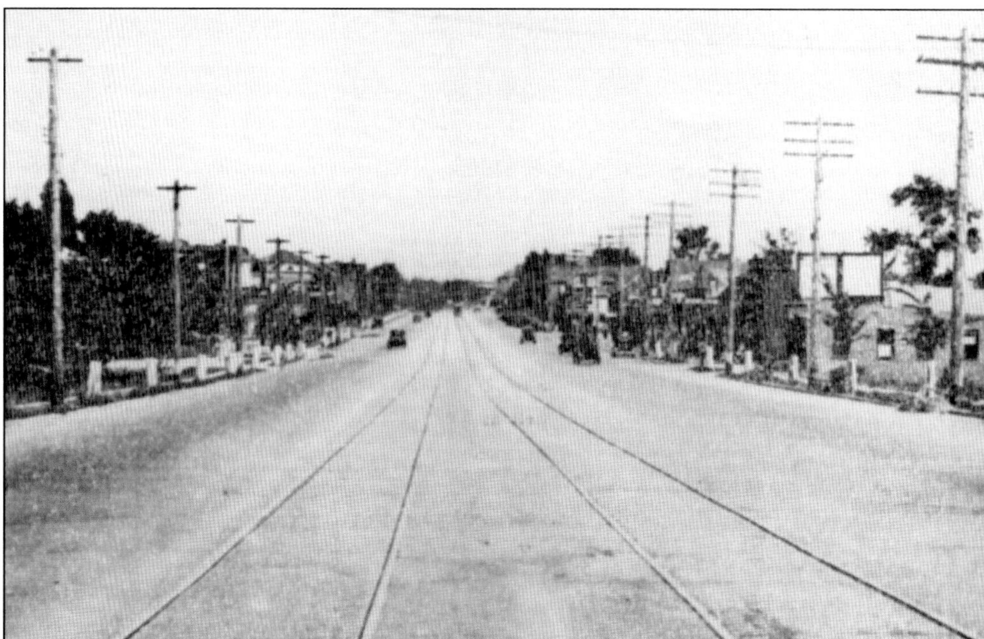

In May 1932, the streetcar line gave permission to pave the track area itself (shown looking east from the District of Columbia border). On completion of that project, the broad paved highway through the center of town was completed and a grand celebration was held. (Courtesy of City of Mount Rainier.)

In 1916, the state legislature enacted a bill that was approved later in a public referendum granting the town power to issue $100,000 in bonds to construct a municipal water and sewer system. The referendum's results were challenged but upheld in court. Construction began, but in 1919, the town sued the contractor, who then countersued. The town ultimately won. In 1922, the system, water tower, and springs were sold to the Washington Suburban Sanitary Commission (WSSC). In this only known photograph of the water tower (below), it is visible above the houses during the dedication ceremony for St. John's Church in 1934. One provision of the sale was that WSSC would supply water to the town's buildings for free in perpetuity. As late as 2015, the long-abandoned wood pipes wrapped in wire continued to be excavated as WSSC performed maintenance. (Right, courtesy of Bryan Knedler; below, courtesy of Walter Plumley.)

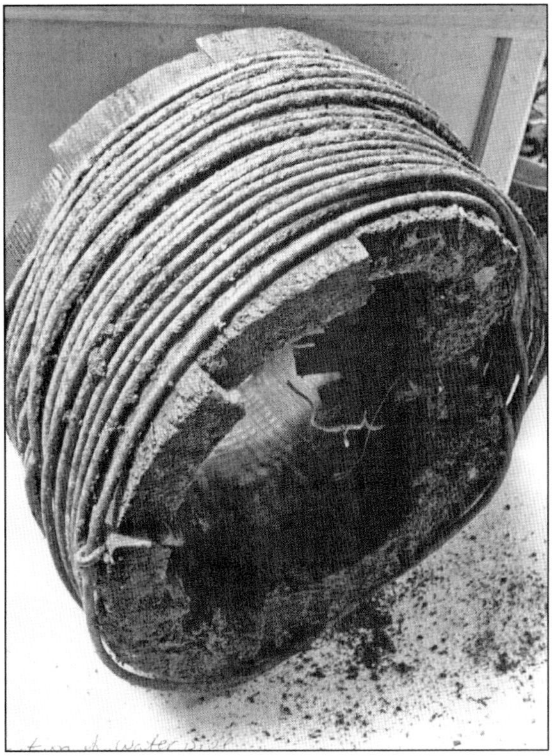

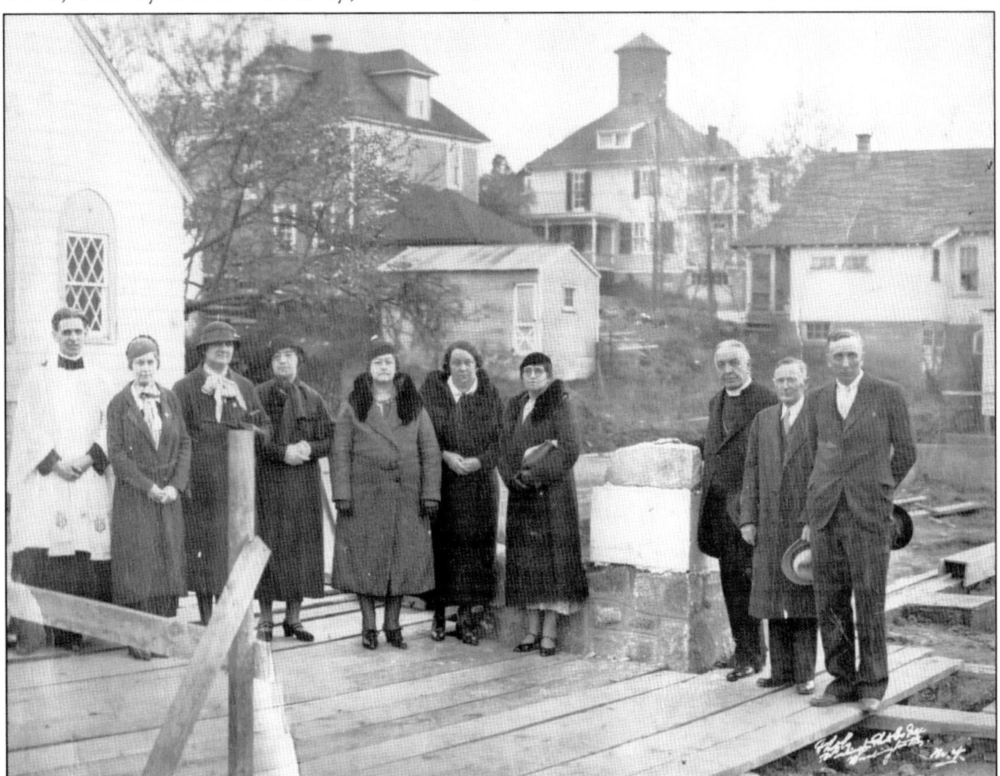

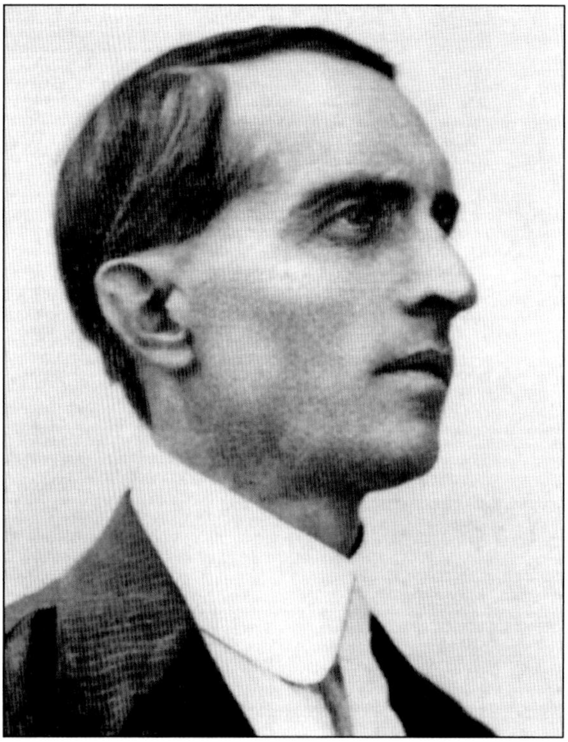

William E. Rider (left) was elected mayor in 1921. Like many others in the community, he was a federal employee, in his case at the US Government Printing Office. Fred Negus (below) was born in England, came to America in 1910, and was elected mayor in 1923. The paid police department was created during his tenure. Prior to that, the town had constables. A referendum to raise the tax rate to support a paid police force failed in 1928, but the issue arose again in 1934 after a county court held that the town's unpaid police bailiff could no longer use the tainted system of accepting part of a fine as a salary. (Both, courtesy of City of Mount Rainier.)

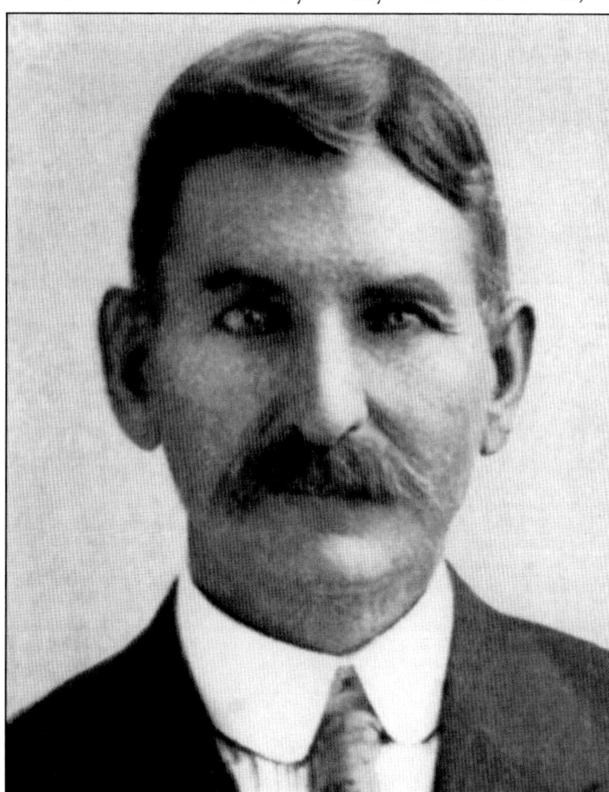

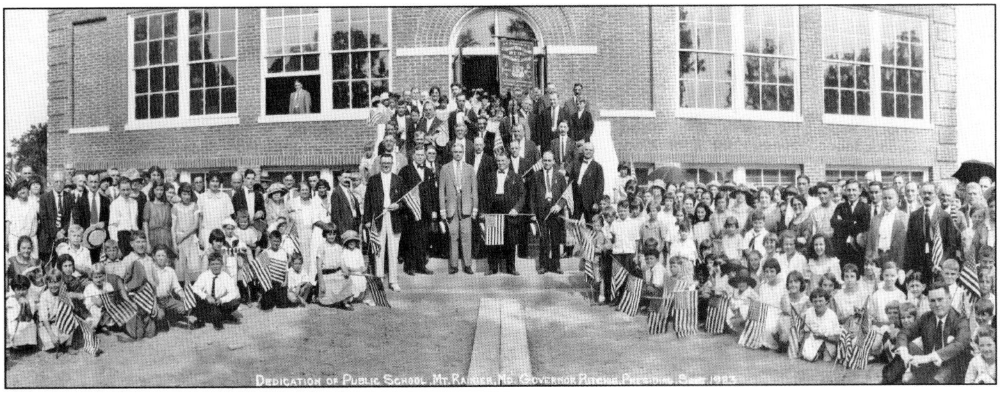

Prior to World War I, Mount Rainier children attended the Brentwood School. With the growth of the population during the war, a new school was required, which opened in 1923 on Thirty-second Street. Former mayor Vanneman was widely credited with securing the state funds of $25,000. A parade preceded the dedication ceremony, at which Gov. Albert Ritchie spoke (above). The building was equipped with electric lights, steam heating, eight classrooms, and an auditorium. The building remained in use until the 1970s, when it was razed and the current school built. The Citizens Association next took up the cause of funding a high school. (Both, courtesy of City of Mount Rainier.)

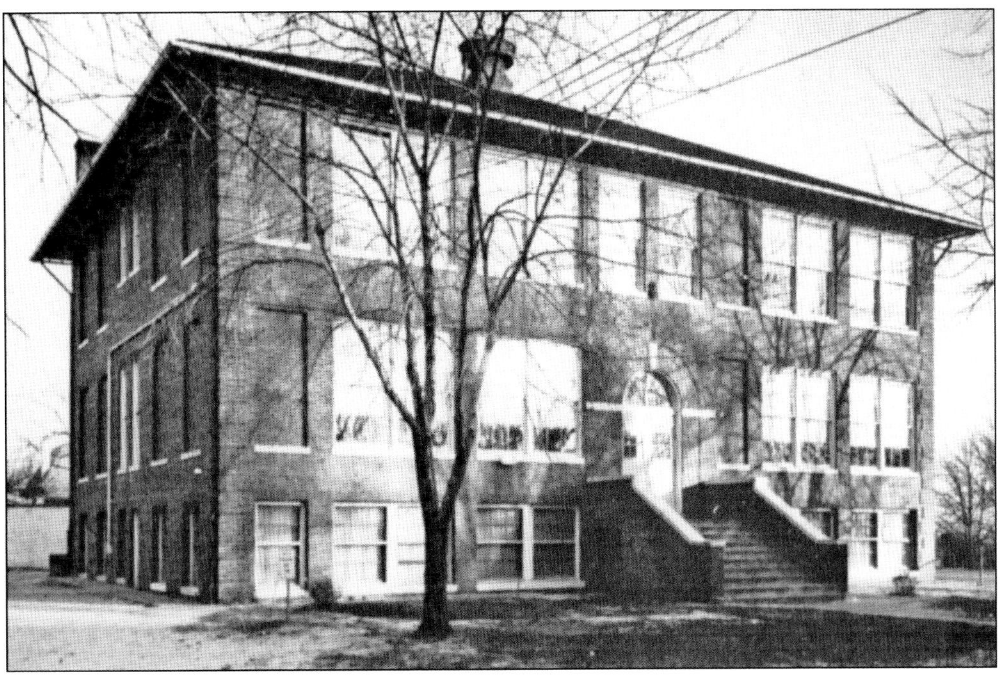

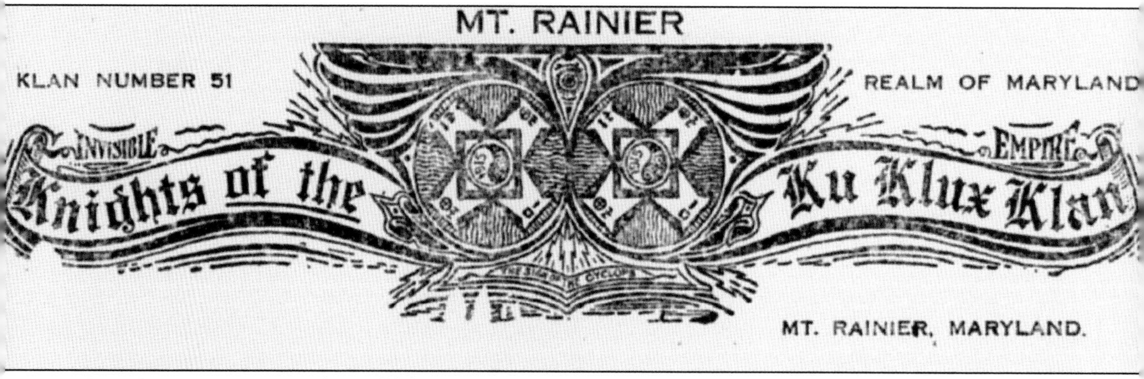

In 1976, new owners of an old house found items in the attic that had belonged to the Mount Rainier Knights of the Ku Klux Klan, including white hooded robes and written meeting records. Although the records provide a glimpse of the activities of at least a small group, it is difficult to determine from this limited cache how much support existed in the community for Klan activities. After all, in addition to its racist doctrine, the Klan was anti-Catholic and anti-immigrant in a town filled with just such people. For example, when the Klan disrupted a school graduation because a Catholic priest gave the invocation and benediction, the Mount Rainier Chamber of Commerce publicly expressed its disapproval, stating that "we do not feel such action in anyway shows the sentiment of a majority of our better-thinking citizens." The klavern's first cross burning lasted only 20 minutes because the volunteer fire department arrived to put out the flames. The Klan letterhead pictured here and other documents now reside at the University of Maryland. (Courtesy of University of Maryland, Hornbake Library.)

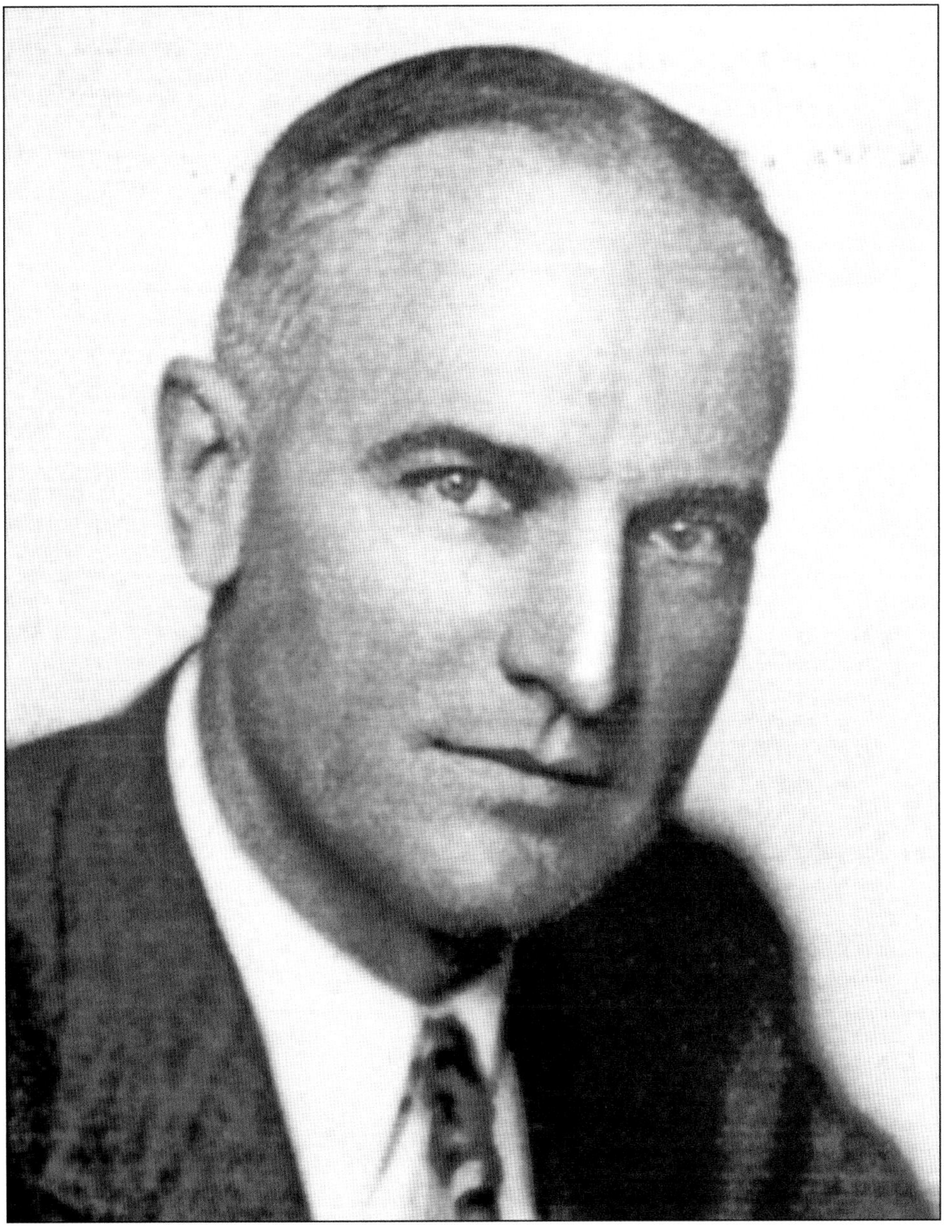

The Klan meeting minutes leave no doubt about the involvement of some local elected officials. Kenneth Bovay (pictured) thanked the members for their support in his election as mayor in 1925. The names of at least three town council members of that era are included in the meeting minutes as Klan members. Participants lived not only in Mount Rainier, but also in Brentwood, Colmar Manor, Cottage City, Hyattsville, and Washington, DC. In 1925, Klan chapters in Hyattsville, Mount Rainier, Capitol Heights, and Laurel sponsored a Fourth of July celebration in Berwyn that according to news accounts attracted 25,000 people from Maryland and neighboring states. Bovay served as mayor only a few months, resigning when he moved out of the town. When the Klan ceased to exist in Mount Rainier is unknown, but the town remained nearly all-white into the 1960s. Mount Rainier was what is known as a "sundown town," meaning that African Americans were not tolerated within the town limits after sunset. (Courtesy of City of Mount Rainier.)

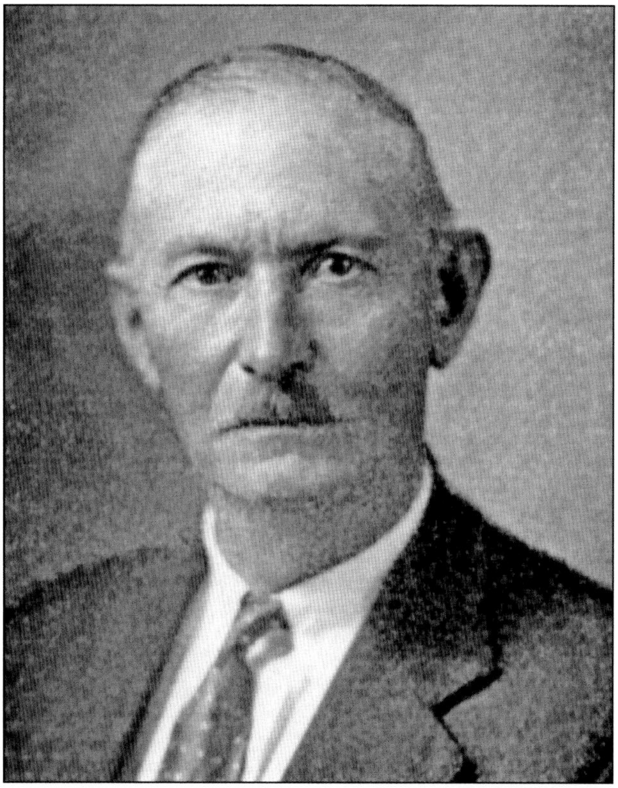

John H. Beall was appointed mayor in 1926 after the resignation of Kenneth Bovay. He served during the Great Depression. His administration employed otherwise jobless men to improve the streets—paving them and the sidewalks, erecting street signs, and planting trees. Beall's motto was "a dollar's worth of service for every dollar spent." He later served as judge for the Prince George's County Orphans Court. (Courtesy of City of Mount Rainier.)

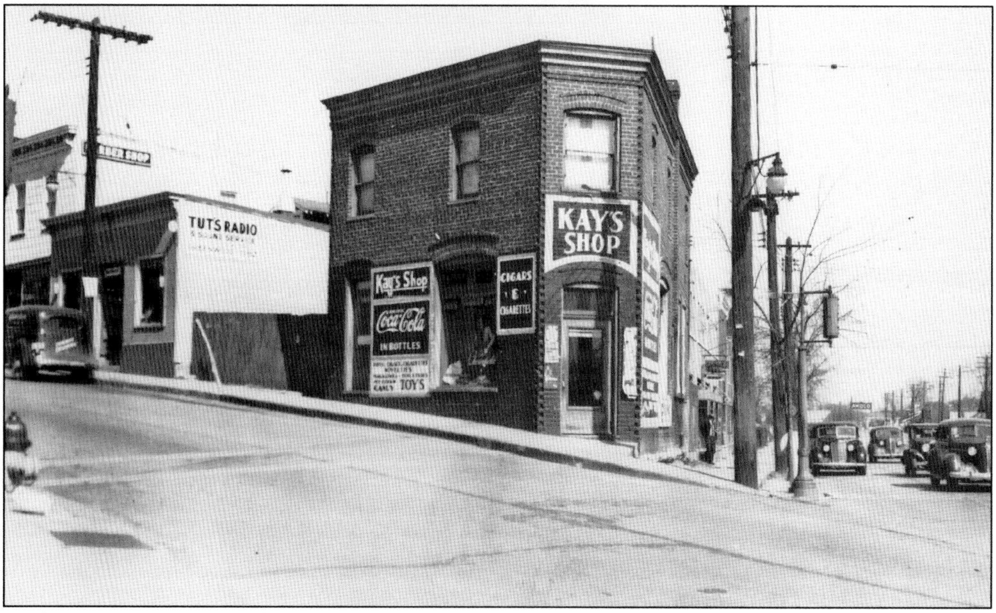

In the 1920s, a brick building replaced the Mikules pharmacy at Thirty-fourth Street and Rhode Island Avenue. The first traffic lights and streetlights were installed on the avenue in the 1920s (both visible on street-side poles) to control the ever increasing numbers of automobiles. The traffic light became a revenue generator, as motorists paid fines for running it. (Courtesy of William Holton.)

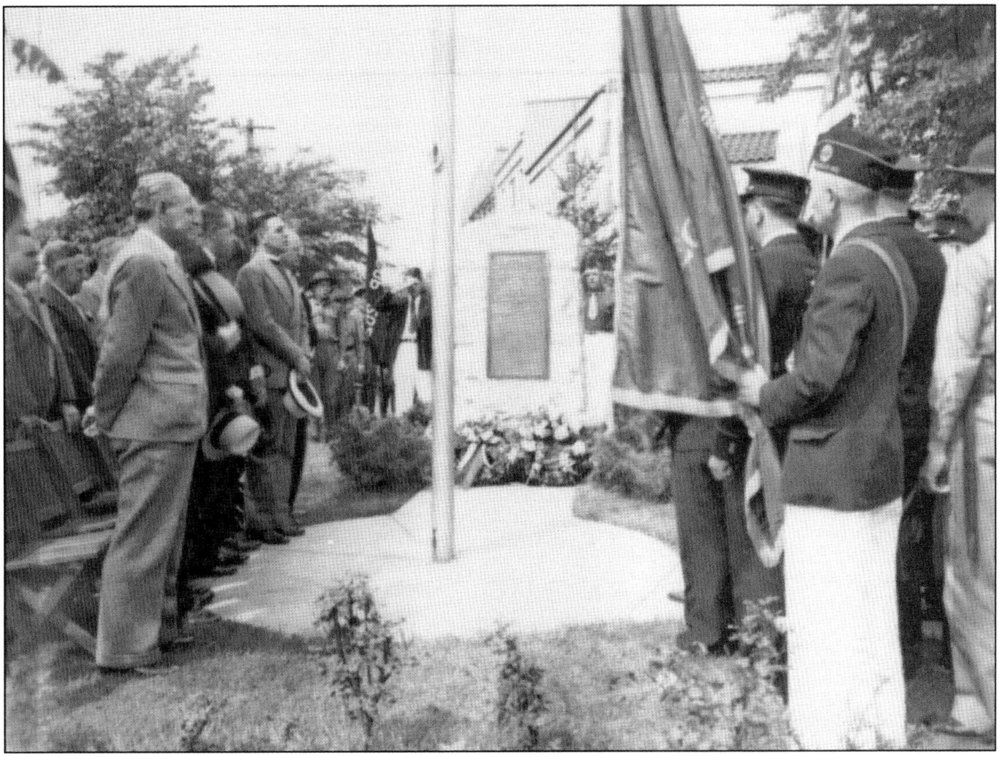

Memorial Park began as a public works beautification project in 1926 and included the planting of barberry bushes, which persisted at the site even in 2015. The small park has been renovated and replanted numerous times over the decades. The granite monument, with names of prominent citizens, was erected in 1938. At the dedication ceremony, Charles Haskins, a member of the memorial committee, said the stone was a reminder "that the princes among us are those who forget themselves and selfish interests to serve their fellow-man." The first names on the memorial were those of three deceased mayors: William Vanneman, Fred Weber, and William Rider. (Above, courtesy of Walter Plumley; right, courtesy of Bryan Knedler.)

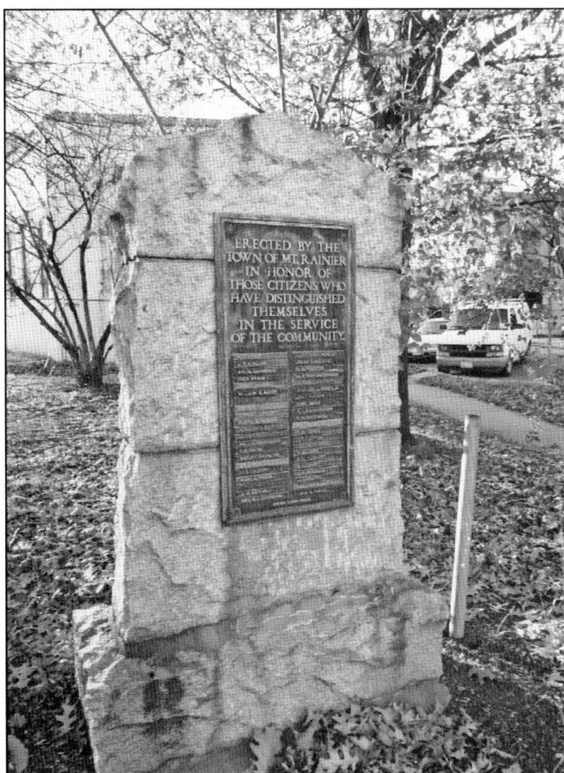

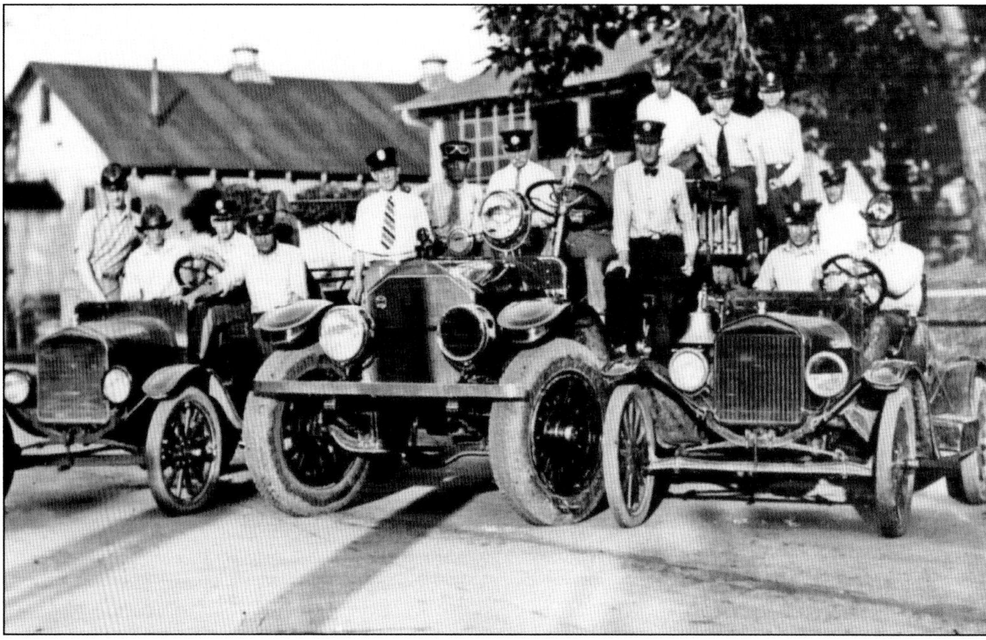

Mount Rainier Volunteer Fire Department (MRVFD) members proudly display their apparatus. From left to right are (first row) Joe McMan, Billy Donohoe, Charlie Alexander (at steering wheel), unidentified, Arthur Bates, Clarence Moore, John Klein, Ed Chase (at steering wheel), unidentified, Chief Karl Young, and George Lee (at steering wheel); (second row) Joe Plumer, Bernie Beal, Harvey Wilson, and Reggie Austin. (Courtesy of Bunker Hill Volunteer Fire and Rescue Co.)

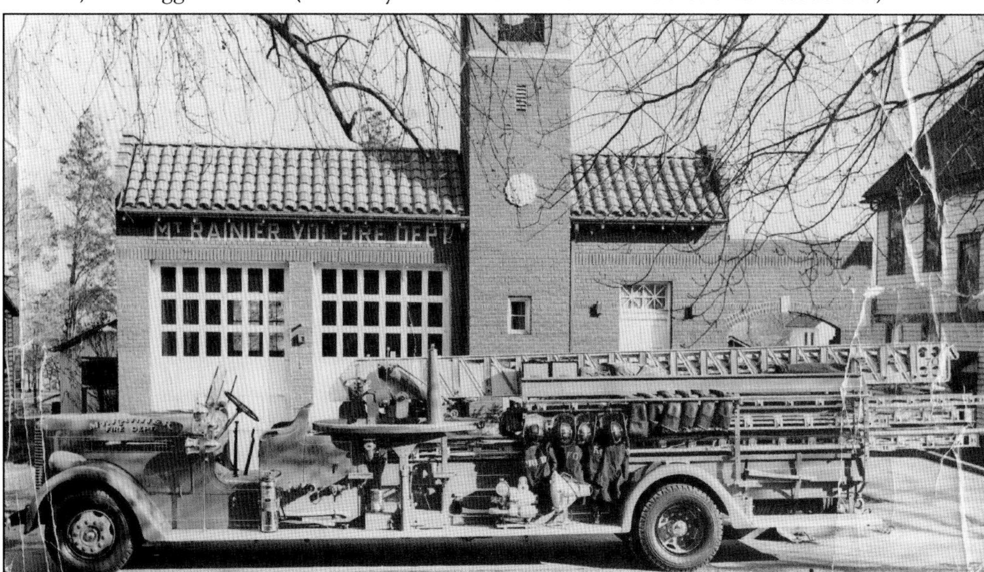

In 1925, a brick building replaced the 1911 frame firehouse at Thirty-fourth and Shepherd Streets. An American LaFrance pumper was purchased in 1926, but it then was replaced in 1935 with a 750-gallon Seagrave single-stage pump (pictured). That apparatus remained in use until 1956. By 1938, it was increasingly difficult to get experienced drivers during the workday, so a paid driver, James Mezzanotte, was put on duty during daylight hours. (Courtesy of Bunker Hill Volunteer Fire and Rescue Co.)

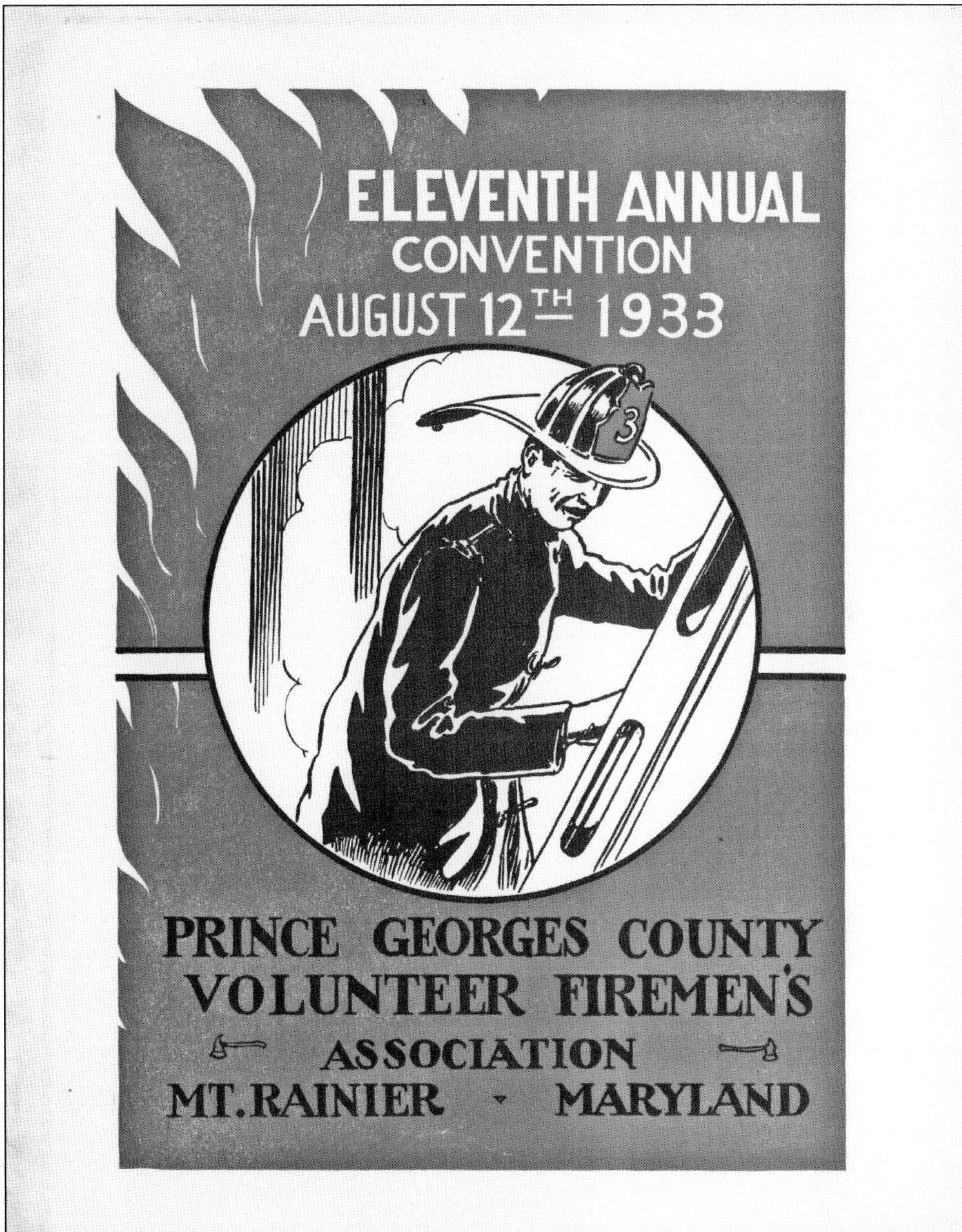

The Mount Rainier Volunteer Fire Department was one of the four founding departments of the Prince George's County Volunteer Fireman's Association in 1922. In 1933, the MRVFD hosted the 11th Annual Prince George's County Firemen's Convention. For many years, the MRVFD was financed from dues paid by members and the proceeds of carnivals and other fundraising projects, such as door-to-door solicitations from residents. In 1929, the state legislature authorized the town to levy a property tax of no more than 10¢ on each $100 of assessed valuation for use of the Mount Rainier Volunteer Fire Department, so long as it was used for equipment and supplies. That tax continued until 1992, when controversy over the purchase of a house adjacent to the fire station resulted in a change to the city charter. (Courtesy of Bunker Hill Volunteer Fire and Rescue Co.)

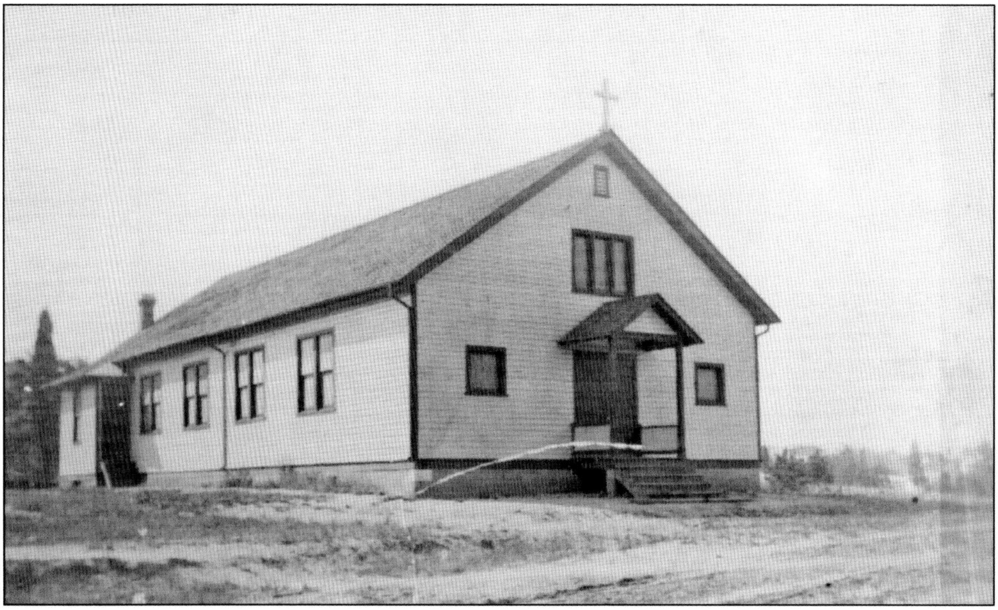

The original Catholic church was built near the intersection of Bunker Hill Road and Thirty-sixth Street in 1908. Prior to that, mass was held at the Fireman's Hall in Brentwood. The organizational meeting was held at the home of Dr. Harry Nalley. Father Malloy, the pastor at St. Francis DeSales on Rhode Island Avenue in the District of Columbia, took charge at St. James and led the efforts to build the present church. (Courtesy of City of Mount Rainier.)

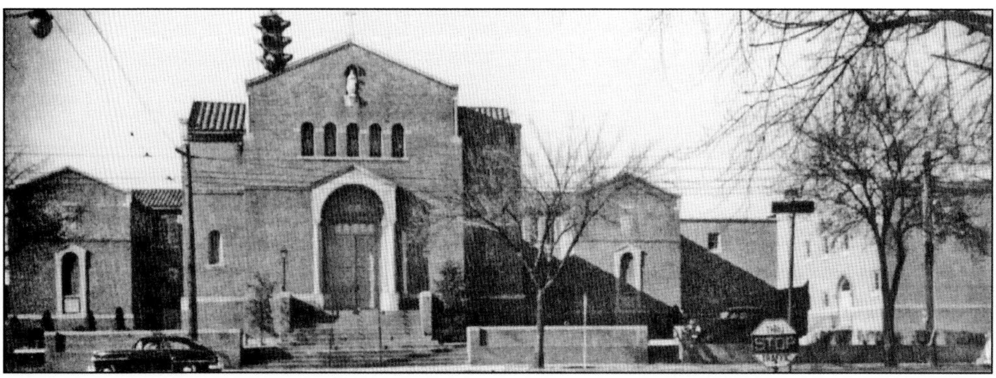

The present-day St. James Catholic Church, designed by the firm of Murphy & Olmsted in the Romanesque Revival style, opened its doors in 1926 on Rhode Island Avenue. The church remained a mission of St. Francis DeSales Church (located at Rhode Island Avenue and Twenty-second Street in the District of Columbia) until 1946. (Courtesy of M-NCPPC.)

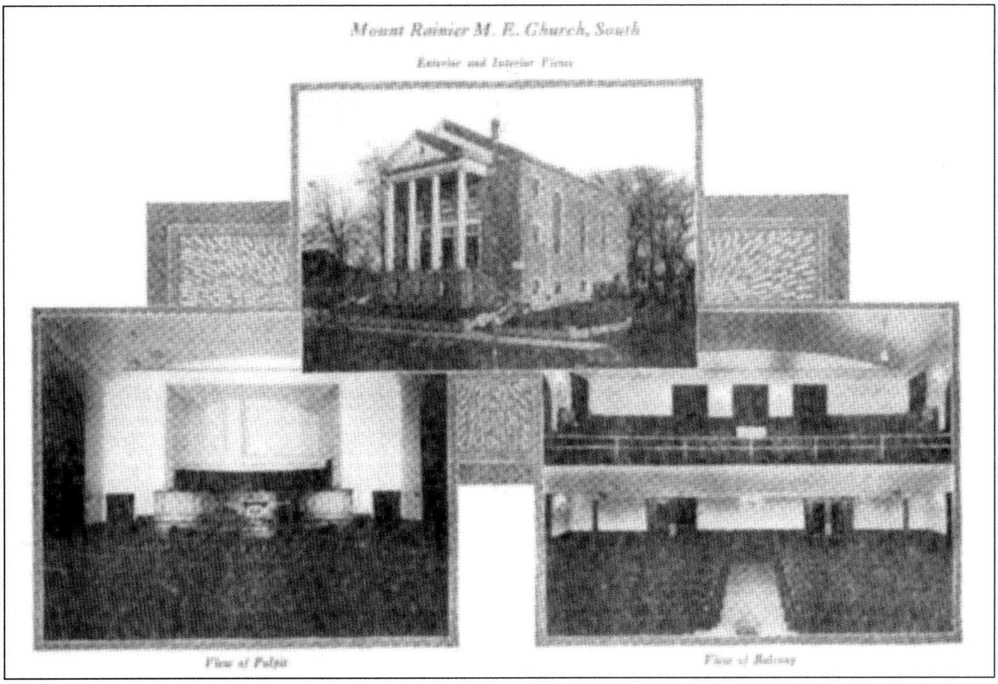

The Mount Rainier Methodist Episcopal Church began as a mission of the Hyattsville Methodist Episcopal Church South and met in a converted barn at Thirty-seventh and Upshur Street in Brentwood. In 1916, a group petitioned the Methodist bishop of Maryland to establish a separate church, which held its first service at Potts Hall in April 1916. In July 1916, the congregation erected a tent and, later that year, a church built of wood on the site of the present church (which was constructed in 1924) on Bunker Hill Road. The stone church was designed by Washington architect Rossel Edward Mitchell, with many features in the Beaux Arts style. In 1955, an addition was made in the Colonial Revival style and included the brick bell tower. (Above, courtesy of PGCHS; below, courtesy of Bryan Knedler.)

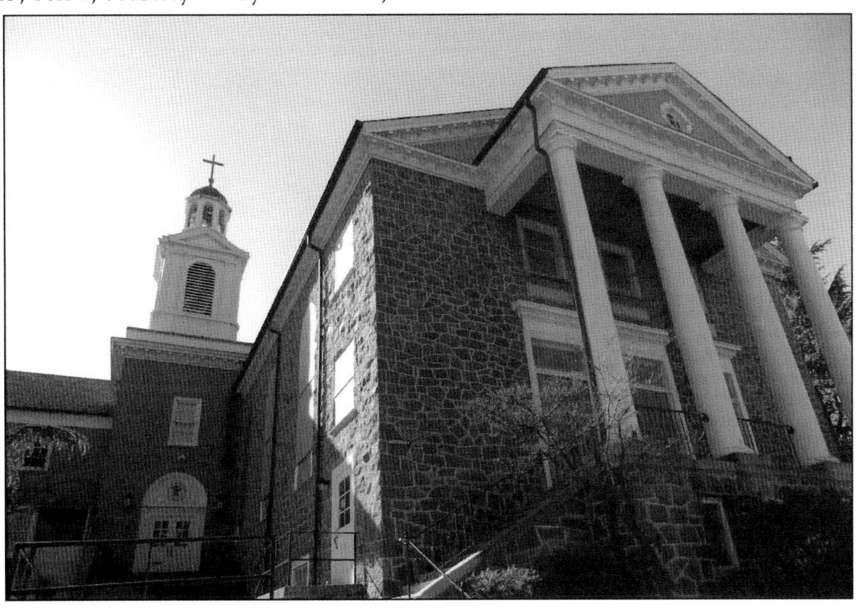

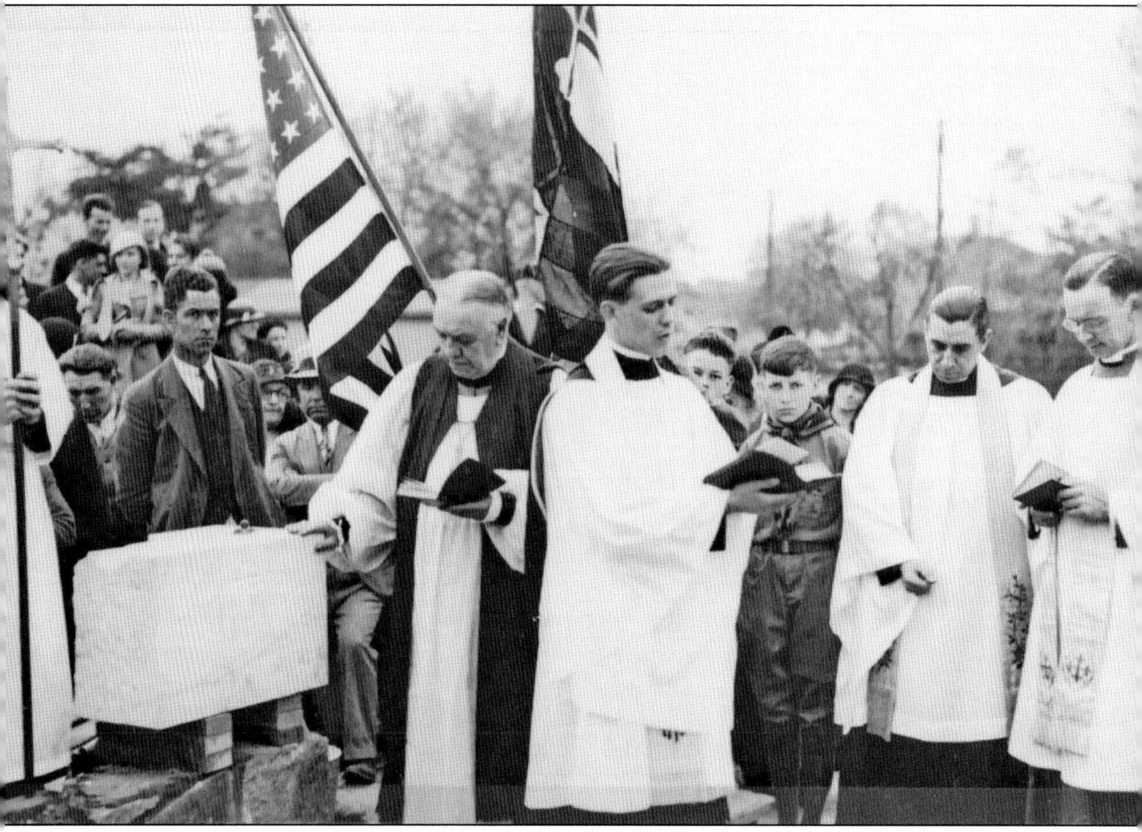

In 1934, the St. John's Episcopal Church congregation built a new brick and stone chapel erected by local construction firm Martin Brothers in an interpretation of the English Country Gothic style. Those attending the cornerstone ceremony included, from left to right, Lawrence Miller, Francis Xander (behind cornerstone), Bishop James E. Freeman, Rev. Walter Plumley, Boy Scout Raymond Wolven, Rev. Clyde Brown (from Hyattsville), and Reverend Canon. Other churches were built around the same time, including Trinity Lutheran Church at Thirtieth Street and Bunker Hill Road in 1937, and First Baptist Church at Shepherd and Thirty-second Streets in 1925. (Courtesy of Walter Plumley.)

Before supermarkets, residents relied on small local stores within walking distance. Neighborhood stores included Gordon's Grocery, 4301 Thirtieth Street; Kaywood Market, 4114 Twenty-ninth Street; the District Grocery, 3100 Bunker Hill Road; and Egan's Market, 4131 Thirty-fourth Street. The former Harry's Market (pictured) has been converted to residential use, as have all the others. (Courtesy of Jimmy Tarlau.)

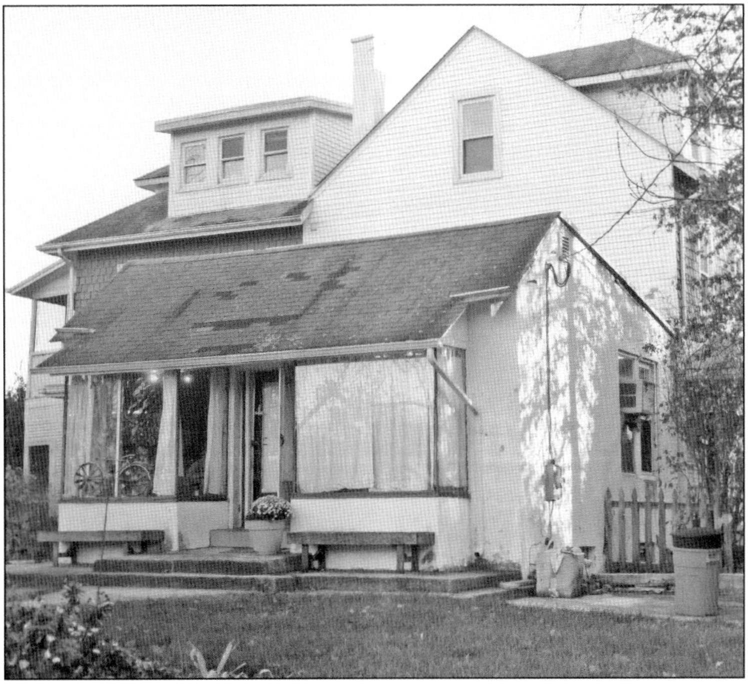

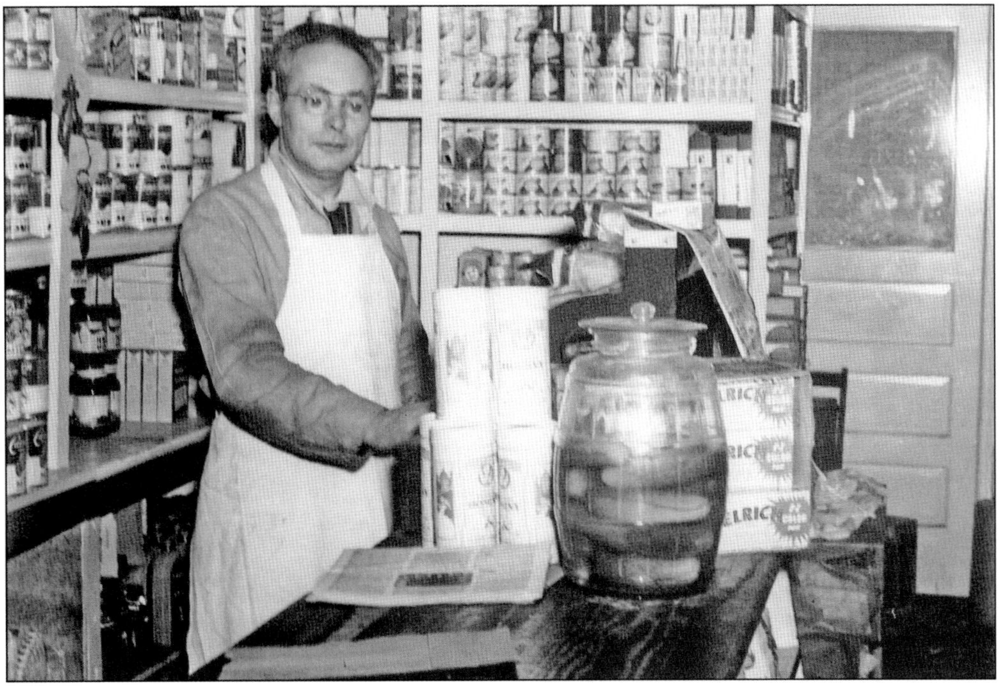

Harry and Leah Weinstein opened Harry's Market at Upshur Street and Rainier Avenue in 1926 as a District Grocery, a local chain of Jewish markets, and lived in the house behind the storefront. Their daughters Vivian and Ruth continued the business until their retirement in 1997. Harry is pictured here in the 1950s. (Courtesy of Jewish Historical Society of Greater Washington.)

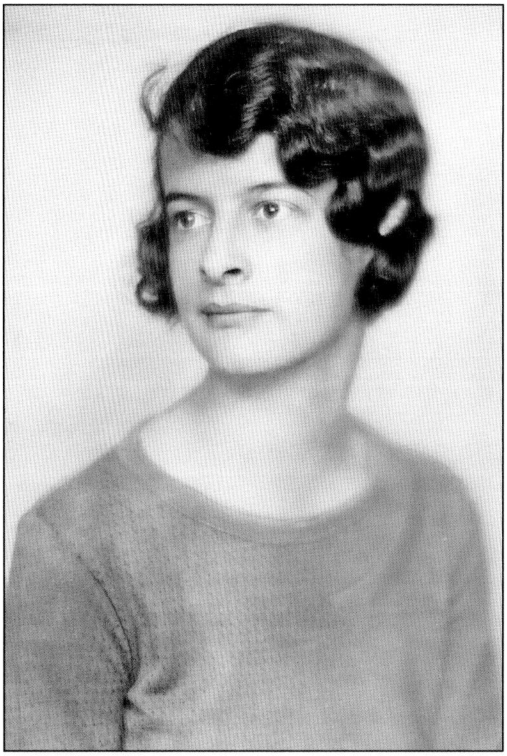

On the night of November 4, 1935, Corinna Loring was murdered on "Lover's Lane" in the lonely Saddleback Ridge (now the Kaywood Apartments area). Her body was found beaten, bitten, and strangled just two days before her planned marriage. The tragic news brought hundreds of people to see the crime scene. The aerial view below shows the location of the Loring home on Beech (now Taylor) Street in relation to the wooded murder site in today's Kaywood area. The sensational murder of the bride-to-be was reported from New York to Los Angeles, Chicago to Miami. The crime was never solved. She was buried in her wedding gown at Fort Lincoln Cemetery. (Both, courtesy of DC Public Library.)

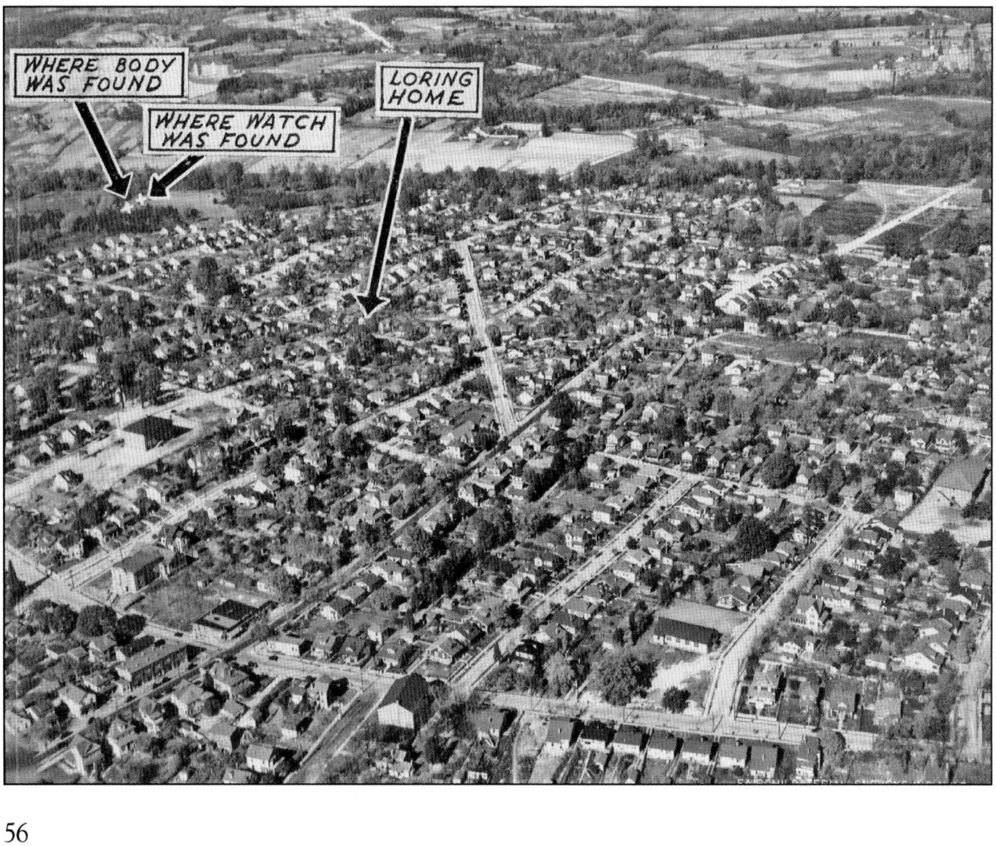

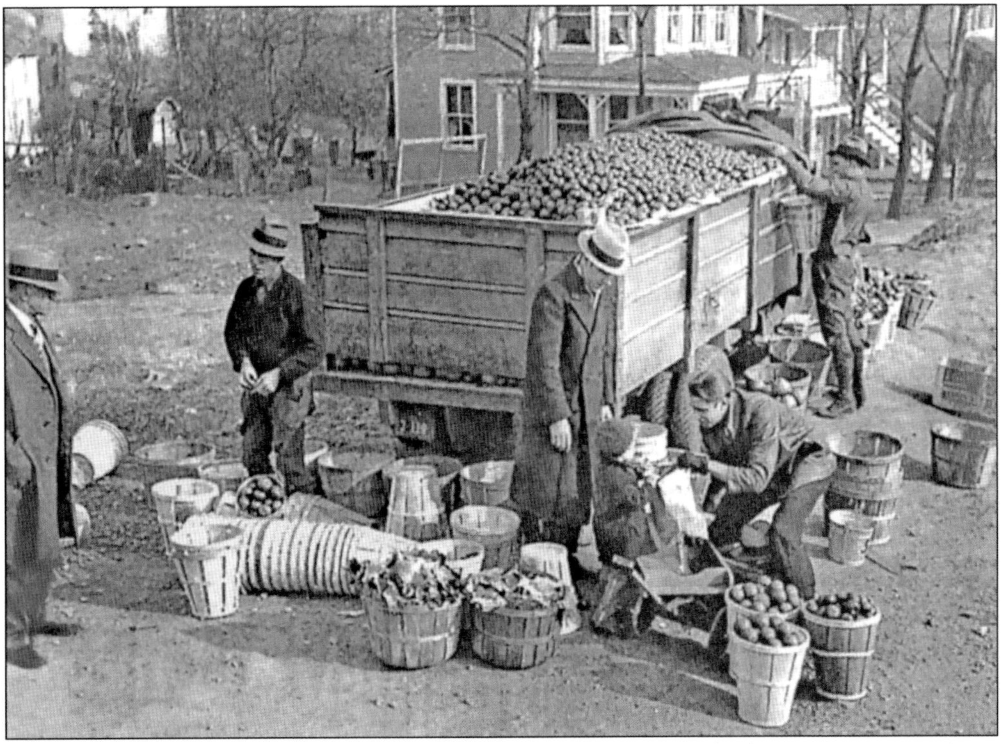

Above, Raymond M. Hollidge Sr. stands over his son as he buys apples from a wagon in 1931, at what today is the intersection of Eastern and Rhode Island Avenues (now US Route 1), but at that time was adjacent to the trolley tracks. By 1939, Nalley's Funeral Home (below) occupied the site. The house visible above behind the apple wagon is located where the Bass Restaurant would later stand. The town in 1932 employed jobless men to build brick pillars adorned with art deco lamps to mark the city limits. The City of Mount Rainier bought these properties in the early 21st century and sold them as part of a mixed-use redevelopment project. (Above, courtesy of Raymond M. Hollidge Jr.; below, courtesy of Debbie Farrell.)

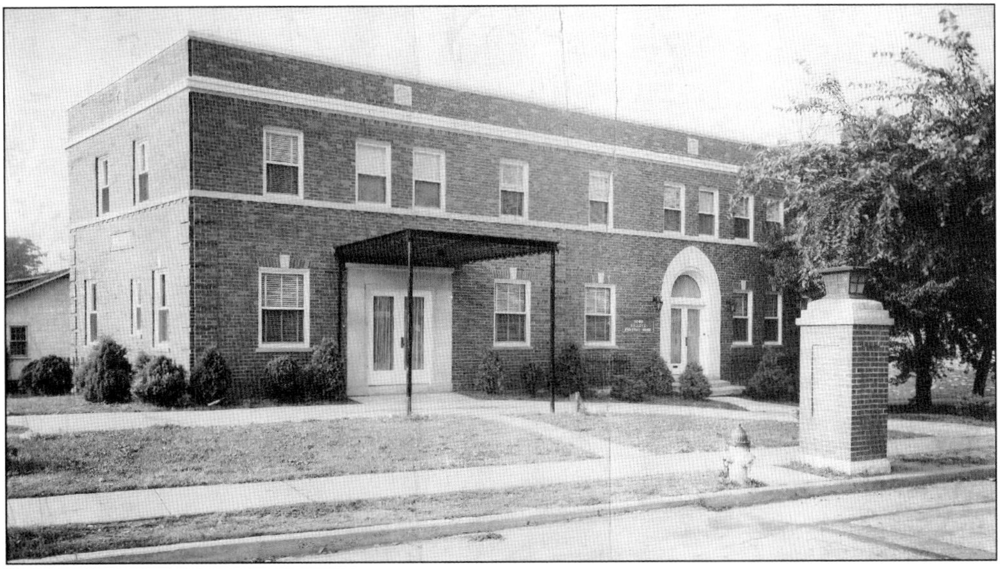

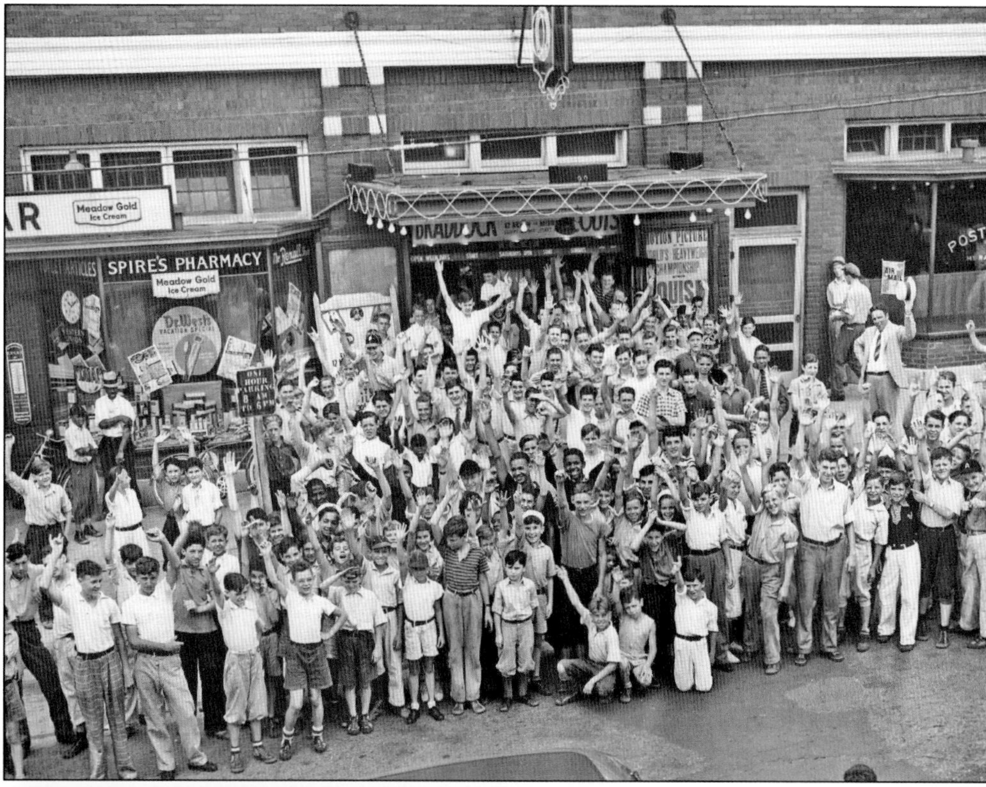

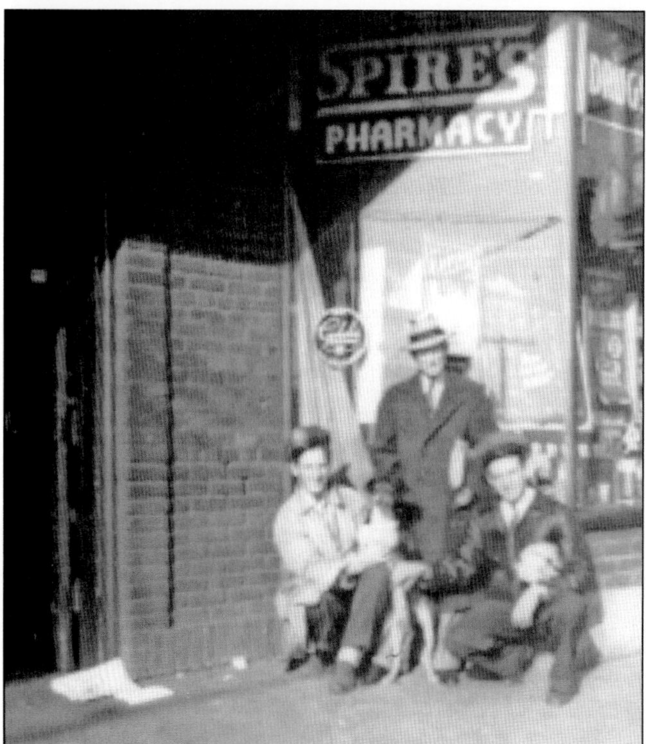

Children wave for the camera after a matinee at the Cameo Theater, 3822 Thirty-fourth Street, in the 1930s. An open-air theater operated by Andrew Crawford had opened at the same location in 1923 and seated 400, making it one of four open-air venues in the area. The enclosed Cameo was built by the Crawford-Spire Theater Corporation in 1927. William Spires moved his pharmacy into a storefront next to the theater. The other storefront served as the town's post office until 1953, when it moved to 3709 Rhode Island Avenue. The photograph above offers rare documentation of black and white children together in that segregated time. (Above, courtesy of Paul Sanchez; left, courtesy of James R. Rice Jr.)

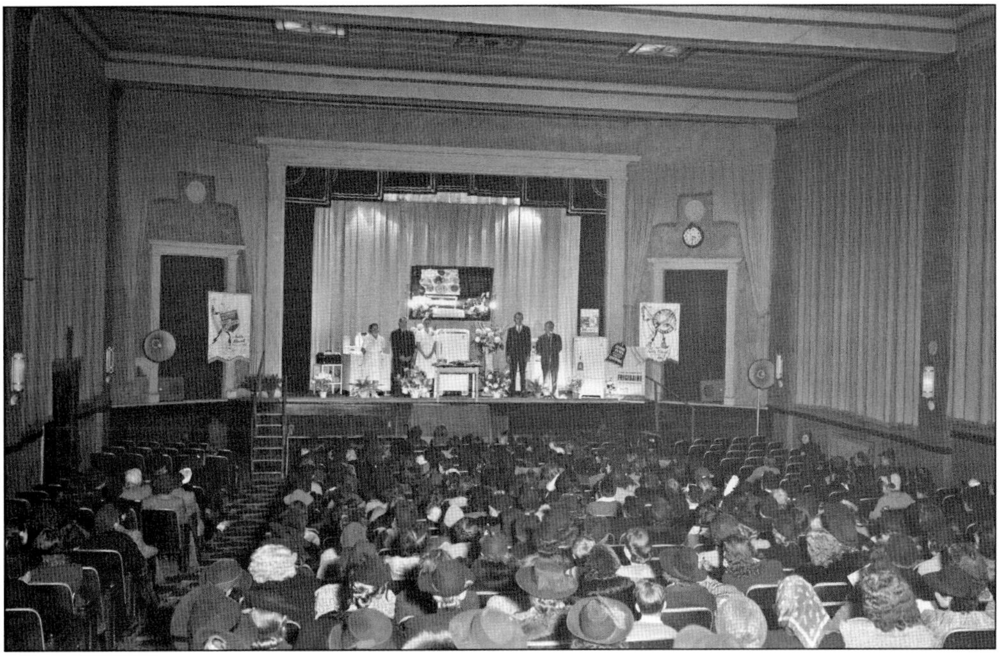

Until the 1930s, many homes were heated with coal and refrigeration relied on the regular delivery of ice blocks. The Electric Institute of Washington sponsored cooking classes around the region—the one seen above took place in the Cameo Theater—to encourage women to embrace new electrical kitchen appliances, including electric stoves and refrigerators. Theodor Horydczak's photograph offers a rare view of the Cameo's interior. He worked as a commercial photographer for clients like the Potomac Electric Power Company and real estate firms. He also supplied Pepco with photographs of typical neighborhood homes and streetscapes, such as the one below of the homes on Date (now Varnum) Street that the utility used to design electrical substations disguised as homes so as to be unobtrusive. (Both, courtesy of Horydczak Collection, Library of Congress.)

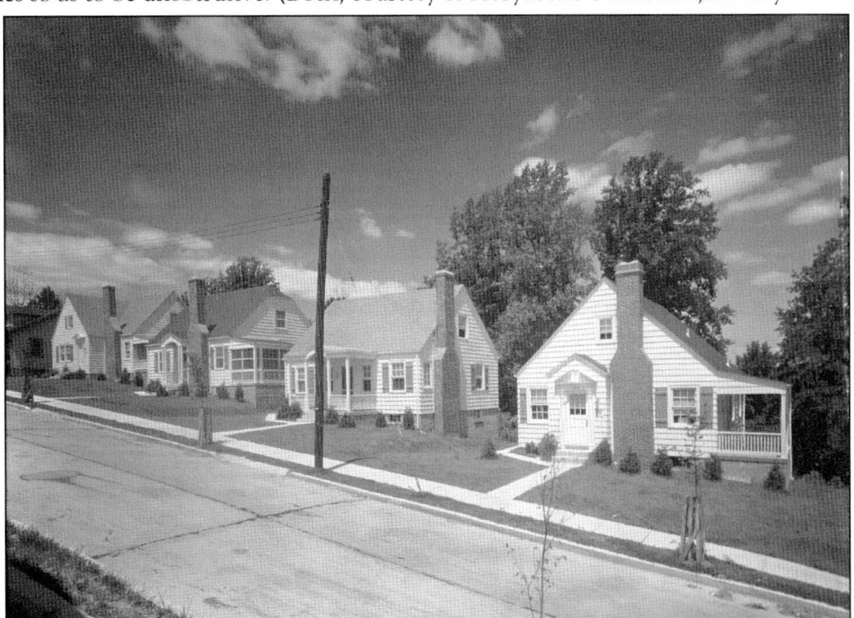

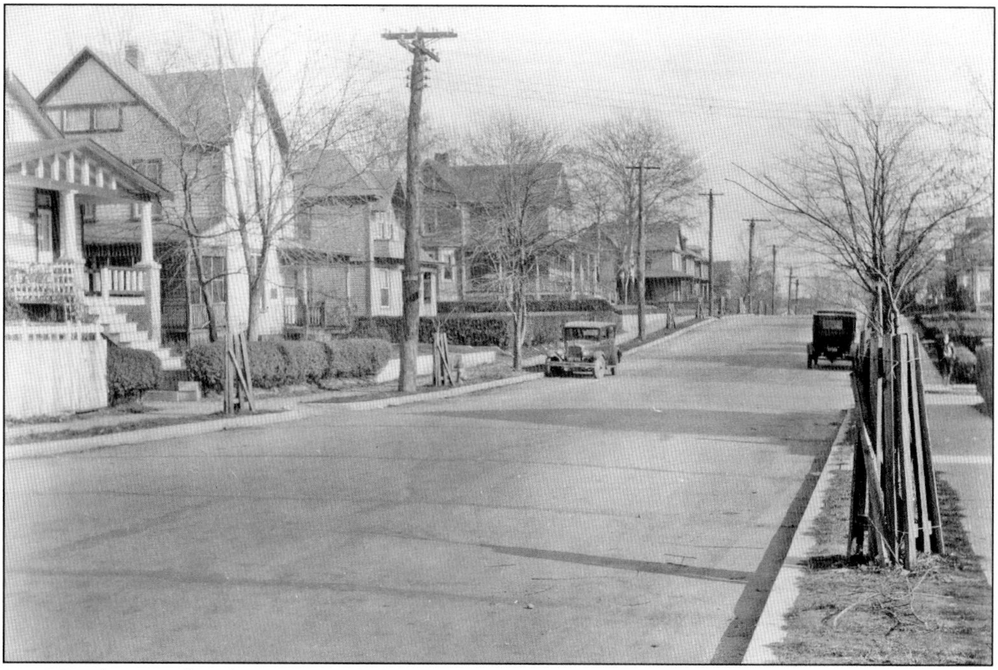

In 1920, the state legislature provided for issuance of bonds for construction of sidewalks, streets, and gutters. Above, this section of Newton (now Perry) Street between Thirty-fourth and Thirty-seventh Streets was the first to be paved. Ross Kimmel, a retired historian for the Maryland Park Service, provided these photographs by Fred W. Besley, a state forester from 1908 to 1942, who was documenting the street tree plantings in 1930. Some of the elms planted at that time still stand, despite the ravages of Dutch elm disease, which was introduced into the United States around 1930. The photograph below shows newly planted street trees in the 3700 block of Thirty-fifth Street. The house at the end of the street is now the site of city hall. (Both, courtesy of Maryland Forest and Park Gift Collection, Maryland State Archives.)

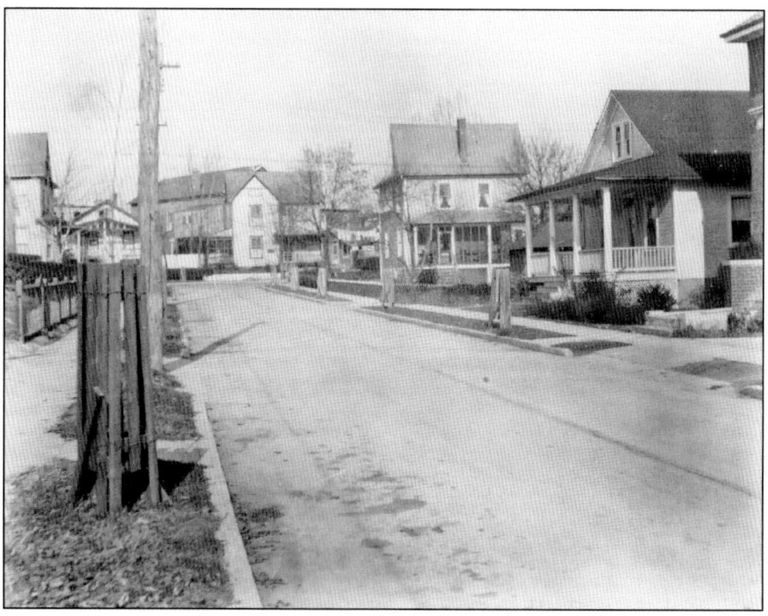

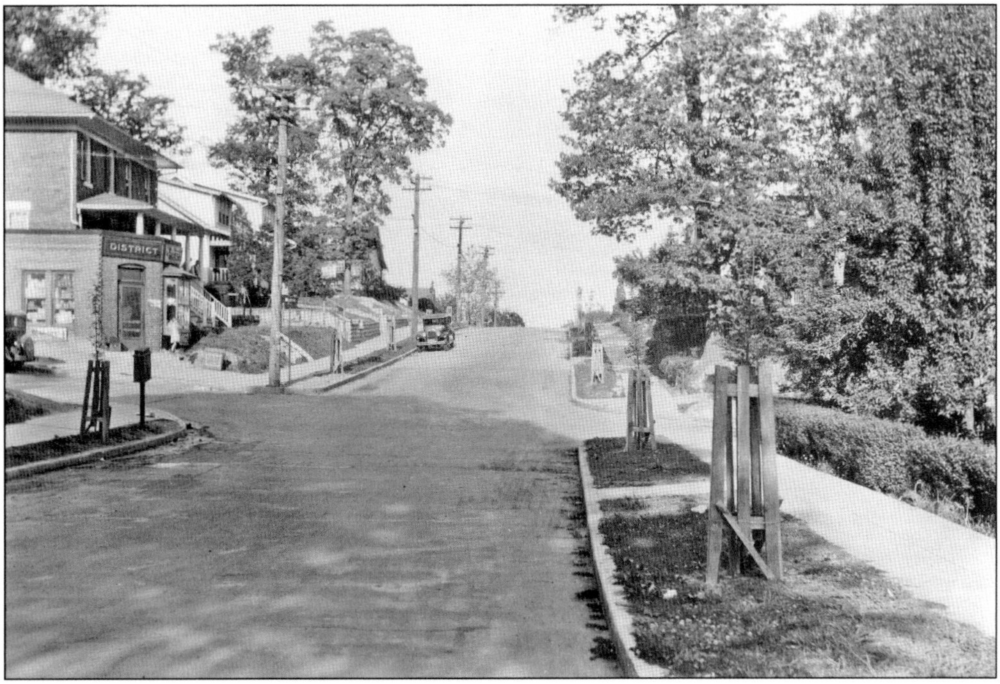

In 1927, the prior road improvement act was replaced with a comprehensive measure for the construction of roads, curbs, sidewalks, and gutters to be financed by town bonds. Abutting property owners were assessed on a front footage basis, with payments to be made in 10 annual installments with interest. These photographs captured the state foresters' efforts to meet the desire for street trees in the 1930s. The photograph above is of the 3100 block of Bunker Hill Road (the District Grocery is visible on the left). The image below shows the 3200 block of Ash (now Shepherd) Street, along which were planted—not coincidentally—ash trees. (Both, courtesy of Maryland Forest and Park Gift Collection, Maryland State Archives.)

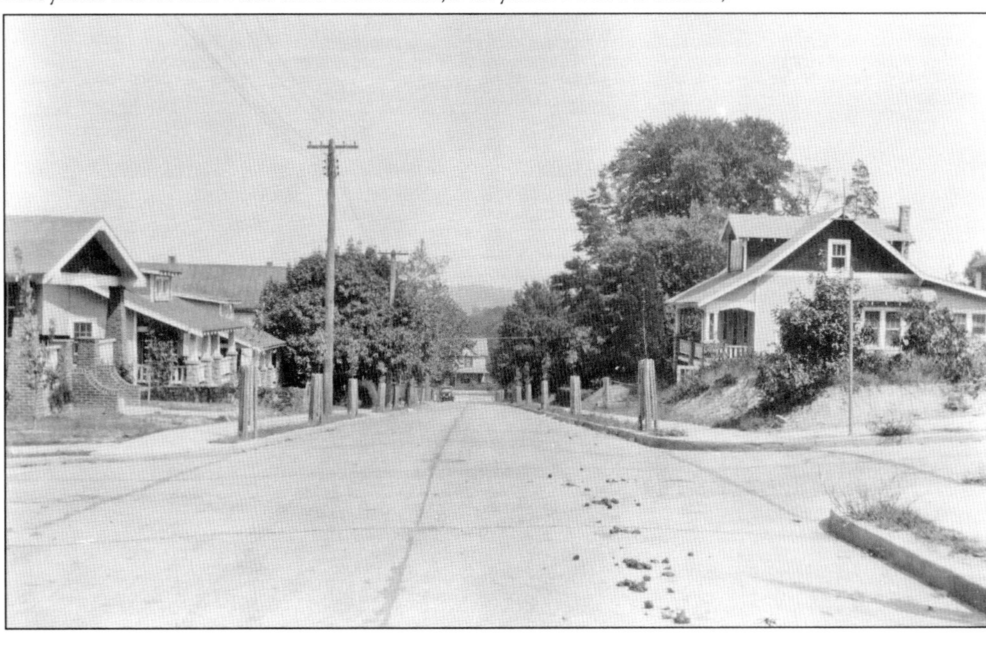

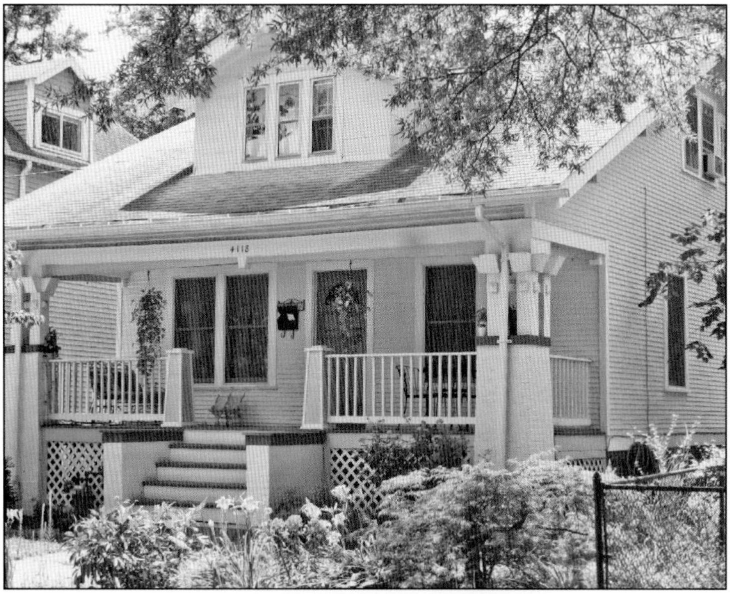

Mount Rainier can boast a number of Sears houses, sold through the Sears Roebuck catalog, with each style given a distinct name; seen at left at 4118 Twenty-ninth Street is a Vallonia model. All components were precut and shipped to the site. Sears did not supply plaster or masonry, but sheet plaster, the forerunner of drywall, was available at extra cost. (Courtesy of Bryan Knedler.)

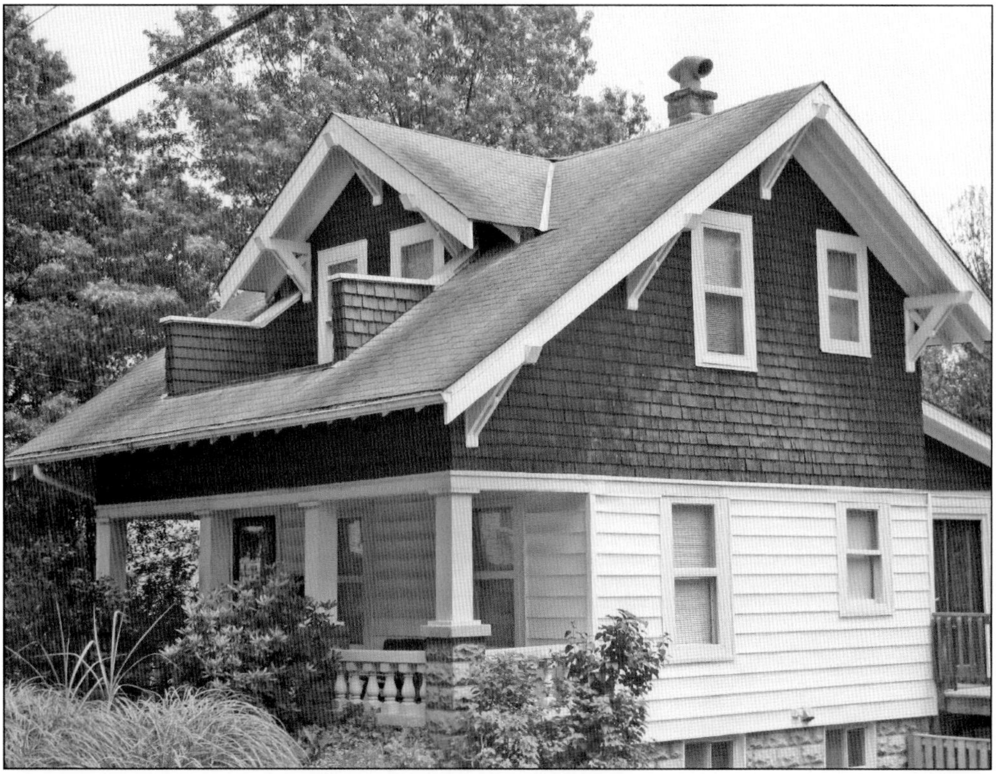

The city's Sears houses vary in age, with some built before 1920. The following homes are identified as Sears houses: 3207 Upshur Street (Windsor model, pictured), 3424 Newton (Winona), 3505 Rhode Island Avenue (Avoca), 3004 Upshur Street (Conway), 3114 Upshur Street (Conway), 3112 Varnum Street (Oak Park), 4115 Twenty-eighth Street (Lakecrest), 4203 Twenty-eighth Street (Conway), 4118 Twenty-ninth Street (Vallonia), 4215 Twenty-ninth Street (Vallonia), 4507 Twenty-ninth Street (Cornell), and 4223 Thirty-fourth Street (Avoca). (Courtesy of Bryan Knedler.)

Three

World War II and the Baby Boom

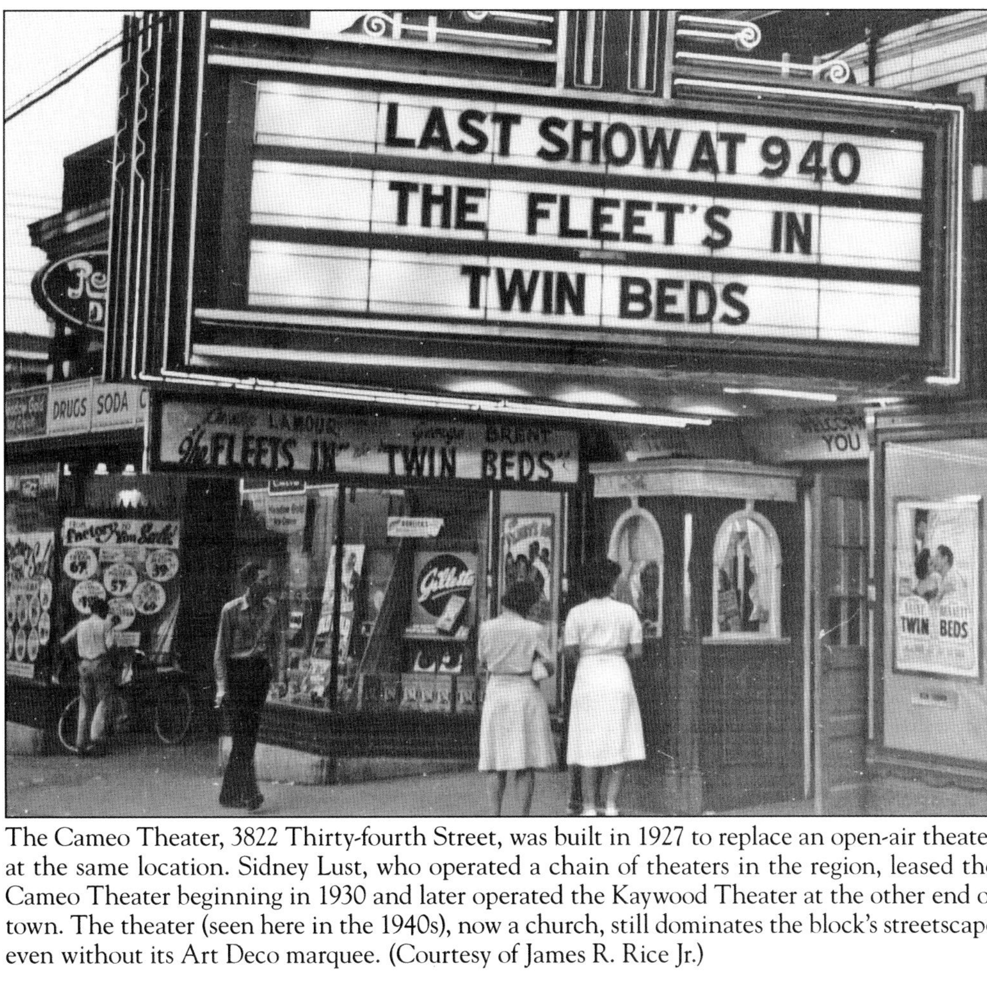

The Cameo Theater, 3822 Thirty-fourth Street, was built in 1927 to replace an open-air theater at the same location. Sidney Lust, who operated a chain of theaters in the region, leased the Cameo Theater beginning in 1930 and later operated the Kaywood Theater at the other end of town. The theater (seen here in the 1940s), now a church, still dominates the block's streetscape even without its Art Deco marquee. (Courtesy of James R. Rice Jr.)

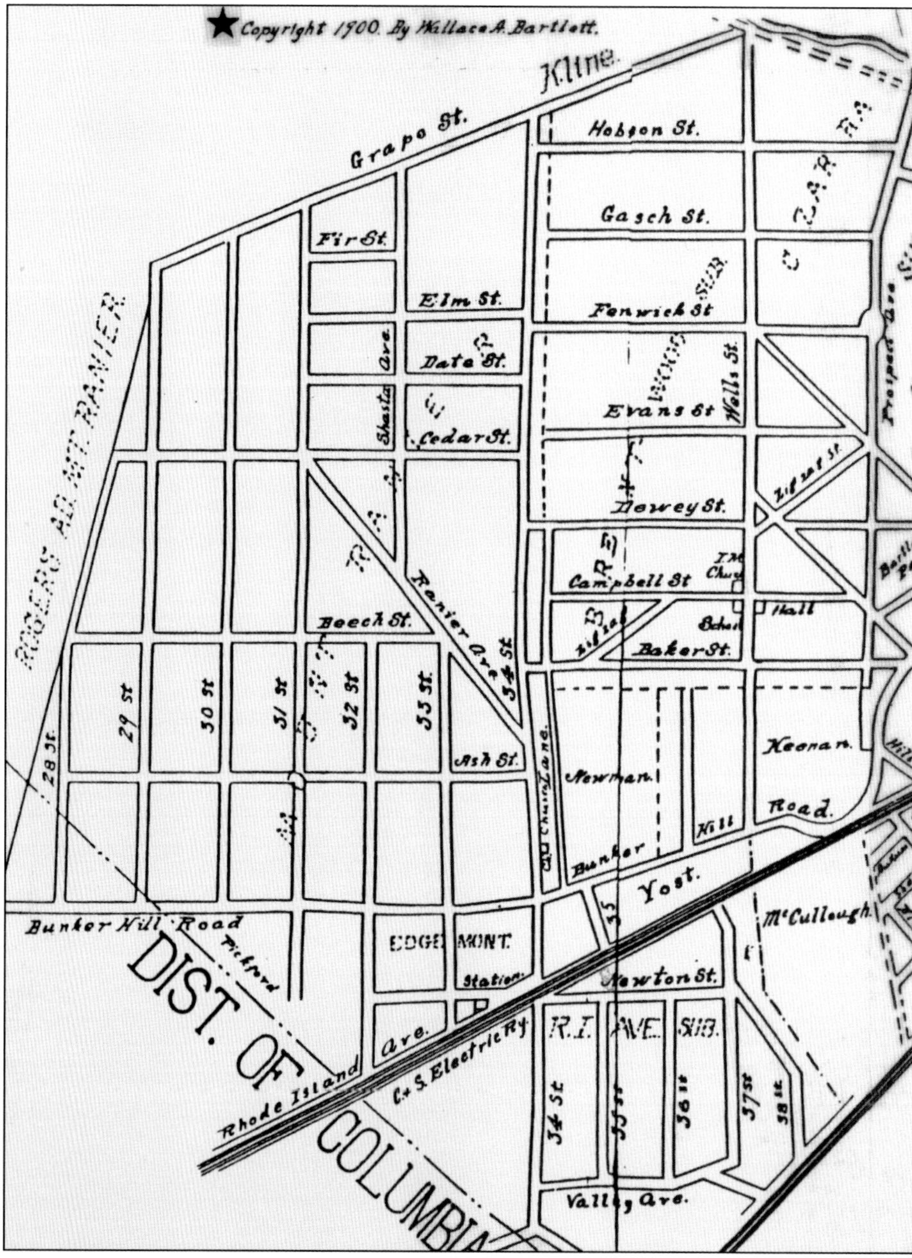

This Wallace A. Bartlett map shows the former street names; a 1940 project renamed them to continue the District of Columbia system, renumbering addresses on each block to match the District's numbering system. Local residents could argue to keep an old name, and did so to retain Bunker Hill Road—the original road of the area and with a rich history—instead of changing it to Randolph Street to correspond to the District's naming convention. For that reason, Mount Rainier to this day lacks a 3900 block of any north-south street. East-west streets north of Bunker Hill originally had botanical names in alphabetical sequence—Ash (Shepherd), Beech (Taylor), Cedar (Upshur), Date (Varnum), Elm (Webster), Fir (Windom Road), and Grape (Arundel Road). Present-day Perry Street was originally called Newton Street. Otis Street was at first known as Valley Avenue, which made sense, given the topography. (Courtesy of City of Mount Rainier.)

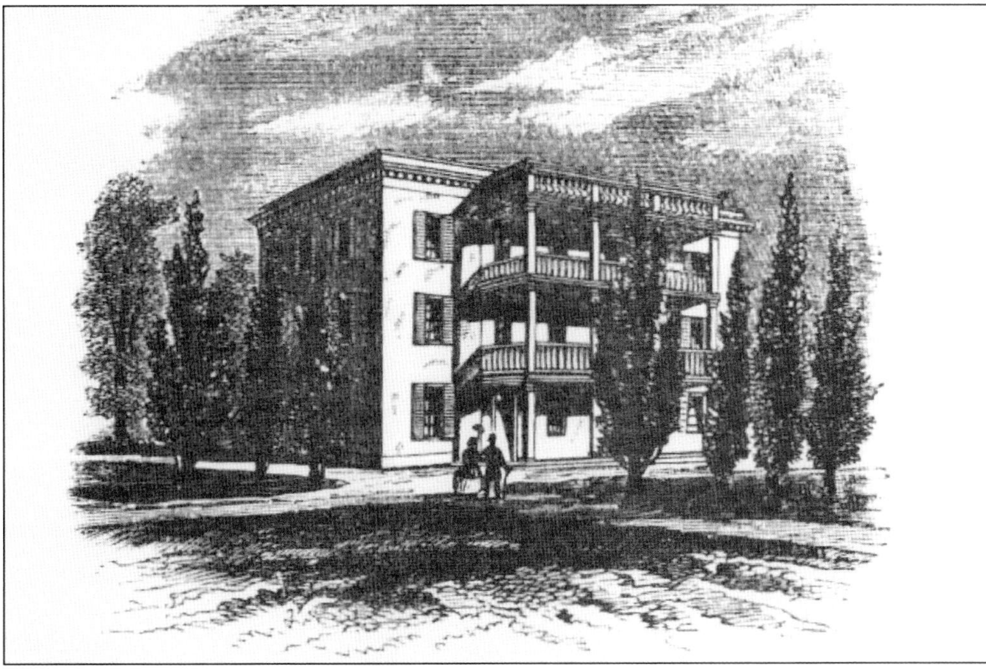

In the 1930s and 1940s, an antebellum mansion just inside Maryland on Bladensburg Road housed a well-known casino: the Maryland Athletic Club, or "Jimmy's Place," after owner Jimmy LaFontaine. The property strategically straddled the border. The casino closed in 1949 after LaFontaine's death. In the mid-19th century, that mansion was the home of John Rives, founder of the *Congressional Globe* (seen above, drawn in 1869 for Benson Lossing's *Pictorial Field-book of the War of 1812*). Prior to Rives owning the farm, it was at the epicenter of the 1814 Battle of Bladensburg. After Rives's death in 1864, he was buried in a vault near the house but then reburied in Congressional Cemetery in the District (LaFontaine is also buried there). Locals remembered that the empty granite sarcophagus with its inscription remained outside the casino for many years. The Cottage City Volunteer Fire Department burned the Rives home/casino in 1955 as a training exercise. (Above, courtesy of Bryan Knedler; below, courtesy of Teresa Wilcox.)

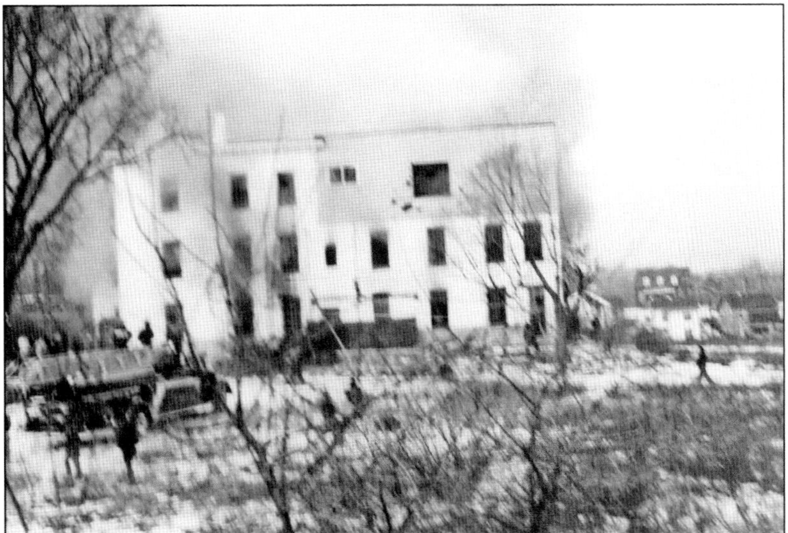

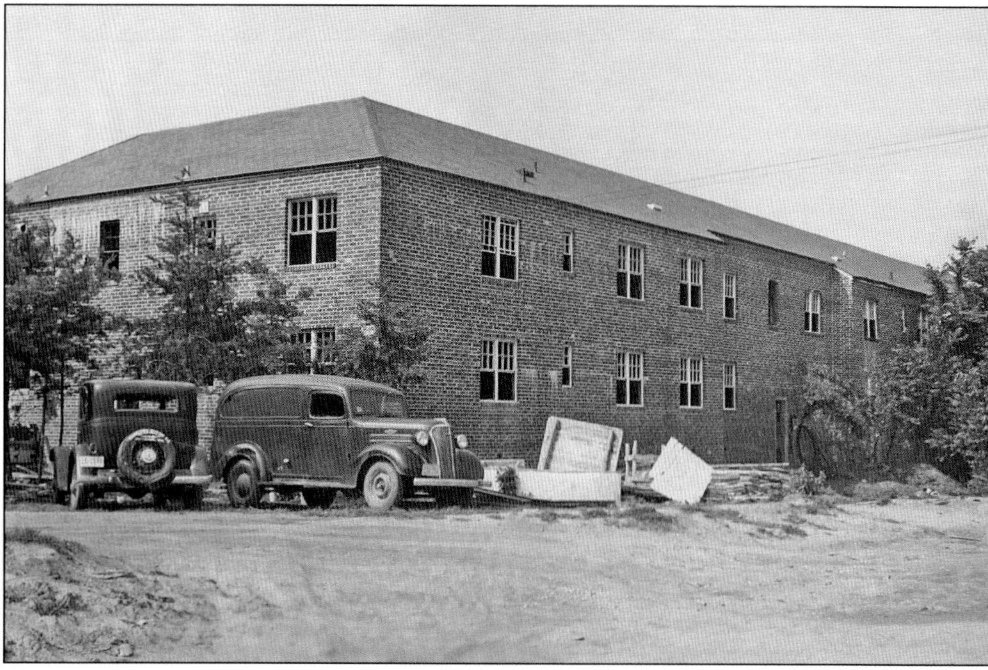

The federal government encouraged the building of more housing for its workforce, which swelled during the Franklin Roosevelt administration. The *Prince Georgean* newspaper editorialized in favor of new apartment complexes, maintaining that the locations might otherwise become "so-called low-cost housing projects such as dominate other sections, or the well-named Alley-Housing projects which now seem to be the vogue in the haste to get living quarters for the incoming people of wartime Washington." Shown here is the construction of Kaywood Gardens, which opened its first units in 1941. The town's 1940 population of 4,830 swelled to 10,989 by 1950. During the 1950s, players of the Senators baseball team lived in the complex. Author and gay rights activist Larry Kramer lived there with his parents in the 1940s. (Both, courtesy of Kay Management.)

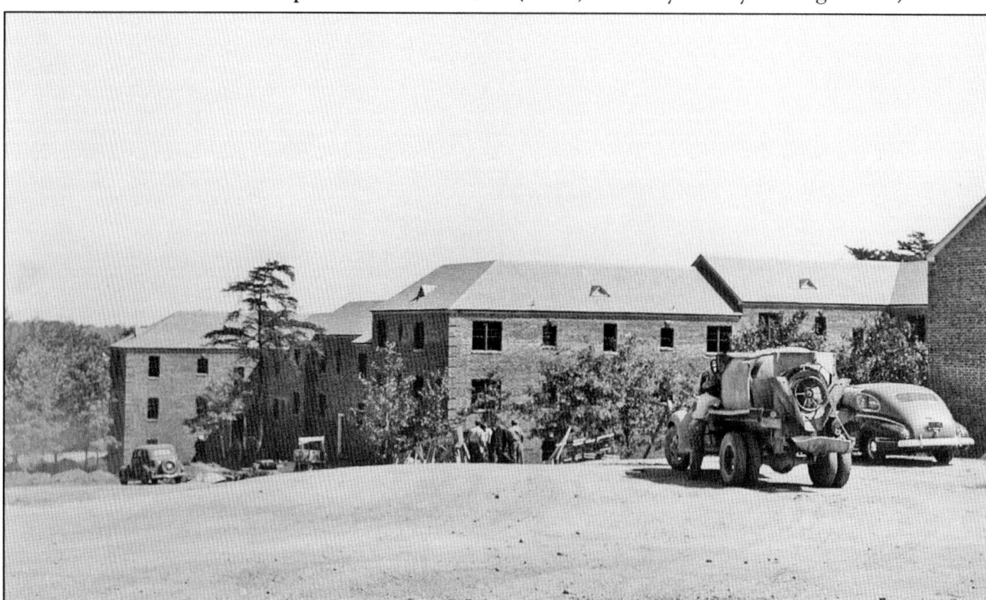

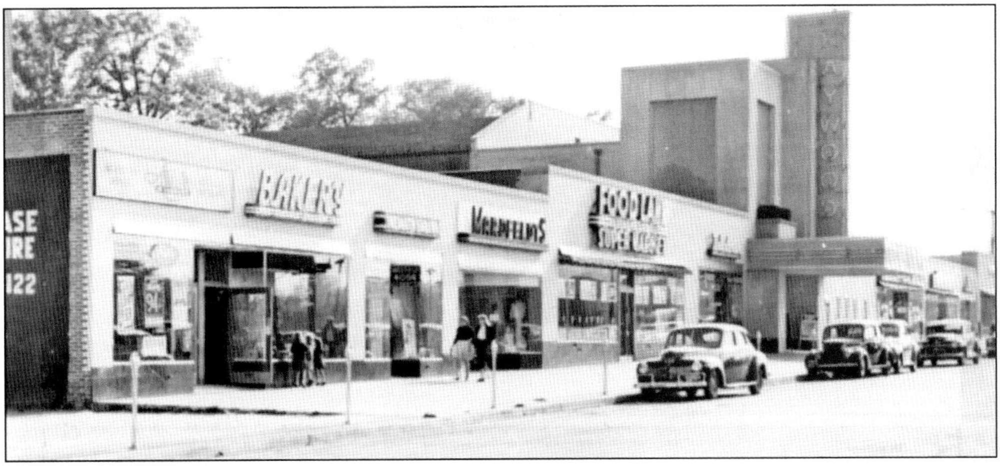

Abraham Kay and Frank Wasserman developed the Kaywood Gardens Apartments in the 1940s. With the building of the complex, a new business district was created on Varnum Street to serve the tenants of the new buildings and as an alternative to Rhode Island Avenue. The new commercial strip included the Kaywood Theater, opened in 1945 and operated by Sidney Lusk. Frank Ackerman was the architect, while the M. Cladny Construction Company was the builder. The All Comedy Show occurred on April 20, 1956. In 1984, the Harvest Church Ministries converted the theater into a church. (Above, courtesy of Clarence Selke; right, courtesy of Becky Livingston.)

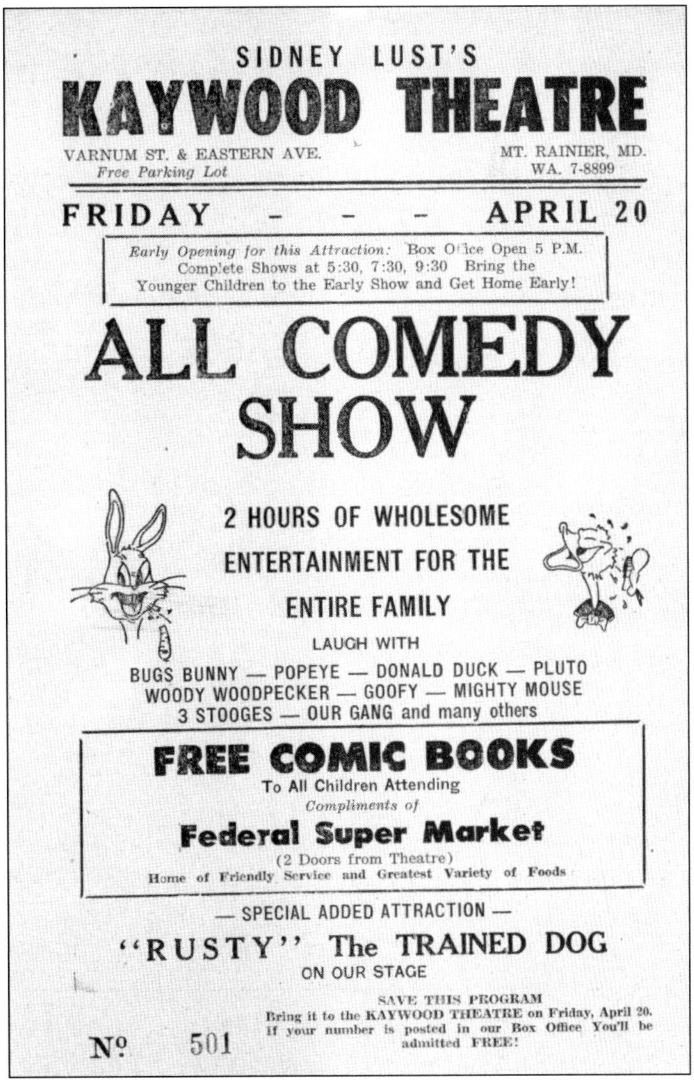

SIDNEY LUST'S

KAYWOOD THEATRE

VARNUM ST. & EASTERN AVE. *Free Parking Lot*

MT. RAINIER, MD. WA. 7-8899

FRIDAY - - - APRIL 20

Early Opening for this Attraction: Box Office Open 5 P.M. Complete Shows at 5:30, 7:30, 9:30 Bring the Younger Children to the Early Show and Get Home Early!

ALL COMEDY SHOW

2 HOURS OF WHOLESOME ENTERTAINMENT FOR THE ENTIRE FAMILY

LAUGH WITH

BUGS BUNNY — POPEYE — DONALD DUCK — PLUTO
WOODY WOODPECKER — GOOFY — MIGHTY MOUSE
3 STOOGES — OUR GANG and many others

FREE COMIC BOOKS

To All Children Attending

Compliments of

Federal Super Market

(2 Doors from Theatre)

Home of Friendly Service and Greatest Variety of Foods

— SPECIAL ADDED ATTRACTION —

"RUSTY" The TRAINED DOG

ON OUR STAGE

SAVE THIS PROGRAM

Bring it to the KAYWOOD THEATRE on Friday, April 20. If your number is posted in our Box Office You'll be admitted FREE!

Nº 501

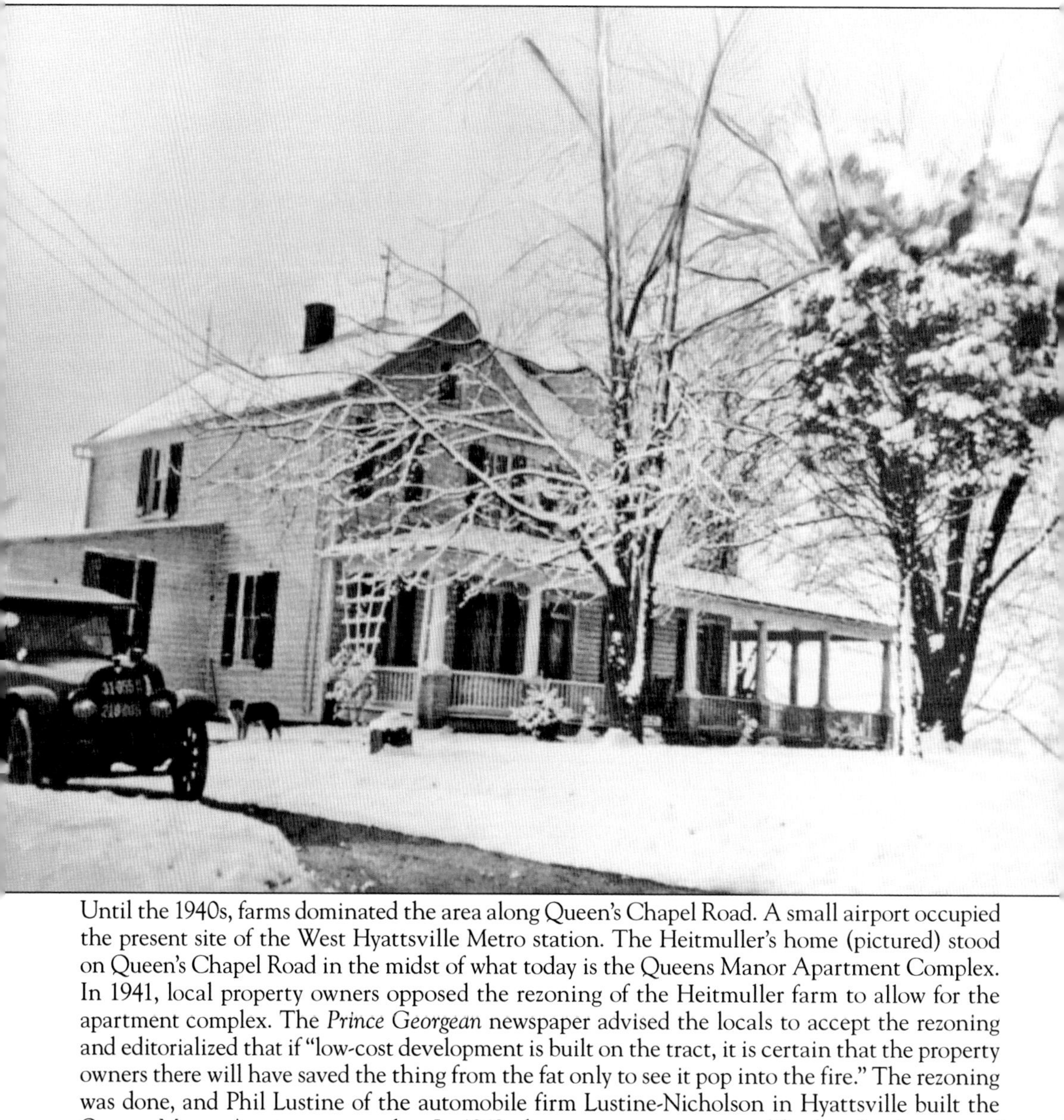

Until the 1940s, farms dominated the area along Queen's Chapel Road. A small airport occupied the present site of the West Hyattsville Metro station. The Heitmuller's home (pictured) stood on Queen's Chapel Road in the midst of what today is the Queens Manor Apartment Complex. In 1941, local property owners opposed the rezoning of the Heitmuller farm to allow for the apartment complex. The *Prince Georgean* newspaper advised the locals to accept the rezoning and editorialized that if "low-cost development is built on the tract, it is certain that the property owners there will have saved the thing from the fat only to see it pop into the fire." The rezoning was done, and Phil Lustine of the automobile firm Lustine-Nicholson in Hyattsville built the Queens Manor Apartment complex. In 1942, the newspaper encouraged further development of the area that would become Lustine's Queenstown project. (Courtesy of Teresa Wilcox.)

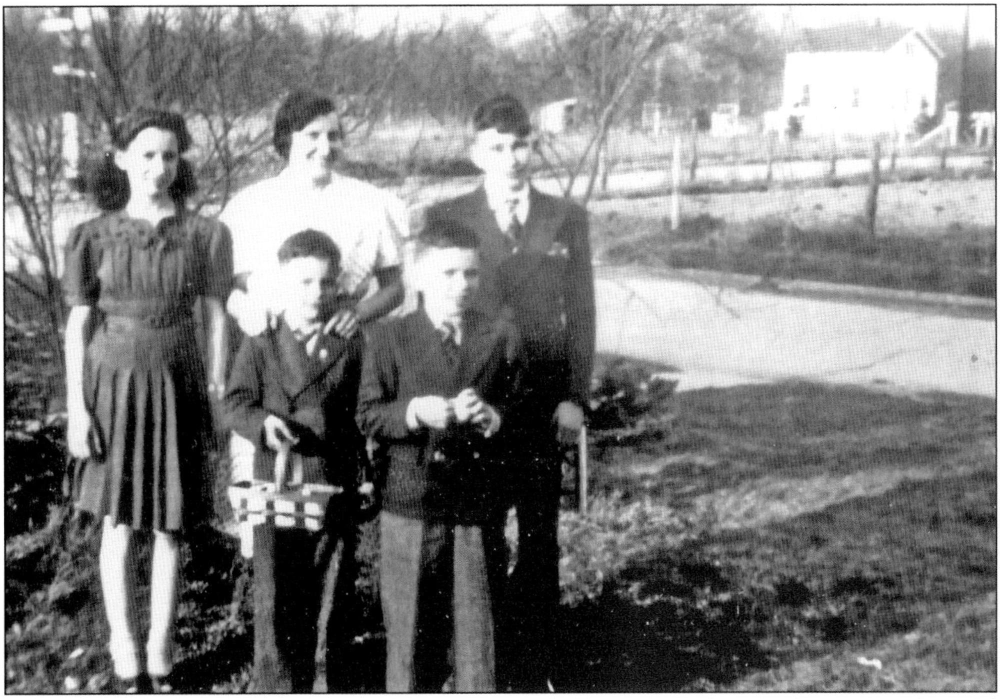

In 1944, the Savage family poses in their finest (probably on Easter) near what now is Arundel Road and Thirty-fourth Street. Before 1950, Thirty-fourth Street did not cross the creek into Queenstown. In 1946, the county commissioners approved the rezoning of 66 acres so that Phil Lustine could build the Queenstown apartment complex. (Courtesy of George Denny.)

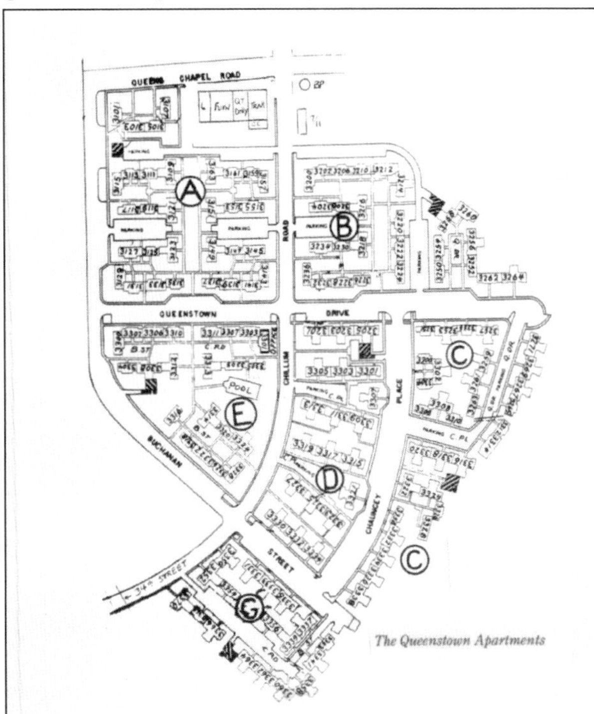

The Queenstown Apartments complex was completed in 1949 on the farmland behind the Savage family. It straddles the Brentwood–Mount Rainier boundary; the line runs through some apartments. The location of the apartment's door determines which town's police department has jurisdiction, where the residents vote, and which town receives the property taxes. (Courtesy of City of Mount Rainier.)

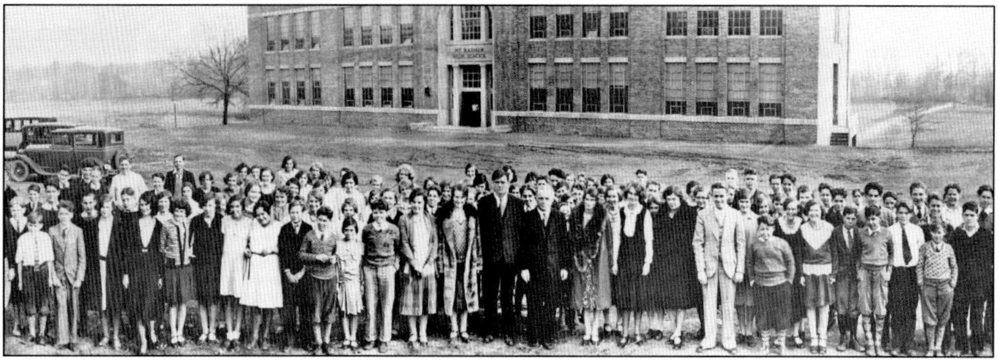

Mount Rainier High School opened in September 1930. During the first year, enrollment was 70 students in seventh through eleventh grade. When the first class graduated in 1933, enrollment had grown to 250 children, making it the fourth largest high school in the county. A junior high was included in the same building, with an enrollment of 80 students in 1932. The building fronted Queens Chapel Road and today is the site of Rainier Manor apartments. This area was part of an annexation of nearly 100 acres in 1929 (including the acreage now occupied by Queenstown and Queens Manor Apartments). Pictured above is the graduation class of 1941. The photograph below is from 1944. (Both, courtesy of Teresa Wilcox.)

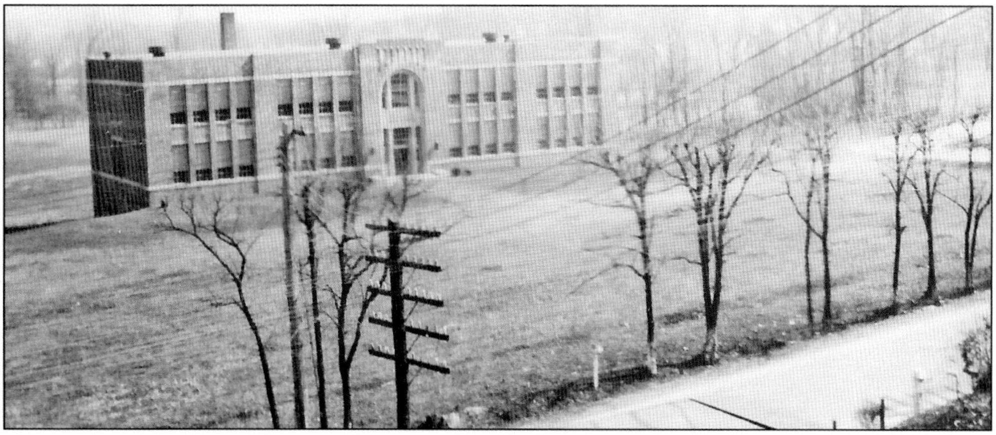

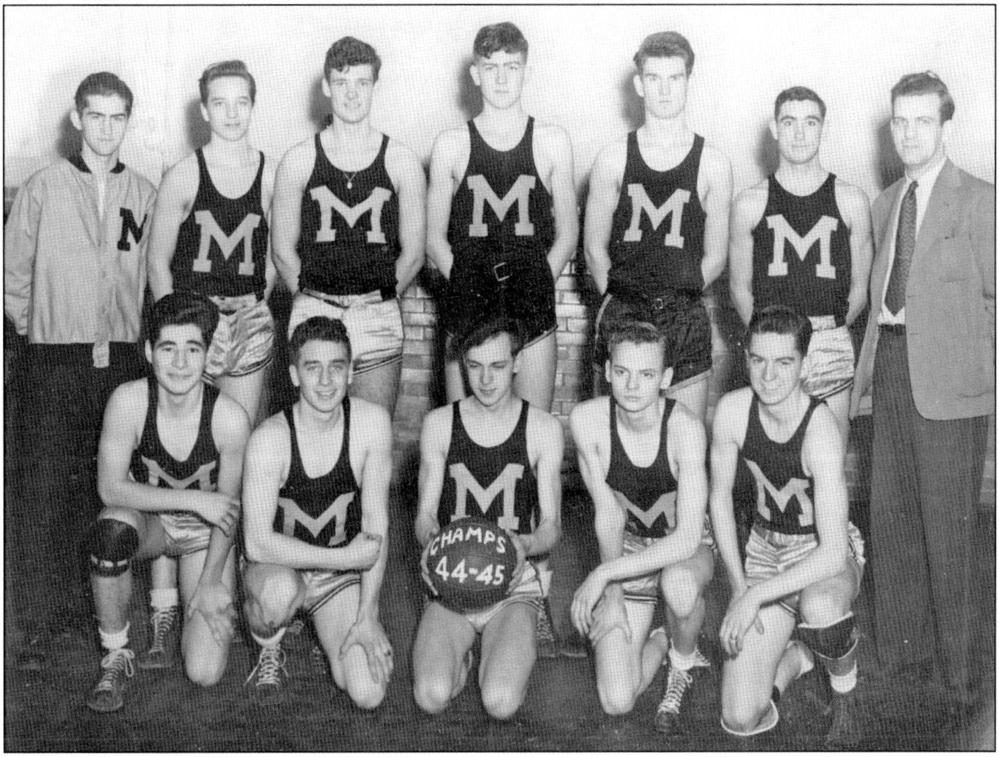

Prince George's County was not prepared for the baby boom after World War II. A *Washington Post* article in 1950 outlined the various problems, in particular overcrowded schools. The high school (a whites-only school; black students were sent to Fairmont Heights Junior-Senior High School) was filled beyond capacity. Classes were held even in the basement locker room. In 1950, the county added the 12th grade for the first time, thus increasing the overcrowding in the schools. Mount Rainier High School had a capacity of 500 students (and only because temporary Quonset huts were used for overflow), but 725 students were enrolled. The last class to graduate from the high school was in 1951, the year that Northwestern High School was completed. Mount Rainier High School then became a junior high. Seen here are photographs of sports teams of the era. (Both, courtesy of City of Mount Rainier.)

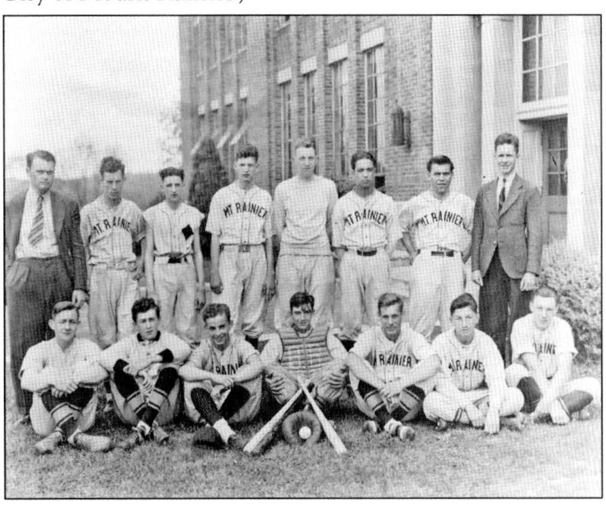

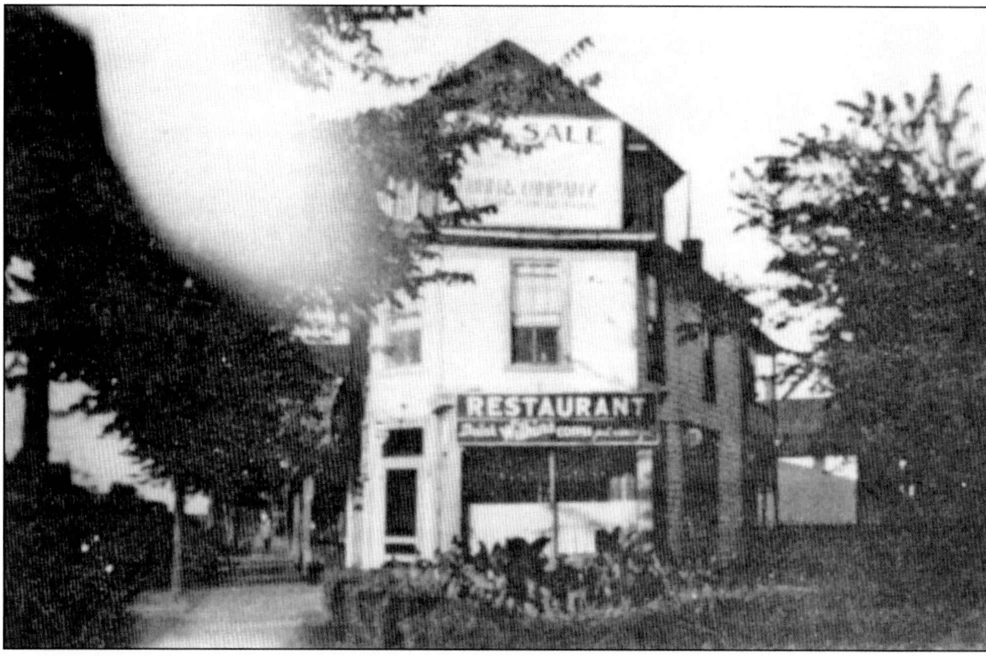

In 1933, the Washington Railway and Electric Company merged with the Capital Traction Company to form the Capital Transit Company. In 1939, a row of dilapidated buildings known as Chinch Row (above) were razed to make way for a new brick streetcar terminal (below and facing page) at Rhode Island Avenue and Perry Street, site of the present bus station and city hall. *The Prince Georgean* newspaper editorialized that the project had the potential to put Mount Rainier on par with Bethesda or Silver Spring as a transit hub. A looped track around the depot made it possible for the new lightweight high-speed cars to serve the town. At the same time, shuttle service was started from Mount Rainier to Beltsville. (Both, courtesy of City of Mount Rainier.)

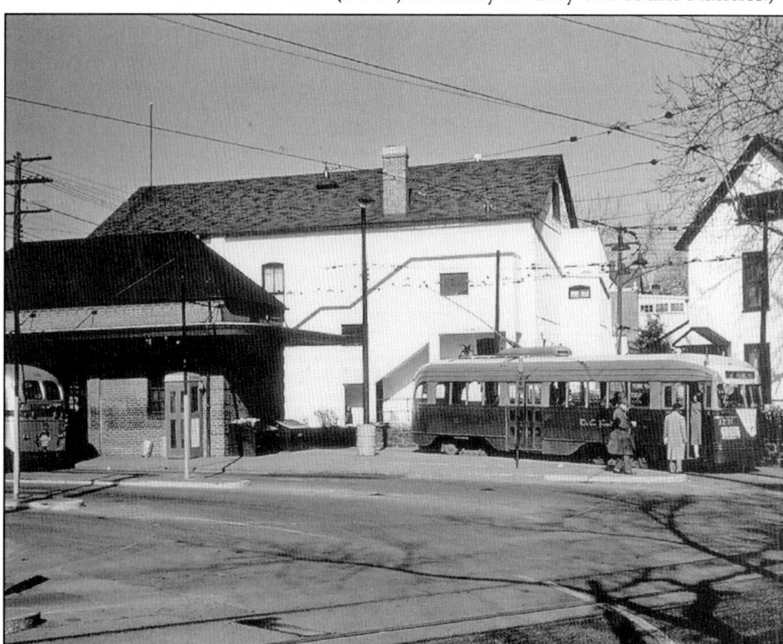

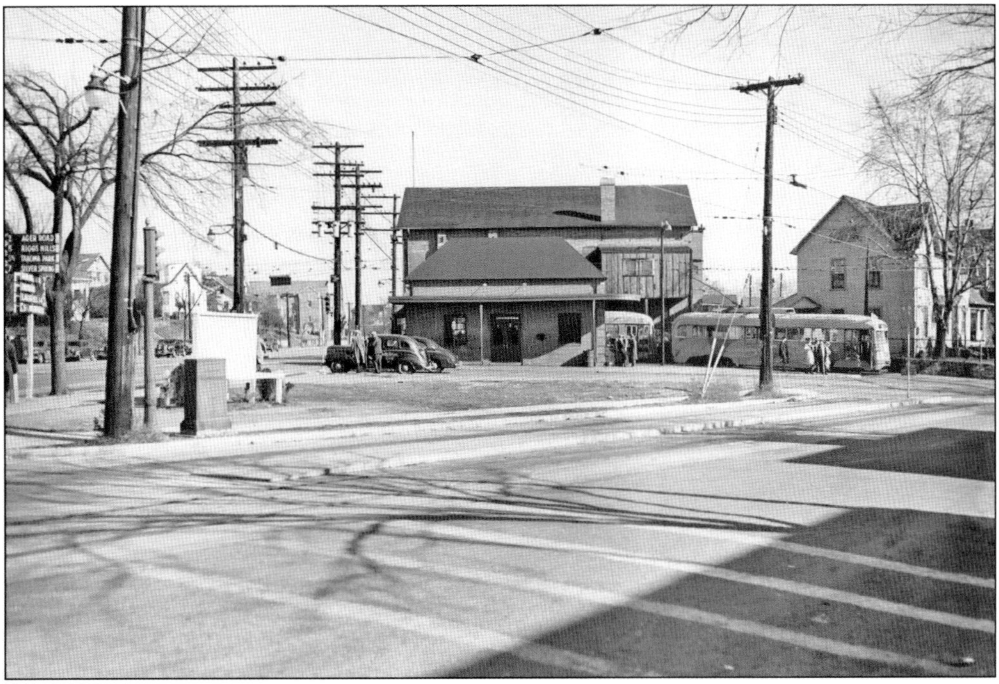

During World War II, a memorial listing the names of local service members was erected near the trolley depot (white square to right of utility pole). In 1945, the Police Boys' Club organized a boxing show in honor of Ray Nalley, the club's former boxing instructor, killed in action in France at age 25. Nalley had been a Golden Gloves champion (1935 through 1936) and was posthumously awarded the Purple Heart medal. In 1948, students at Mount Rainier Elementary adopted the French village of Bohars, raising money to buy supplies for the people left destitute after heavy Allied bombings. In the image below, the first-grade class marches down the 2800 block of Upshur Street with a collection box on wheels. A ton of canned food and 50 crates of clothing were sent to Bohars. (Above, courtesy of Washington Star; below, courtesy of Marilyn Mowat.)

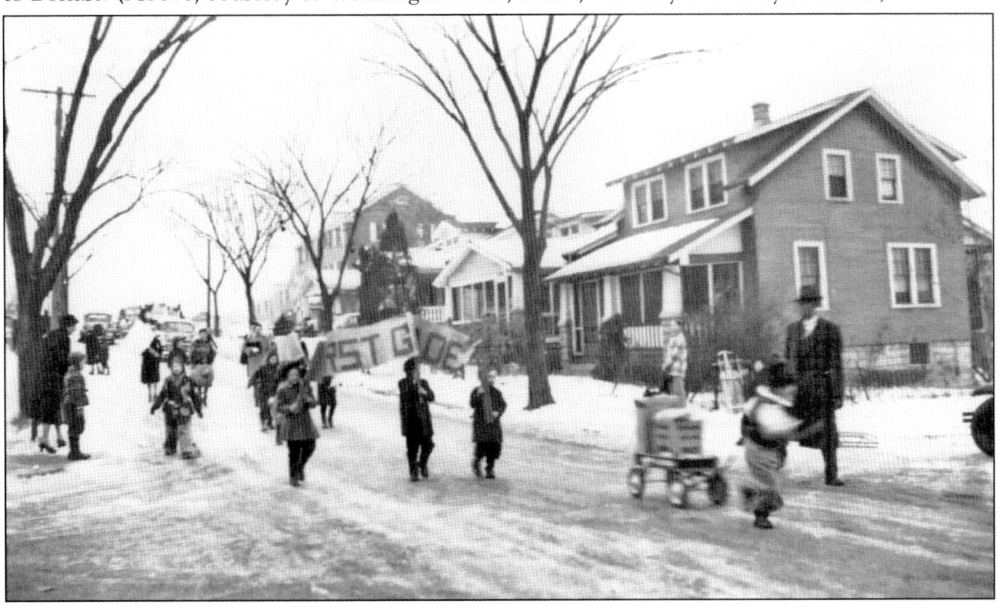

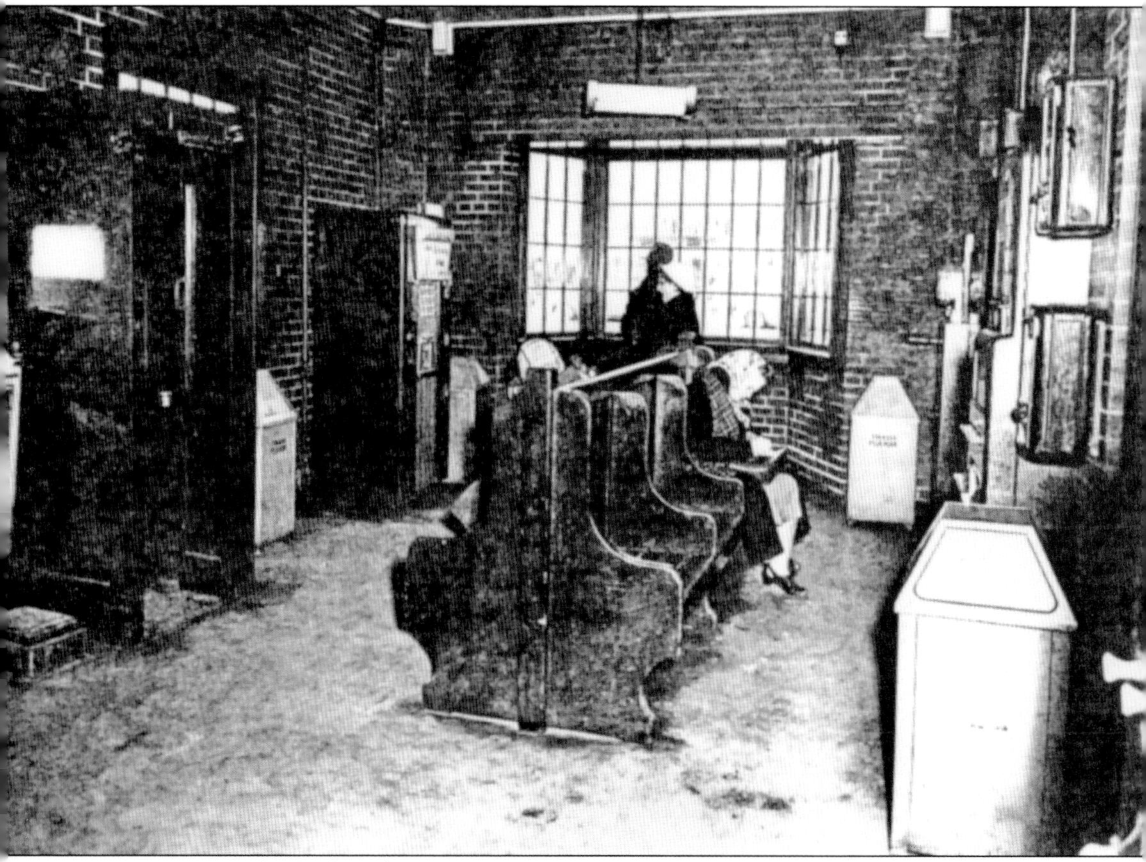

As a streetcar suburb of Washington, DC, Mount Rainier has long been tied to transit history. Here, women wait for the streetcar inside the Mount Rainier terminal. For several years after the new terminal's construction, bus service was limited; that changed in 1946 when several feeder bus lines were routed through the Mount Rainier terminal, thus connecting the streetcar line with bus service. A prolonged series of strikes by operators in 1955 resulted in the passage of legislation cancelling the franchise of Capital Transit. A new franchise was granted to the DC Transit System in 1956, but a condition of the new franchise agreement was the conversion of all rail service to bus routes. On September 8, 1958, the last streetcar rolled out of the Mount Rainier terminal. The terminal itself became a dilapidated nuisance and was razed in 1980. (Courtesy of City of Mount Rainier.)

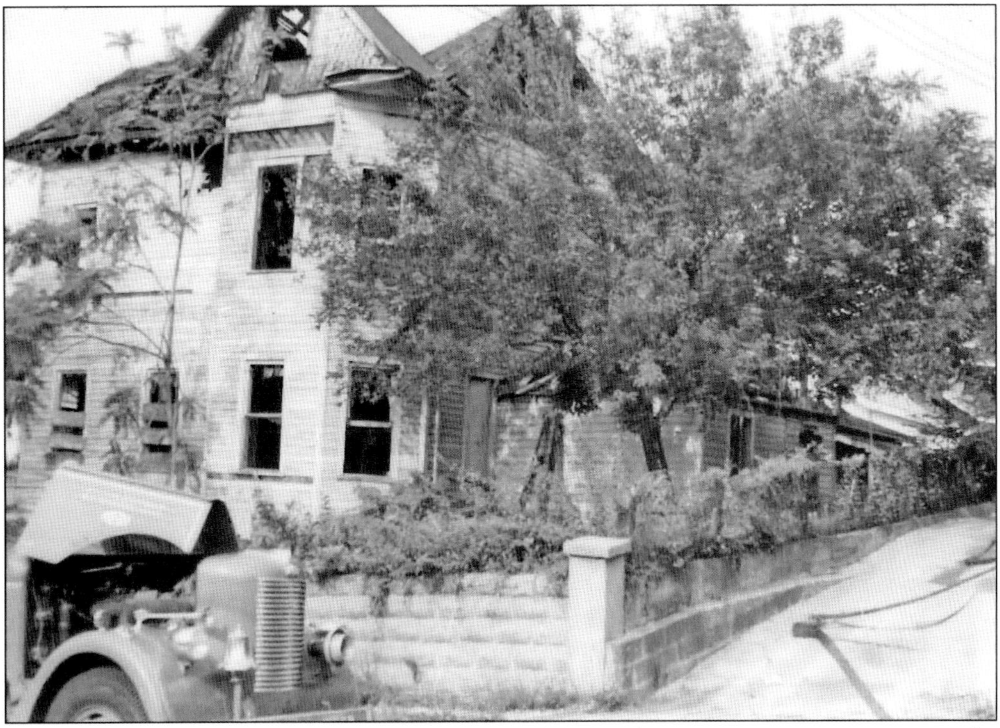

Undoubtedly, the most enduring, widely known, and disputed Mount Rainier story concerns the 1949 exorcism. The 1973 film *The Exorcist* is based on the novel by William Blatty, who retold the story he remembered from a 1949 newspaper account of the exorcism of a Lutheran boy by Father Edward Hughes of St. James Catholic Church. Local lore places the boy's home at 3210 Bunker Hill Road, now a small park with a gazebo adjacent to the elementary school playground (below). In the 1960s, the volunteer fire department razed the dilapidated house (above). The Georgetown street steps made famous in the movie are a tourist attraction, but occasionally, people are seen photographing the Bunker Hill Road site, even though an investigative reporter has determined that the whole episode actually occurred on Fortieth Avenue in nearby Cottage City. However, exorcising Mount Rainier's urban legend is likely to be devilishly difficult. (Above, courtesy of Bunker Hill Volunteer Fire and Rescue Co.; below, courtesy of Jimmy Tarlau.)

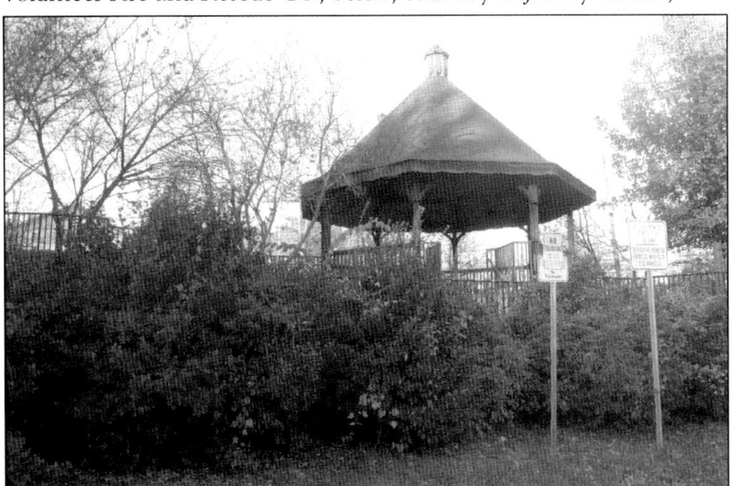

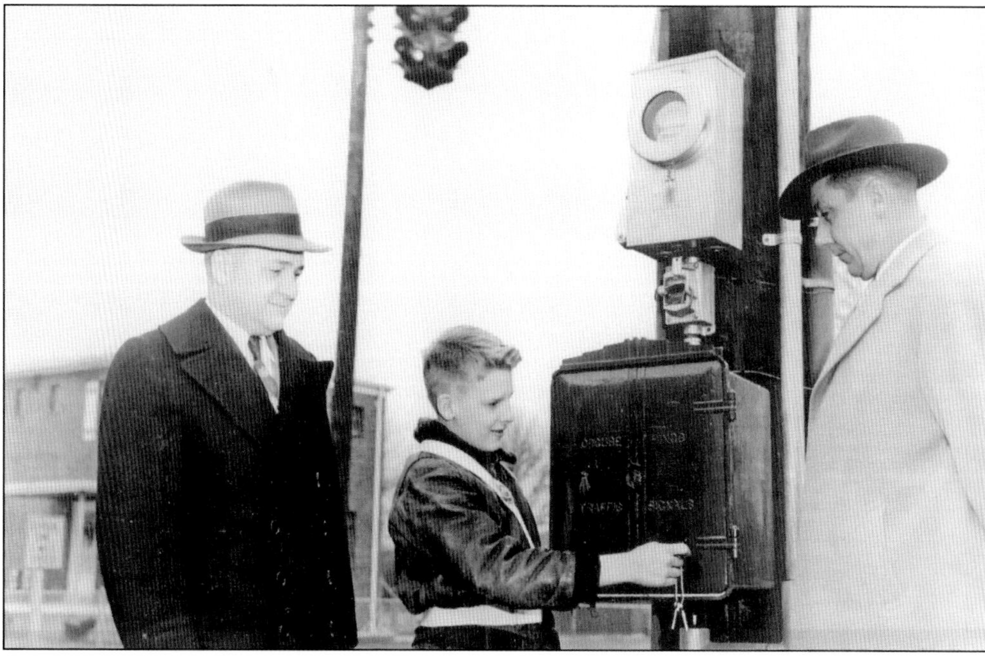

Thomas S. Stone Elementary School opened in September 1950 with approximately 500 children. In 1951, Brentwood and Mount Rainier cooperated to install a traffic signal outside the school. Above, safety patrol member Jimmy Zulick had the honor to flip the switch with Brentwood mayor James Russell (left) and Mount Rainier mayor Herbert Reichelt looking on. The school received wide publicity because of its inexpensive construction and was visited by educators from other systems and other countries. The school was named to honor the county examiner of schools, who served more than 20 years beginning in 1877. Overcrowded from its first day, it was enlarged in 1953 and again in 1956. As the 2010 photograph below attests, the school remains overcrowded and depends on temporary pods as classrooms. (Above, courtesy of City of Mount Rainier; below, courtesy of Jimmy Tarlau.)

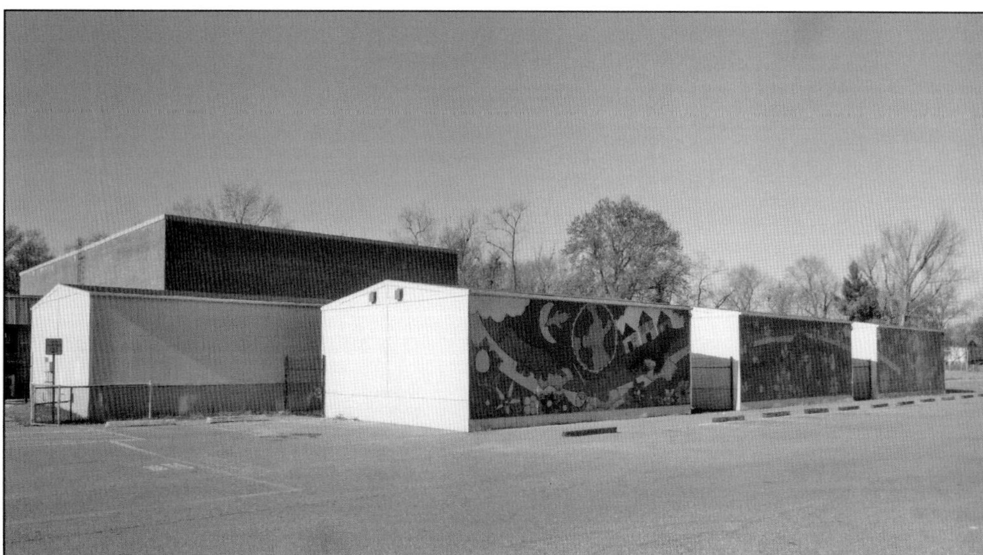

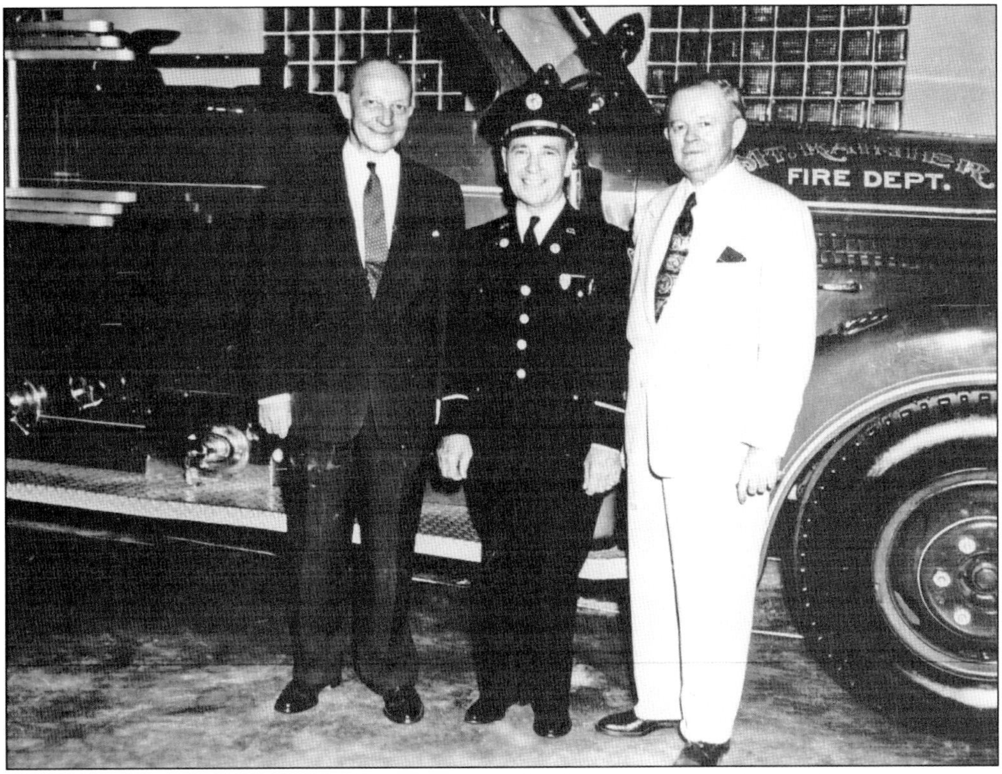

During the first years of World War II, volunteer fire department members took turns staying at the firehouse during the night as a safeguard against any potential sabotage. In 1938, the MRVFD had hired a man for daytime duty, and in 1942, a second man was hired and the town had a fire department open 24 hours a day, seven days a week, for the first time. As the town grew, a third piece of equipment was needed, and the firehouse was expanded to accommodate it in 1950, as seen below. The dedication (above) was attended by Gov. William Preston Lane (left) and comptroller Millard Tawes (right), who stand with Chief Karl Young (center). Homeowners further benefited from the expanded department in having lower fire insurance rates available. In 1959, a third man was hired, giving the town the distinction that year of being the only department in the county that never failed to answer an alarm. (Both, courtesy of MRVFD.)

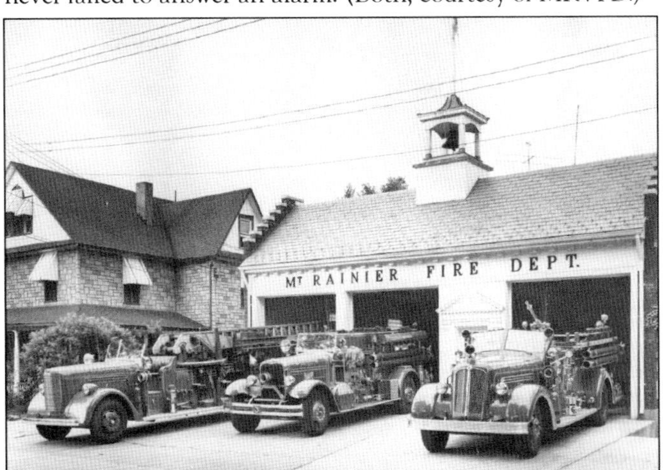

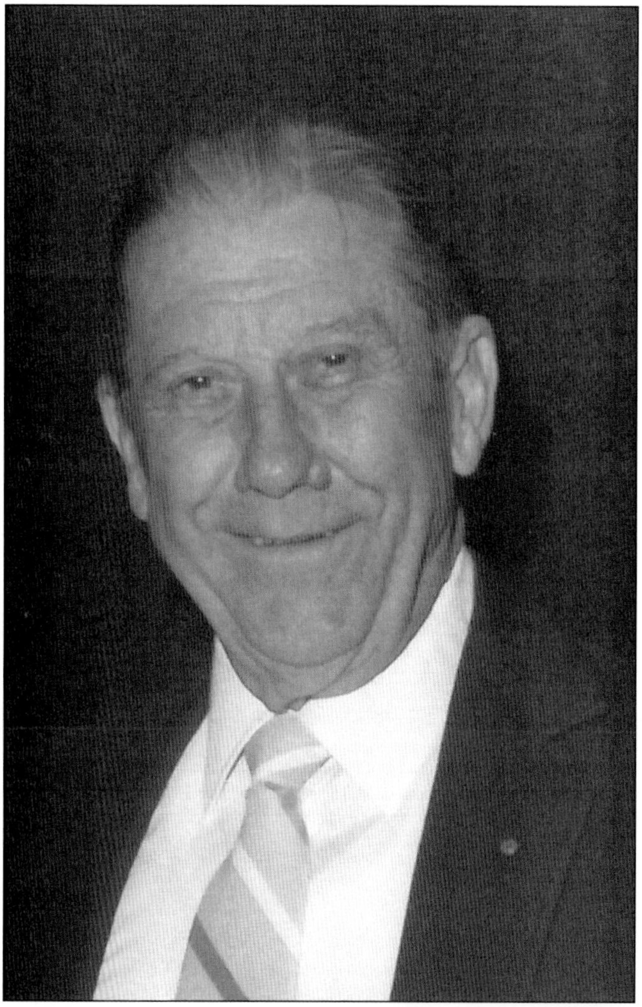

Herbert Reichelt, a Mount Rainier native, graduated from McKinley Technical High School in the District of Columbia and became a master plumber. He received a law degree after serving in the Navy during World War II. During the mayoral campaign of 1949, Reichelt promised to rid the town of "undesirable elements" and known gamblers. Reichelt defeated incumbent mayor Floyd B. Mathias and appointed Chief John Wise (seen below with his department in 1950) to replace longtime chief Eugene Plumer. This was the second time Plumer had been fired; Mayor Pruitt removed him in 1940 for insubordination, but he was rehired by Mayor Mathias. Reichelt was elected in 1955 to serve on the Prince George's County Board of Commissioners. He served as president of the Maryland Municipal League and the Maryland chapter of the National Association of Counties. (Left, courtesy of Maryland Municipal League; below, courtesy of City of Mount Rainier.)

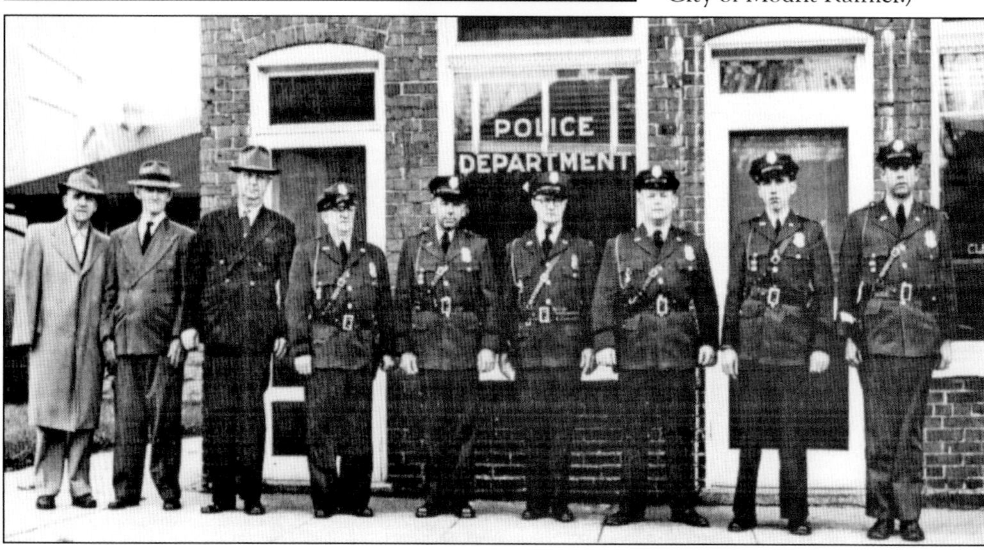

In 1952, a library next to city hall was dedicated in memory of former fire chief Karl A. Young. Though the library was small in square footage, the celebration was big—a reminder of the importance of public libraries. The Bladensburg High School marching band led a parade from the Kaywood apartment complex to the new library. Mayor Reichelt presided over the ceremonies. Speakers included Maryland governor Theodore McKeldin, University of Maryland president H.C. Byrd, and Congressman Lansdale Sasscer. In the 1970s, the library offered not only books, but also entertainment for children in the form of puppet shows. (Both, courtesy of PGCMLS.)

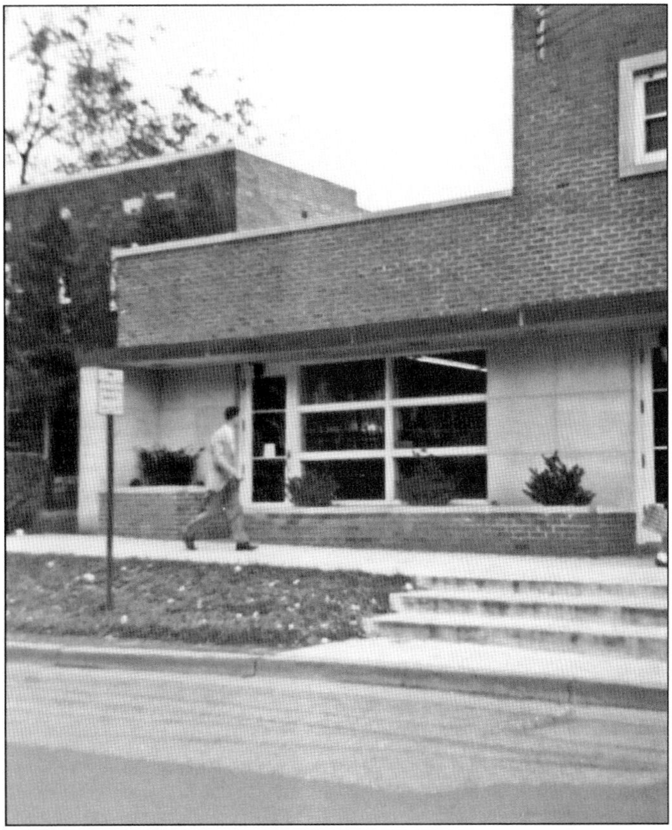

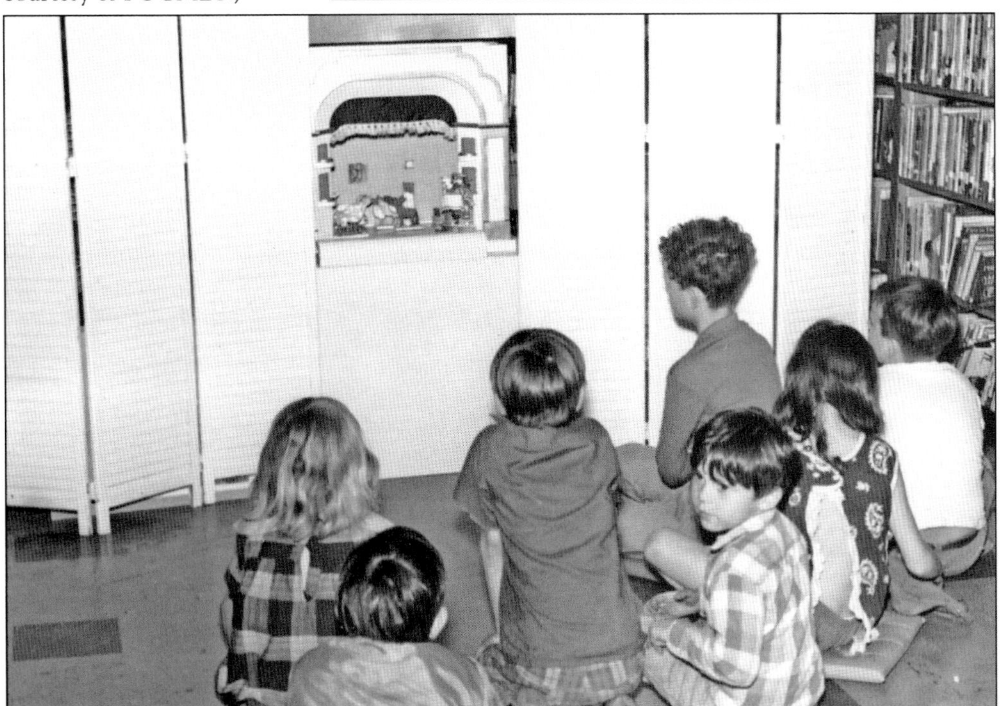

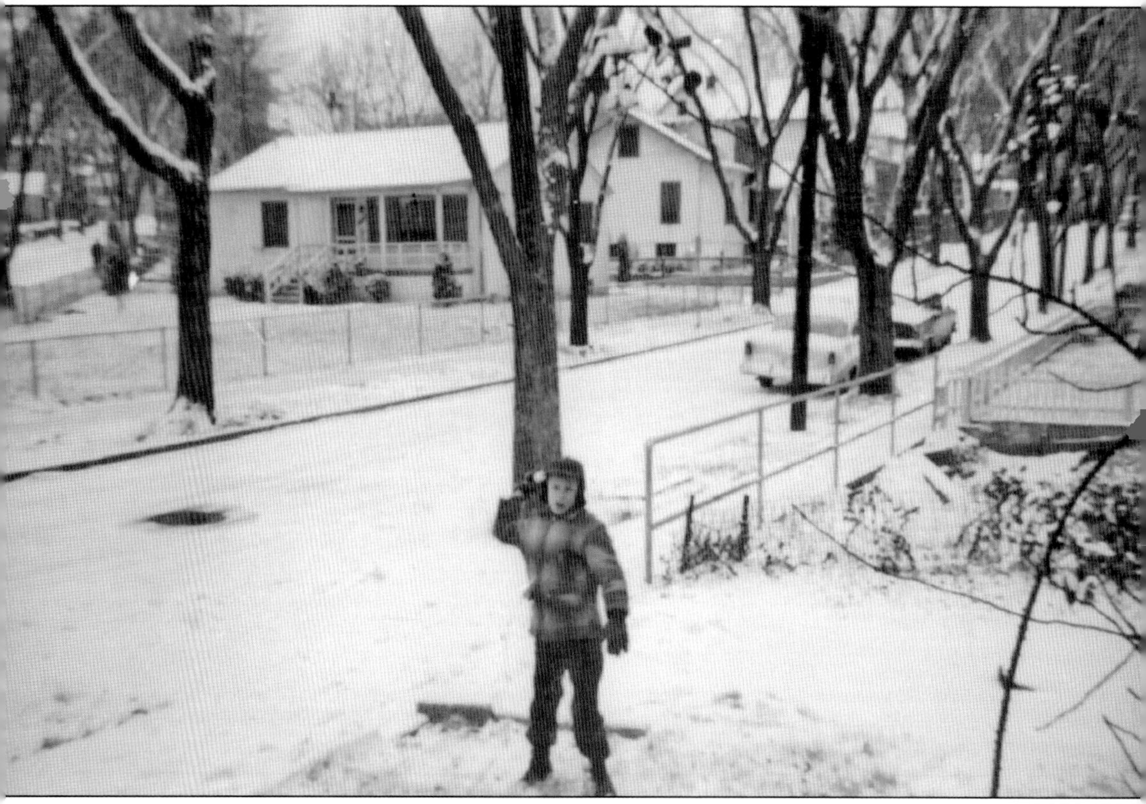

Young Cary Dawson aims a snowball at the photographer, who is capturing a winter scene at the intersection of Rainier Avenue and Thirty-second Street. In the 1950s, several small streams ran through the town, including the one passing under this intersection. Becky Livingston, who grew up in Mount Rainier, recalls that in the 1950s this "brook ran in a bed of varying widths and depths from at least Thirty-first to Thirty-fourth and thence under the roadway into Brentwood. A small park at Upshur Street is located over that point in the valley between two hills. The length of the brook between Thirty-second and Thirty-fourth could become rushing during storms or it could be merely a trickle during dry years." These small streams were channeled into storm sewer lines in later years to eliminate mosquito breeding sites. This particular stream is still evidenced by the winding path that follows its course below the surface from Thirty-first to Thirty-second Streets behind the homes facing Rainier Avenue. (Courtesy of Lawrence Dungan.)

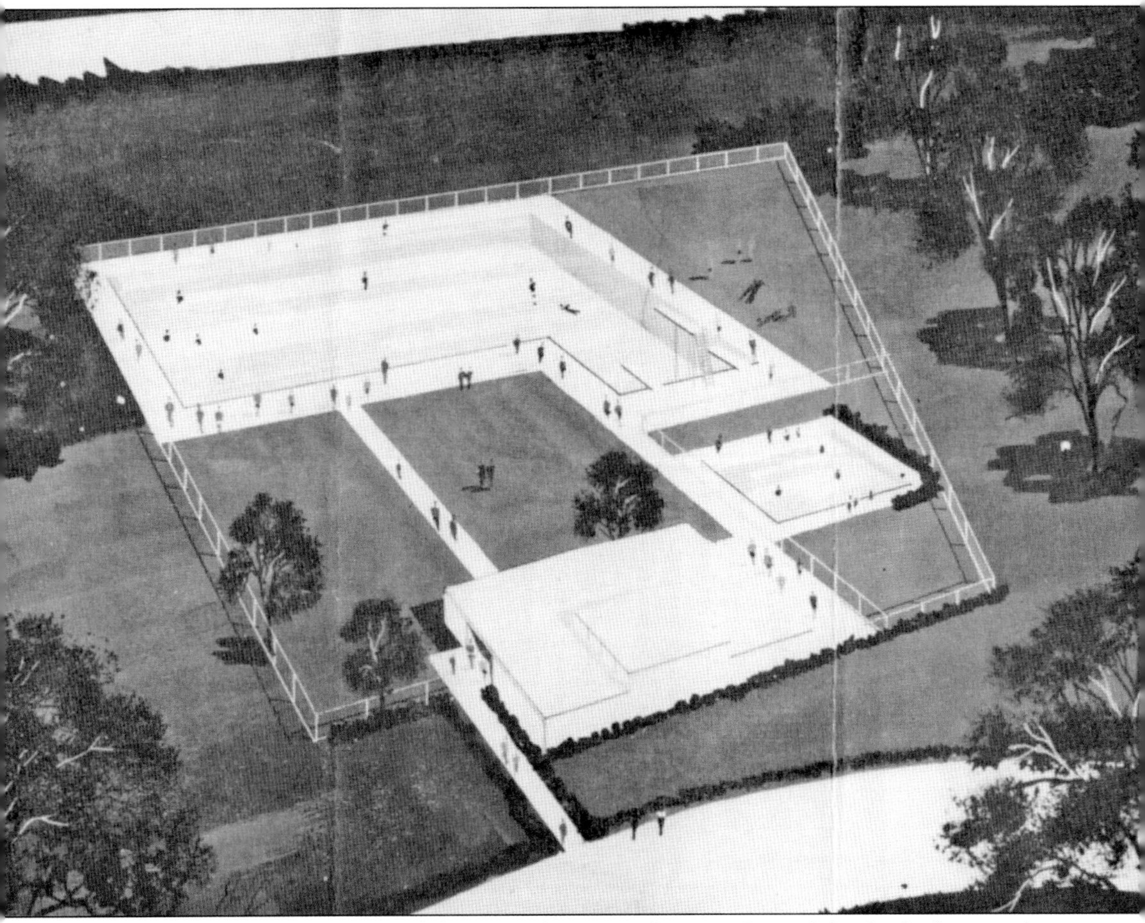

A membership brochure promoted the privately operated Prince George's Pool, which opened on Buchanan Street in 1956. H. Mitchell Jernigan, president of the Mount Rainier-Brentwood Teen Club, pitched the idea of a swimming pool to the club's board of directors in 1953 to give children an alternative to using the contaminated Northwest Branch swimming holes. As was common for many swimming pools of that era, it had a whites-only membership policy. After being rejected for membership in 1974, Raymond Bowlding, with the support of the NAACP, filed charges with the US Department of Justice and the Maryland Commission for Human Rights. The pool changed its policy in 1975; however, Bowlding did not join, fearing retribution against his children at the pool. He died in 1994. In 2015, the Bowlding family attended the ceremony dedicating a new pavilion. A plaque on the building says, "In honor of Raymond Bowlding, whose courage and perseverance led to the integration of PG Pool in 1975." (Courtesy of PGCHS.)

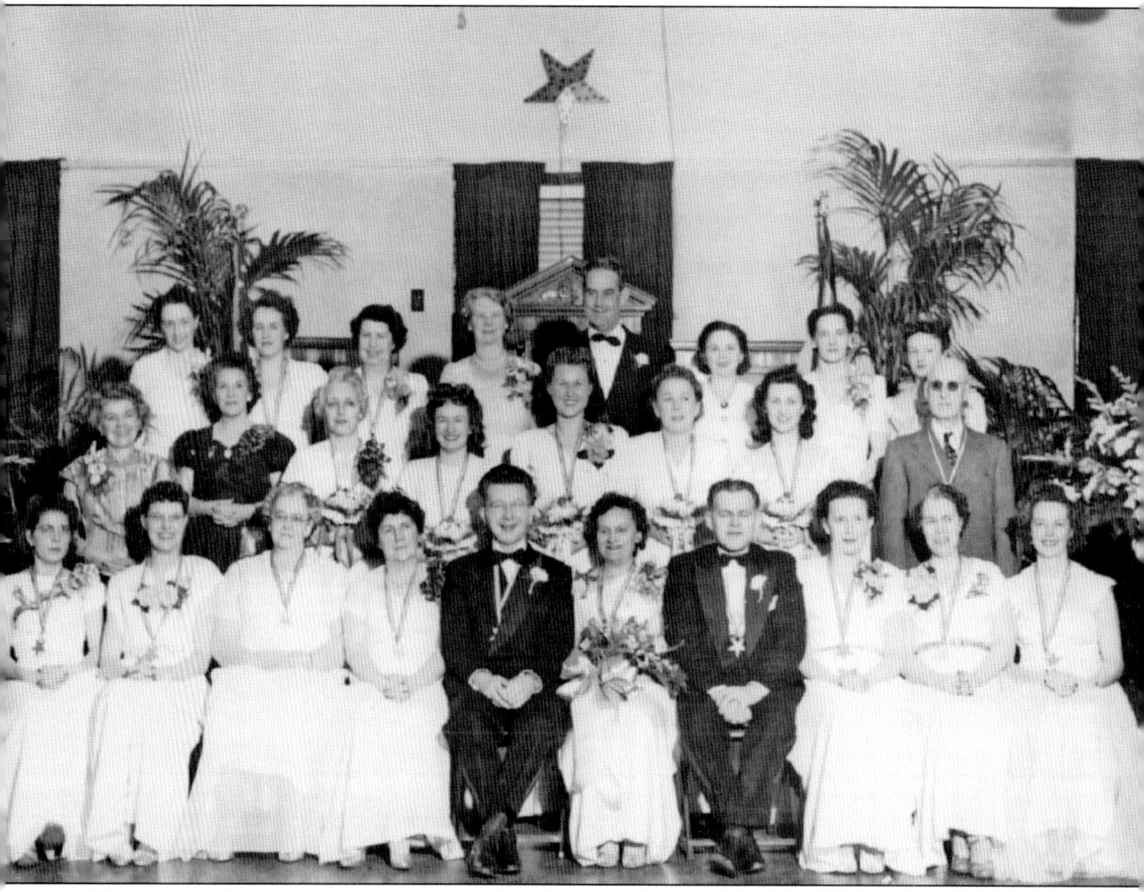

This picture shows the 1947 installation of leaders of the Adah Chapter No. 25, Order of the Eastern Star. The chapter was organized in 1915 and purchased Star-Potts Hall in 1921. Civic organizations supported the growth of Mount Rainier from its earliest years. The volunteer fire department (founded 1911) in particular has close ties to the city's history. In the 1920s, the Mount Rainier Civic League supported beautification efforts. The Citizens Association (founded in 1950) supported various causes, including the building of the library. Other organizations have included the Woman's Christian Temperance Union (chapter created 1921), American Legion Post No. 110 (1934), Mount Rainier–Brentwood Lions (1946), Civil Defense Organization (1957), Mount Rainier–Brentwood Boys Club (1932), Boy Scouts (1912), West Gate Lodge No. 220 of the Masons (1930), and Order of the Odd Fellows (1914). In the early 1940s, a park and playground committee organized the creation of two baseball diamonds, a basketball court, and a clubhouse at the site of today's Thomas Stone Elementary School. In 1984, the Mount Rainier Jaycees admitted the first woman in Maryland as a member. (Courtesy of Adah Chapter No. 25, Order of the Eastern Star.)

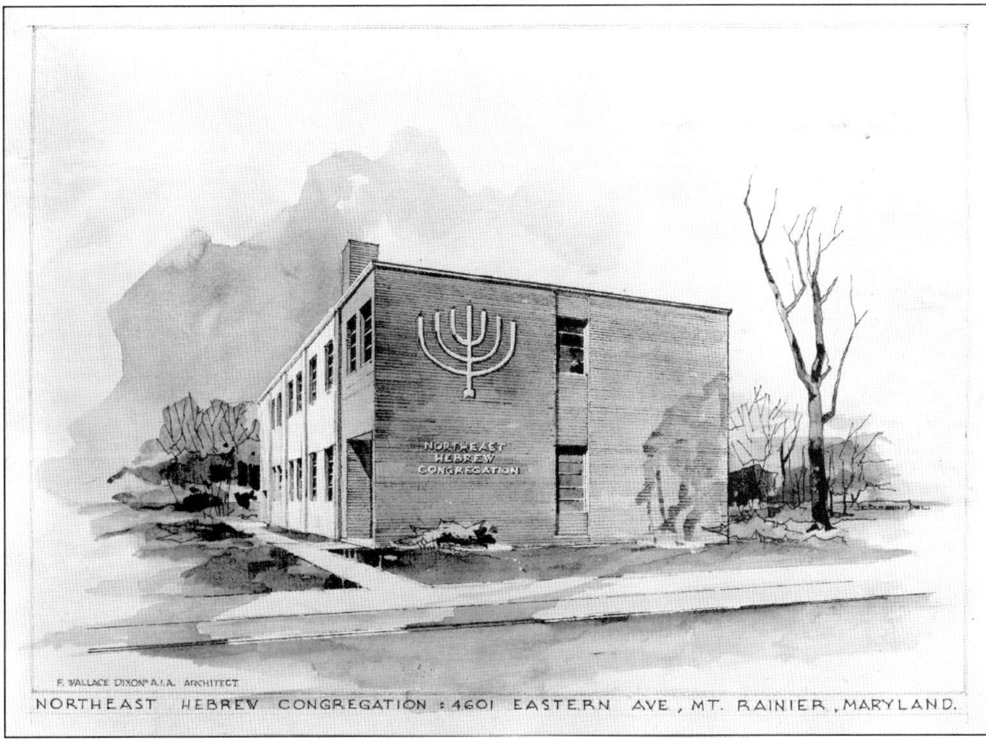

The Washington Bridge Unit purchased the Quonset hut at 3801 Eastern Avenue (below) in 2000 for its large membership of duplicate bridge players. The club is a unit of the Mid-Atlantic Section of the American Bridge Association, which was founded in 1932 by African Americans, who at that time were denied membership in the American Contract Bridge League. The Quonset hut, built in 1946 by American Legion Post No. 110, also served the Beth Torah Congregation, which leased it in 1951 for services until they moved in 1952 to a new synagogue at 4601 Eastern Avenue (above). Beth Torah began in 1945 as the Northeast Hebrew Congregation, the first Conservative Jewish congregation organized in Prince George's County. In 1969, the former synagogue became the Washington-area headquarters for Nichiren Shoshu Soka Gakkai of America, which provides outreach for Nichiren Shoshu Buddhism. (Above, courtesy of DC Public Library; below, courtesy of Bryan Knedler.)

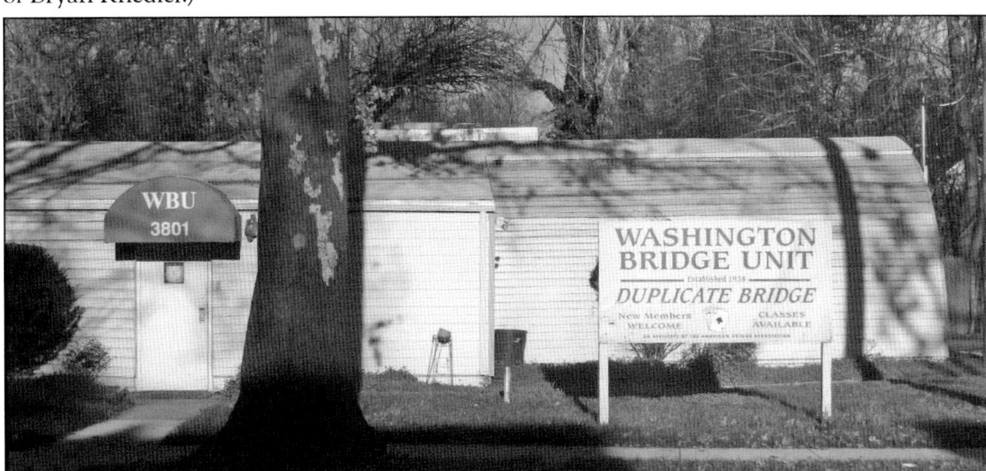

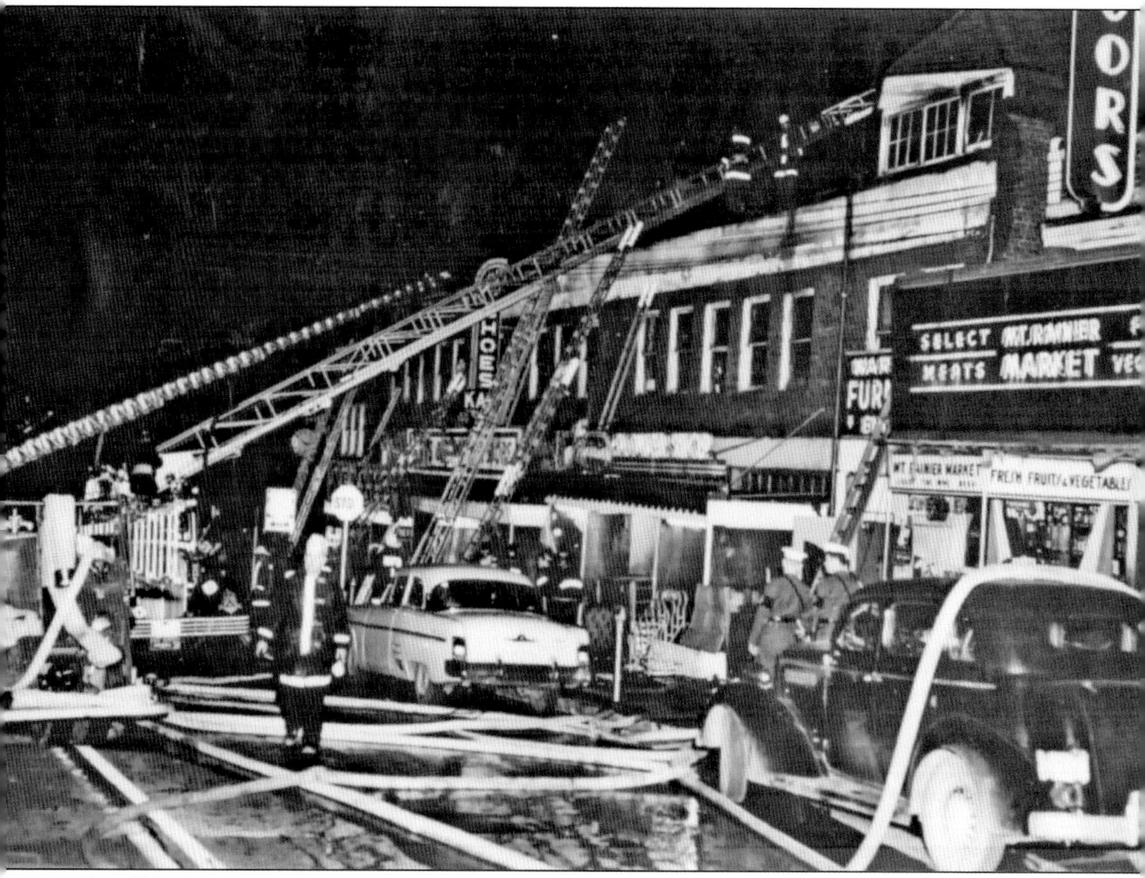

Small businesses on every town's main street, like the Mount Rainier Market (adjacent to the 1955 fire that destroyed the Melody Dance Studio, located on the 3800 block of Thirty-fourth Street) were threatened by more than fire—suburban malls and "super" markets catered to an automobile-crazed world. In 1954, an estimated 9,000 people attended the opening of the Giant supermarket on Queens Chapel Road in the Queens-Chillum Shopping Center. The celebration was hosted by the grocery chain's television star, cowboy Pick Temple. A real-life queen visited the Queens-Chillum center in 1957: the United Kingdom's Queen Elizabeth II and Prince Philip had been to see an American football game at the University of Maryland and were on the way to the White House via Queens Chapel Road. The queen made an impromptu request to see the newfangled American supermarket. The royals mingled and asked questions for about 15 minutes. (Courtesy of City of Mount Rainier.)

Four

Mid-Life Crisis

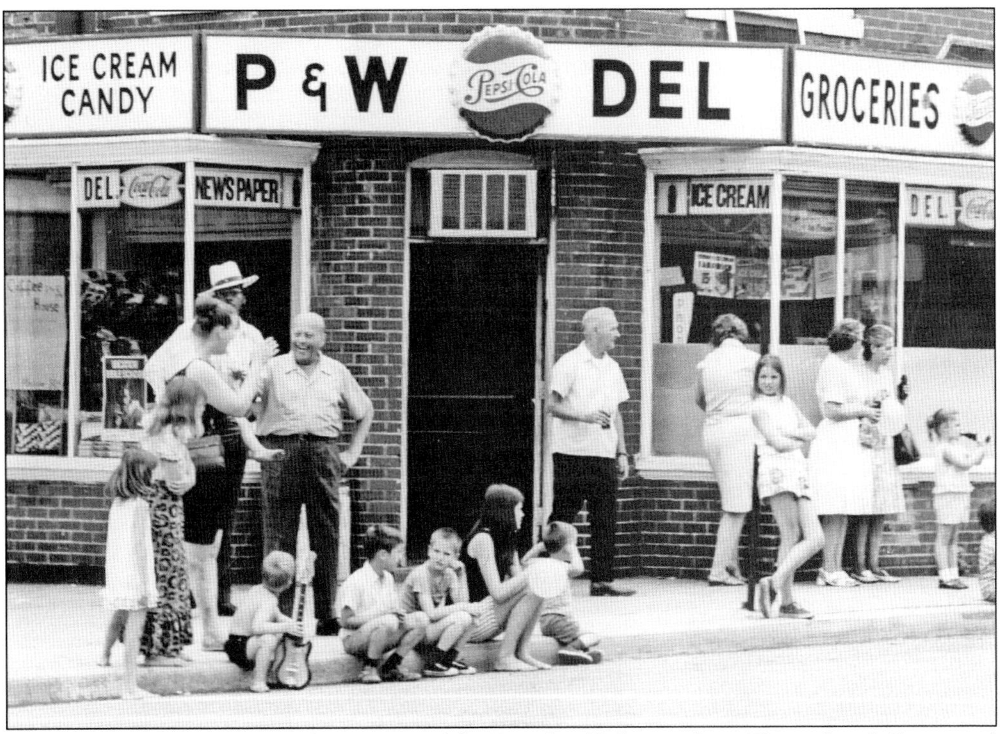

In 1971, residents anticipate the passing of the Fourth of July parade at Thirty-fourth Street and Bunker Hill Road. The transition from segregated town to a multicultural city began in the 1970s with the steady decline of the nearly 100 percent white population in 1960 to 61 percent in 1980. (Courtesy of Joseph Howell.)

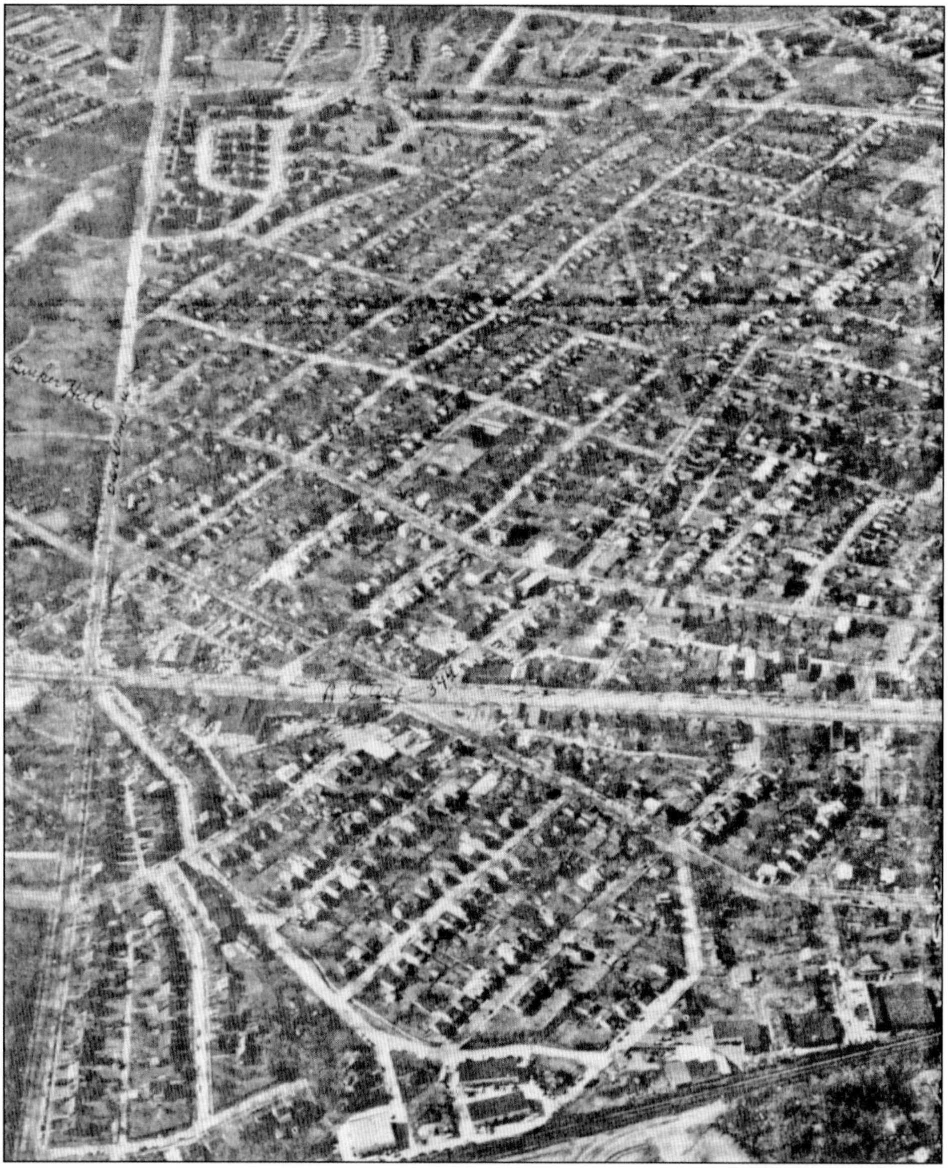

Crossing Eastern Avenue (seen here at left) can be a challenge in heavy traffic, but it could have been much worse. The planners of the interstate highway system intended that Interstate 95 would slice through the Prince George's County suburbs and stream valleys, through the District, and into Virginia. In one plan, coming south from Baltimore, the interstate would run through the University of Maryland, then along the Northwest Branch and Sligo Creek stream valleys, through the north side of Avondale, and then toward Fort Totten, before heading south along the CSX tracks through Brookland. Another more southerly path would have brought it down along Queens Chapel Road, into the Kaywood neighborhood at the northern end of Mount Rainier, and on into Brookland. If that version of Interstate 95 had been built, a proposed connector between it and Route 50 would have created a four-lane highway down Eastern Avenue and over Fort Lincoln. Protests erupted in the 1960s against the proposed freeways, and Congress instead funded construction of the Metrorail system. Pictured is an aerial view from 1960. (Courtesy of City of Mount Rainier.)

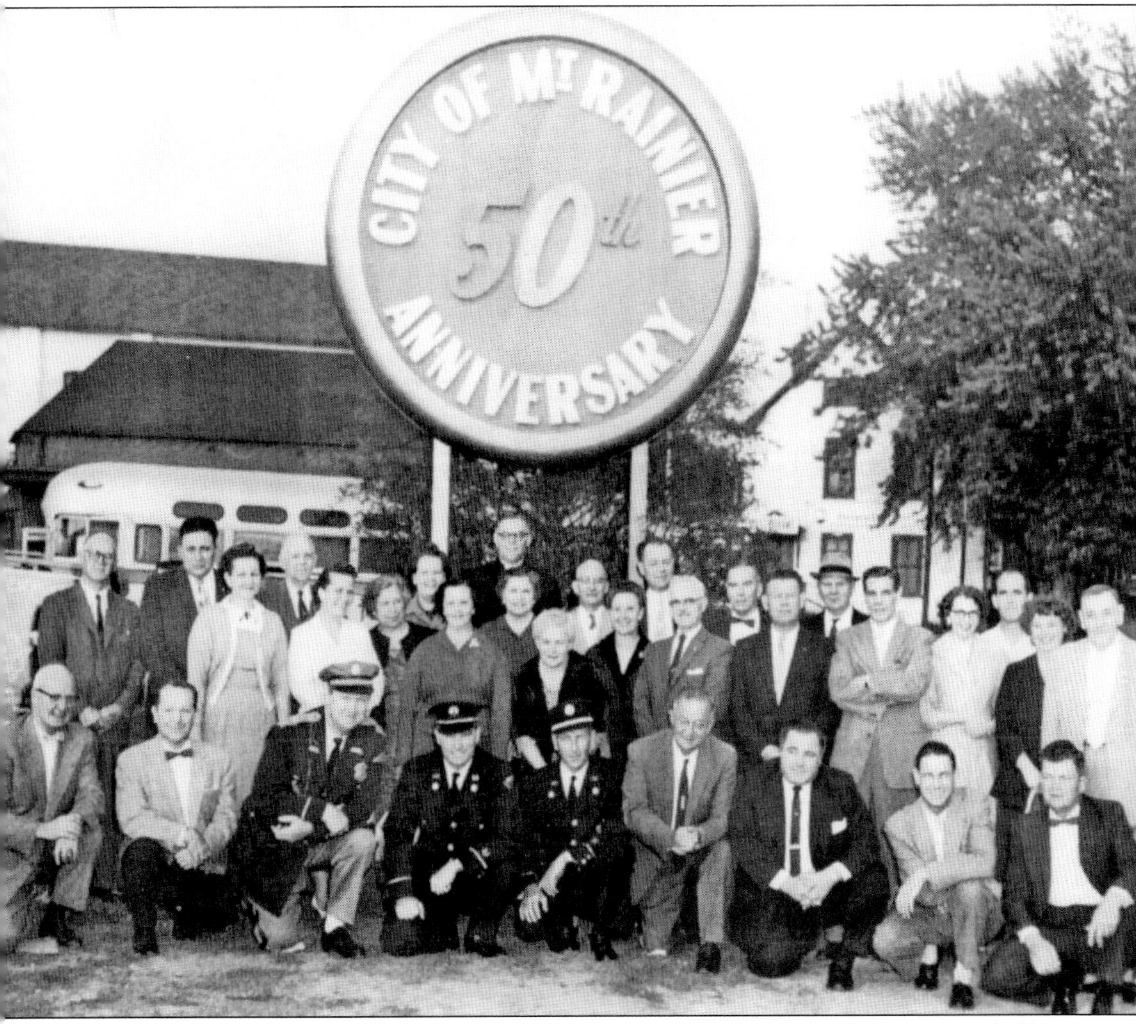

The Citizens Association organized many of the centennial events in 1960. A banquet was held at the Junior High School, and a large parade marched through the streets. The association presented a framed copy of the original charter to the city. American Legion Post No. 110 presented an American flag that had flown over the US Capitol. City leaders posed in front of the bus depot for a commemorative photograph. The house in the background later became the site of the current city hall. From left to right are (first row, kneeling) Vernon Eackles, Lancaster Lowry, Mount Rainier Police Department chief Thomas Alsop, MRVFD captain Karl A. Young Jr., MRVFD chief Francis Xander, Mayor Frederick Richardson, Councilman Dominic DeSarno, Councilman Jack Bransom, and Councilman Roy Callaway; (second row, standing) J.R. Venning, W. Burcher Brown, Ruth Fenwick, Oscar Harlow, Ann Smiley, Rose Camelot, Doris Brown, Mary Lowry, Bruna Giannetti, St. John's Episcopal Church reverend Elwyn Brown (behind Bruna Giannetti), Wilhelmina Richardson, postmaster Francis Leverone, Eva Leverone, George Dressel, George Giannetti, Ennis Almond, Gurney Thompson, Joseph Goliwas, Linus Clarke, Edith Callaway, Fred McDonald, Mary Bransom, and Richard Sturges. (Courtesy of James R. Rice Jr.)

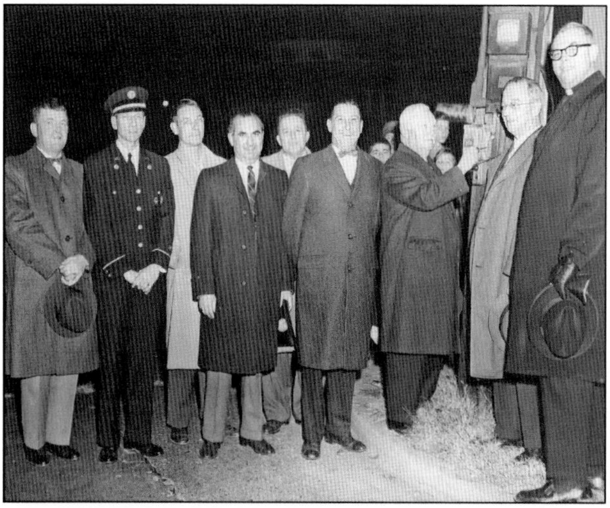

A distinguished group throws the switch for the annual Christmas tree lights in the 1960s. From left to right are Councilman Roy Callaway, MRVFD chief Francis Xander, Councilman Jack Bransom, Councilman Dominic DeSarno, Councilman Burcher Brown, former mayor Herbert Reichelt, unidentified (at the switch), Mayor Frederick Richardson, and Rev. Elwyn Brown. An automobile struck and killed Mayor Richardson in April 1968 outside the County Services Building in Hyattsville. (Courtesy of City of Mount Rainier.)

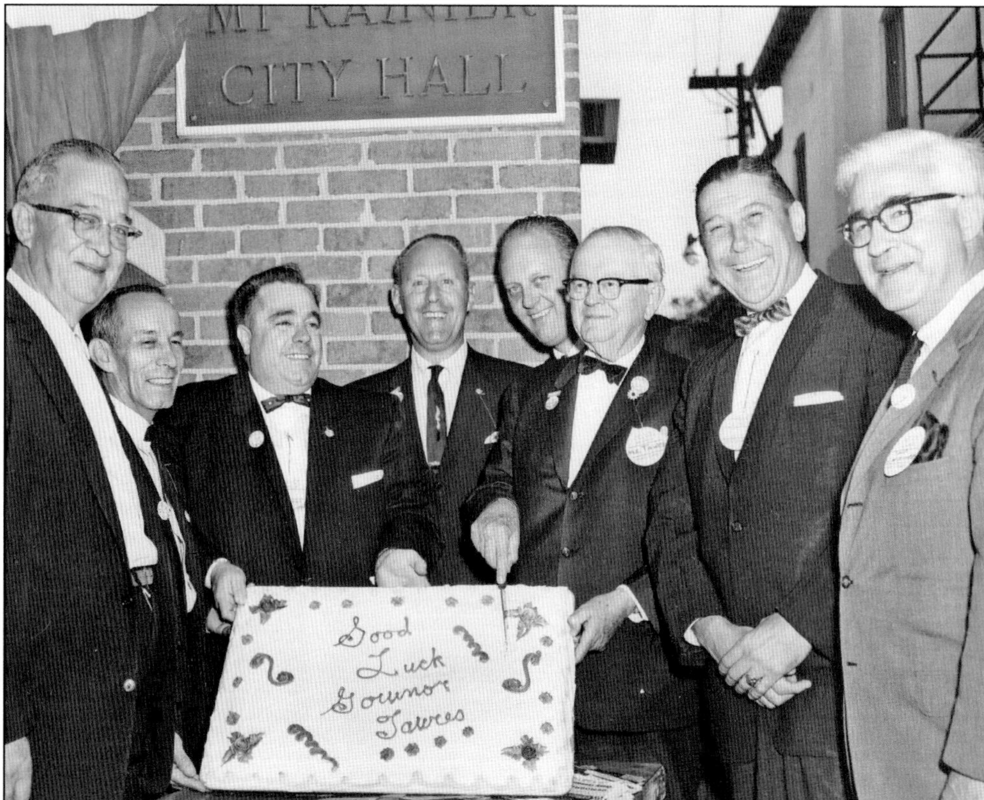

During Gov. J. Millard Tawes's administration, Maryland became the first state south of the Mason-Dixon line to enact a public accommodations law, and he issued directives prohibiting discrimination on the basis of race, creed, or color in state employment and by contractors doing business with the state. In this 1962 photograph, locals in support of Tawes's reelection include, from left to right, Mayor Richardson, Alex Gonzalez, Dominic DeSarno, Comptroller Louis Goldstein, unidentified, Tawes, Herbert Reichelt, and unidentified. (Courtesy of Maryland State Archives.)

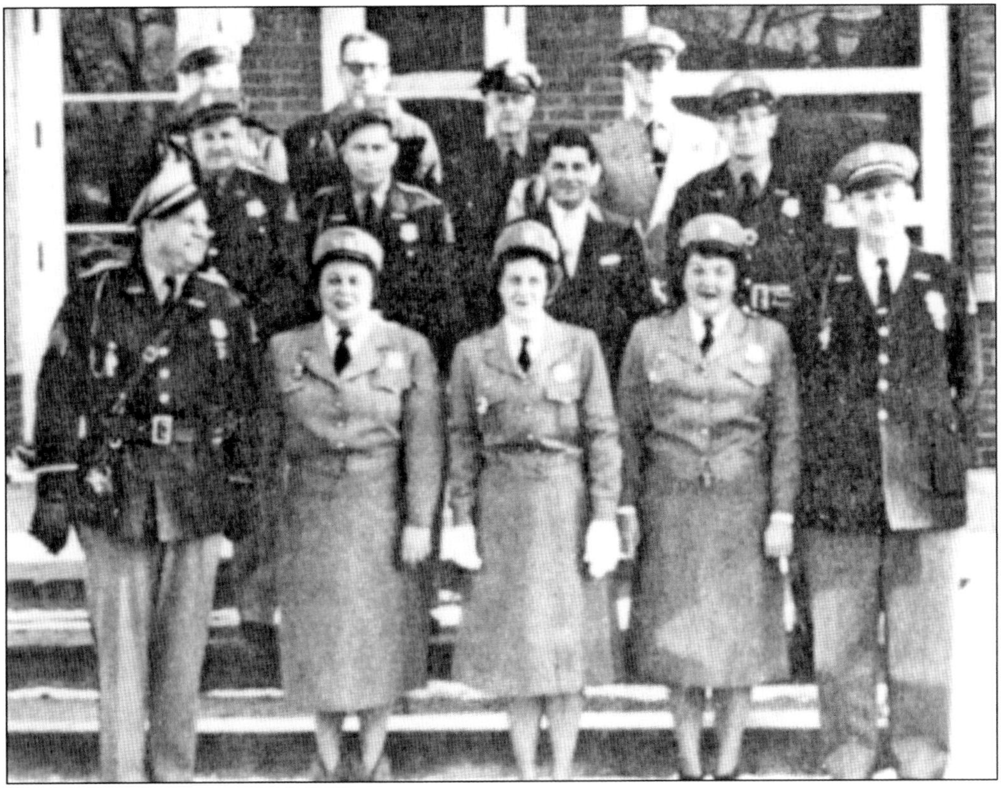

In 1960, the police department poses in front of city hall. From left to right are (first row) Sgt. C.W. Smith, Mrs. A. Bolton, Mrs. F. Manuel, Mrs. A. McCloskey, and Chief Tom Alsop (served 1958 to 1975); (second row) R. Carr, F. Glascock, C. Booth, and J. Suite; (third row) R. Van Ness, R. Orton, C. Reiser, and B. McLean. (Not pictured are P. Farrell, J. Earnest, J. Rainey, and R. Greaner.) Chief Alsop poses with his car below. The department was headquartered in a space that became cramped as the department grew, situated on the second floor above the city offices and accessed by a narrow, creaking staircase. (Both, courtesy of City of Mount Rainier.)

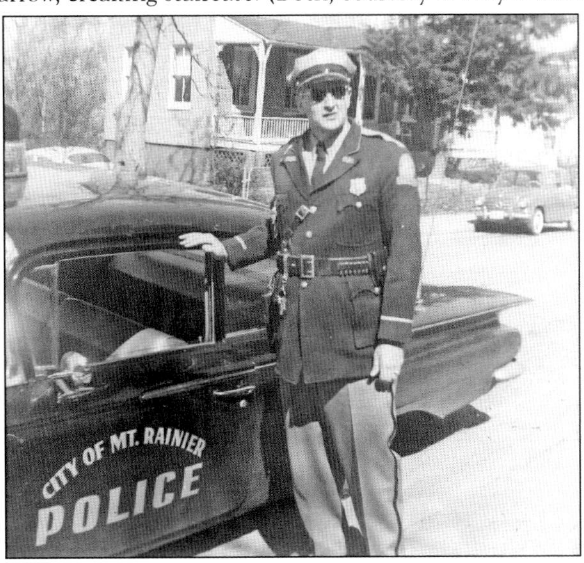

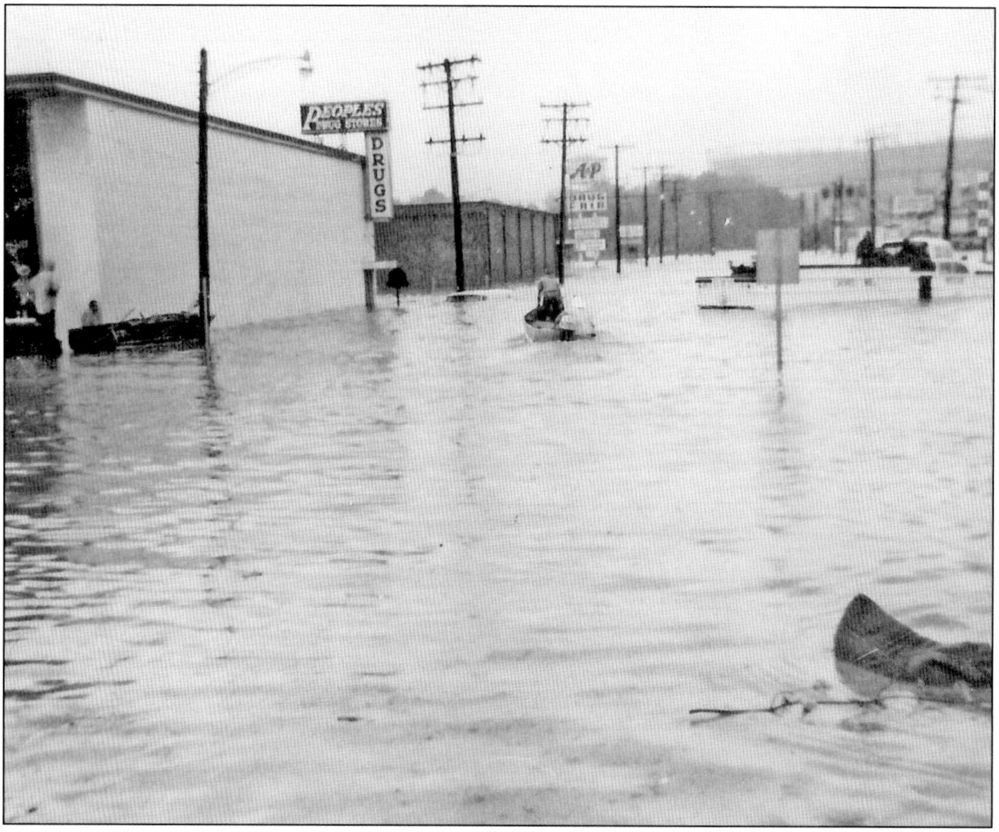

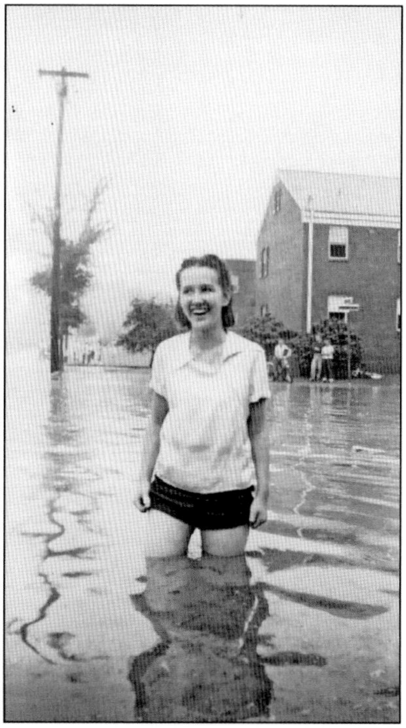

Mount Rainier is fortunate to have green parkland on its west (Barnard Hill Park) and on the east (the Northwest Branch of the Anacostia River). But for many years, the river brought misfortune with periodic flooding. Over the decades, as more upstream areas were paved, the storm water runoff increased and resulted in the flooding of the Queenstown and Queens Manor Apartments. Queenstown was inundated in January 1967. The photograph above shows the Queens-Chillum Shopping Center looking north up Chillum Road from Queens Chapel Road. Hurricane Agnes flooded the area again in September 1975. In 1984, the Washington Suburban Sanitary Commission received $5 million to build the earthen levees and concrete flood walls to protect Queenstown. After Hurricane Katrina in 2005, the Army Corps of Engineers required the county to reinforce and extend the flood protections. At left, lifelong resident Marilyn Mowat wades in an earlier flood around 1950 in the Queens Manor Apartment complex. (Above, courtesy of George Denny; left, courtesy of Marilyn Mowat.)

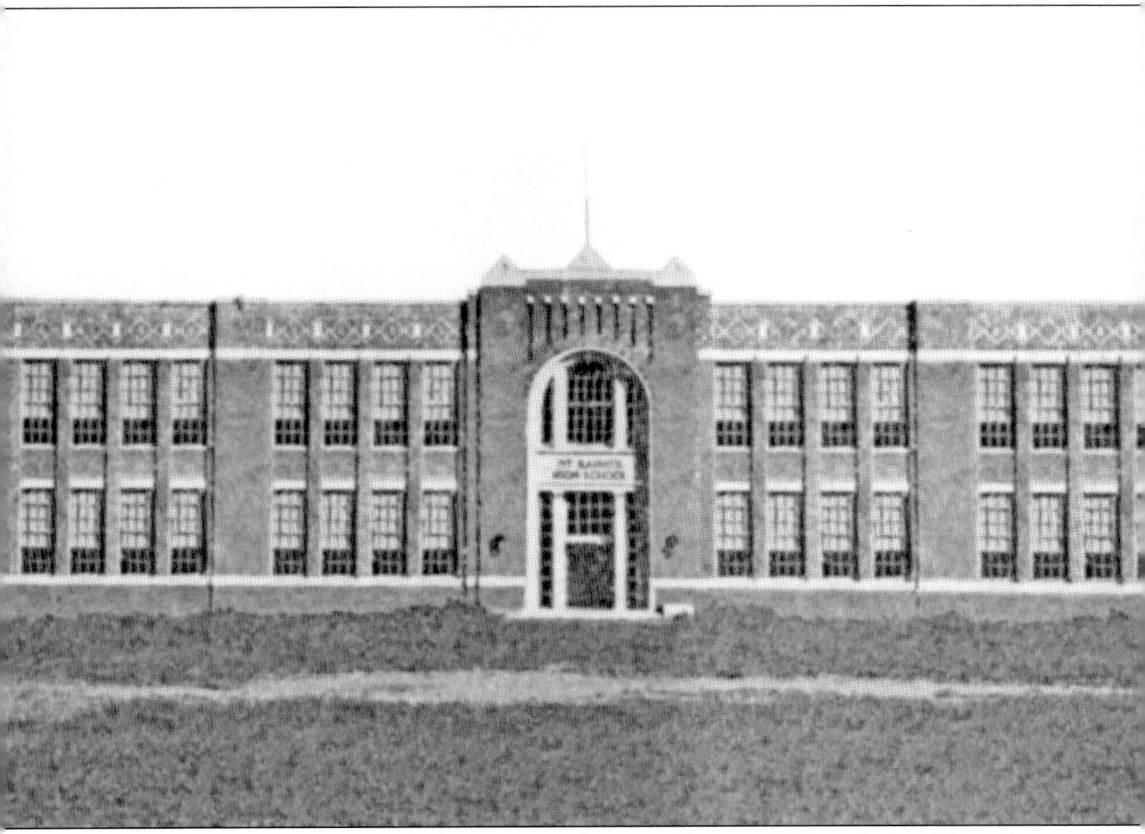

The high school became a junior high in 1952, with an enrollment of 725 pupils. In 1972, realizing that the town lacked facilities and programs for teenagers and through the junior high school principal's efforts, the Maryland–National Capital Park and Planning Commission's Department of Parks and Recreation sponsored a drop-in program on a part-time basis. A year later, the M-NCPPC and the Prince George's County Board of Education reached a joint facility-use agreement, part of which was to provide a full-size staff. The drop-in center operated seven days a week from 3:00 p.m. to 10:00 p.m. There were 90 recreational classes available for all community residents, an extension of the county library, and a multipurpose lighted athletic field. In 1976, girls participated for the first time in interscholastic sports. In the 1980s, the old school was sold to a private developer and was razed in 1992 to make way for the Rainier Manor apartments. (Courtesy of City of Mount Rainier.)

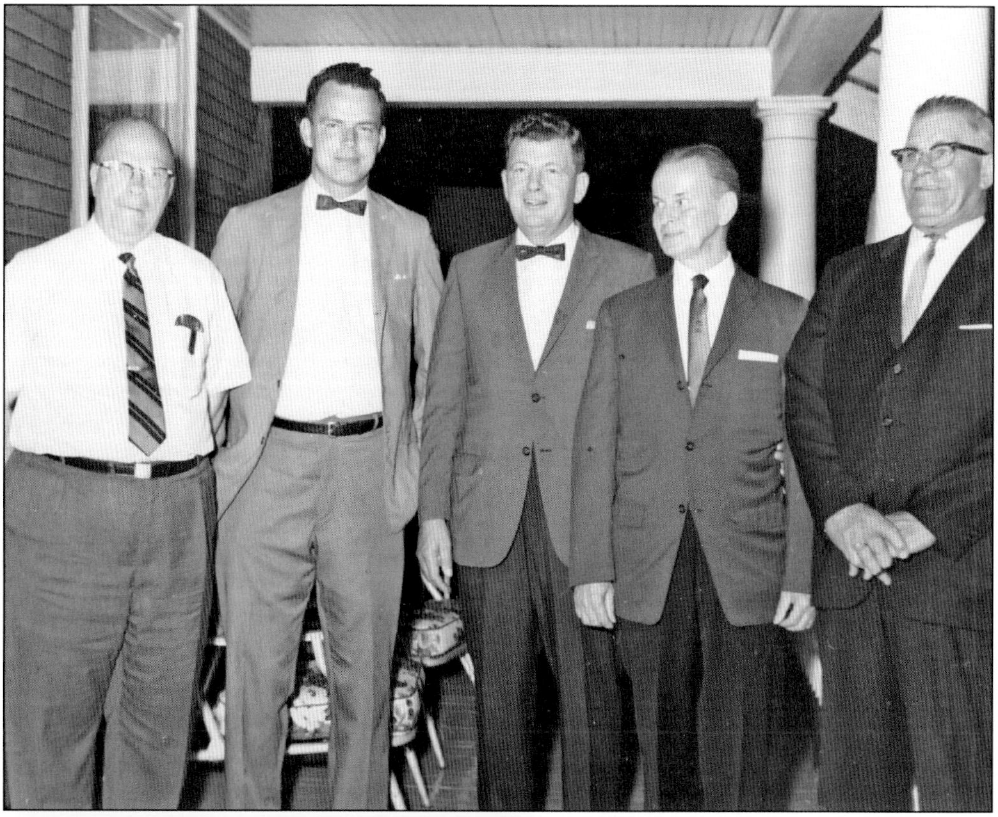

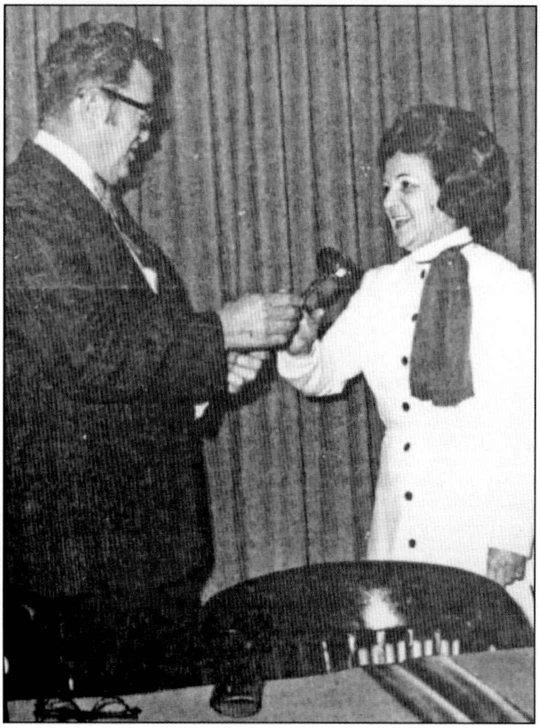

In 1969, the city council members (above) were, from left to right, Cedric Samuel, Ray Tanner, Mayor Roy Callaway, Jerome Richards, and Joseph Plumer. In 1975, the council rejected a $200,000 community improvement grant from the US Department of Housing and Urban Development, claiming the money might hurt the city. The rejected grant monies included funds for street repairs and rehabilitation of existing housing. Councilman Samuel said the grant might have required the city to accept urban renewal and public housing projects. Officials said rejection of the grant was proof of the independent, self-supportive status of the predominately blue-collar community. Residents who had lobbied to get federal money were outraged; this became a political issue in future elections. In 1977, Callaway presented the gavel to the first woman mayor, Linda Nalls. (Both, courtesy of City of Mount Rainier.)

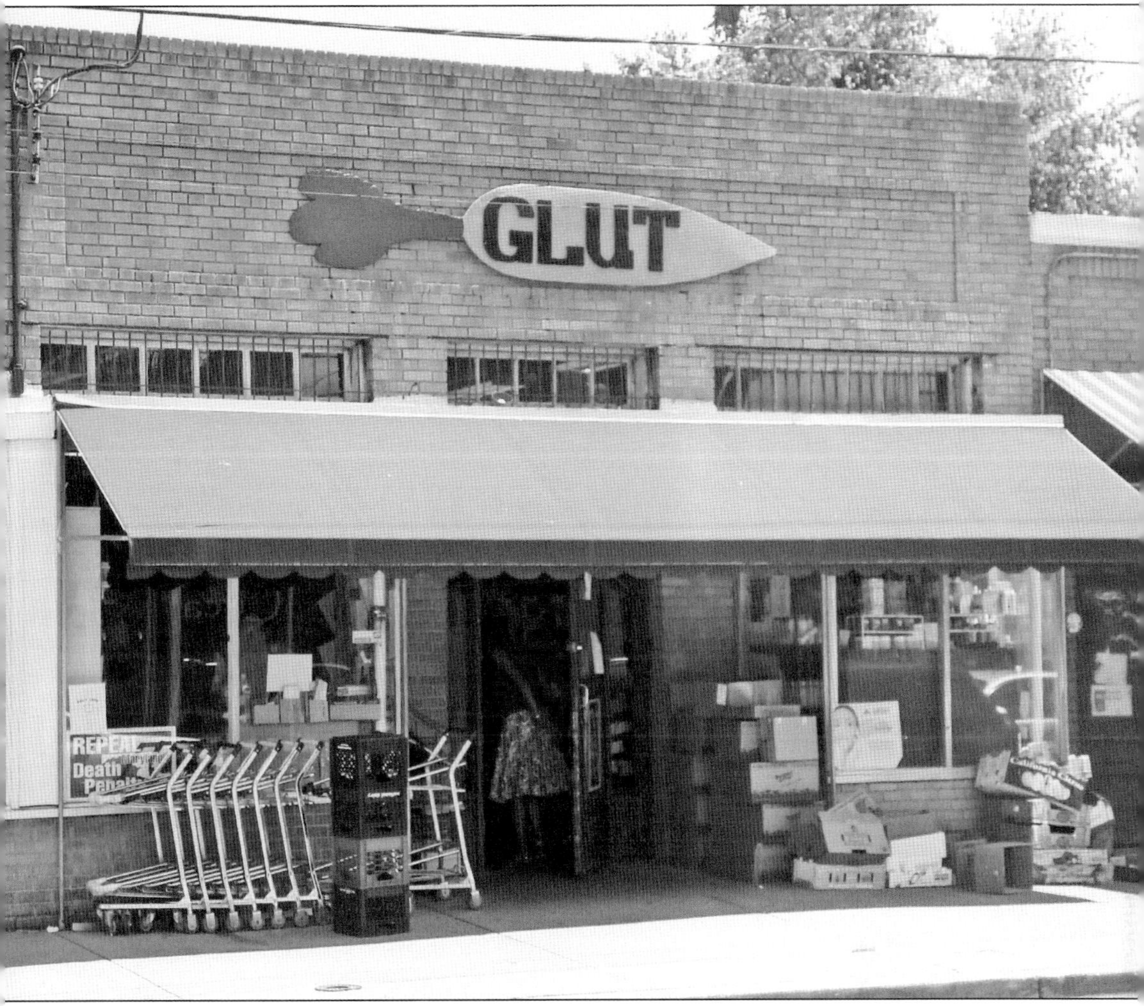

The Glut Food Co-op celebrated its 45th year in 2015. Glut has traditionally supported peace, environmental, and social justice movements. This commitment is rooted in its 1969 founding by conscientious objectors during the Vietnam War. At the time, food co-ops, alternative newspapers, and free health clinics were an integral part of a movement that went beyond opposition to the war. In lieu of military service, the members created a buying club to provide affordable, wholesome food. In 1971, having outgrown the church basements that it had been using, Glut moved its operations to a larger space, a rented storefront in Mount Rainier. Eventually, it expanded beyond co-op members and opened its doors to the general public. Finally, the building at 4005 Thirty-fourth Street was purchased, and in the 1990s, properties at 4001 and 4003 were added. The co-op became an anchor business and also attracted many new residents, who became aware of Mount Rainier through visits to the store. (Courtesy of Robert Page.)

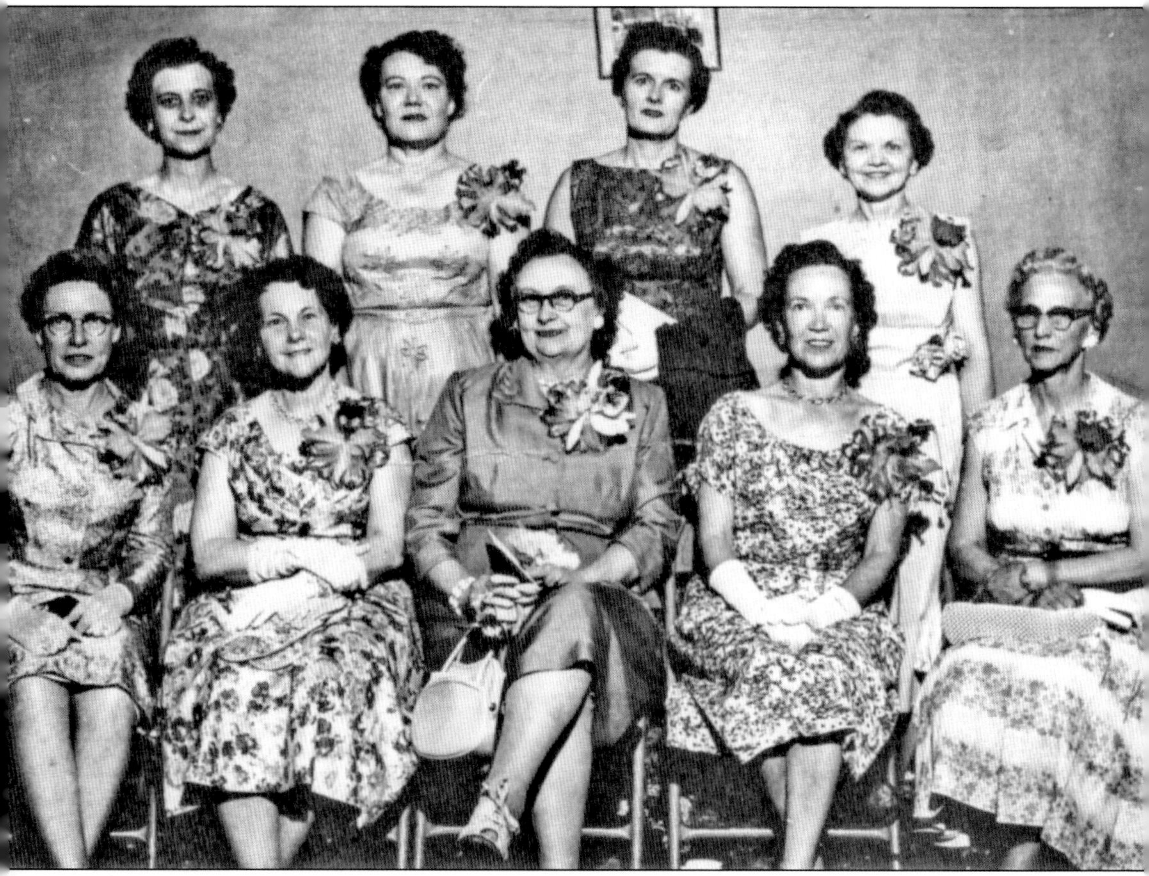

The Cora B. Wood Senior Center, located at 3601 Taylor Street, is named to honor Wood, a civic activist (second from left in first row). The center (in the former Brentwood Elementary School) sits partially in Mount Rainier. In the 1970s, local seniors lobbied for a health center. They succeeded when county executive Winfield Kelly and the County Council agreed to fund a center, which opened in 1974 at St. James School in Mount Rainier under the management of the National Institutes of Health. In 1976, the Prince George's Hospital Center took over management, and in 1981, services moved into the Taylor Street location. Over the years, the seniors have successfully protected the center. They opposed the hospital's proposal to move from Brentwood to the hospital itself. In 1994, they were informed that the center would be closed on Tuesdays and Thursdays. Pres. Bill Clinton happened to be scheduled for a visit, and as he arrived at the center with media in tow, the seniors hoisted placards in protest of the reduced hours. Three weeks later, the proposal was rescinded. (Courtesy of George Denny.)

The Queen Anne–style Bellman House, located at 4012 Thirty-third Street, is a county historic site. Built on a high point, its octagonal tower affords a vista view of the surrounding area. The house was built by Oscar and Bertha Bellman in 1905. Oscar was founder of the Bellman Heating Company. It remained in the family for 56 years. Winfield M. Kelly Jr. (right) and his wife, Margaret, lived there in the early 1960s. He served as Prince George's County executive from 1974 to 1978 and later as Maryland's secretary of state. In the 1980s, future mayor Fred Sissine and his wife, Deborah, purchased the home and restored it. (Right, courtesy of Maryland State Archives; below, courtesy of Jimmy Tarlau.)

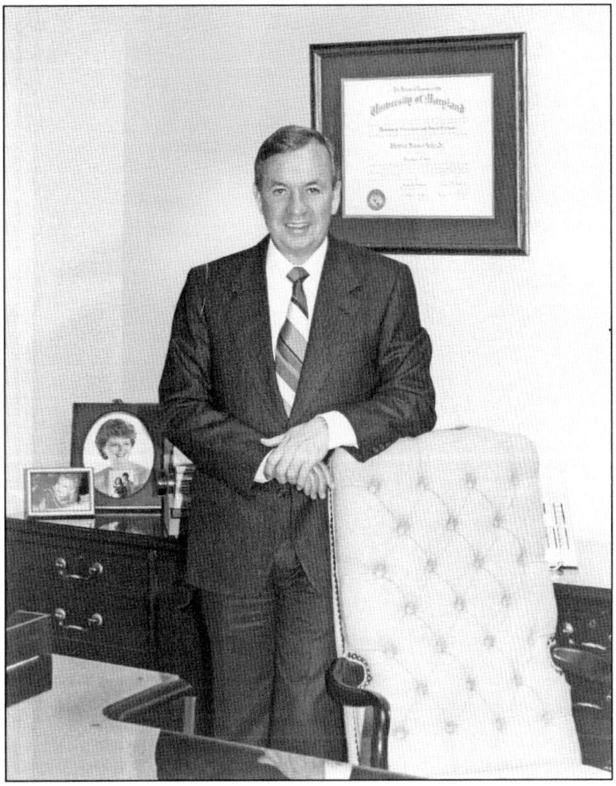

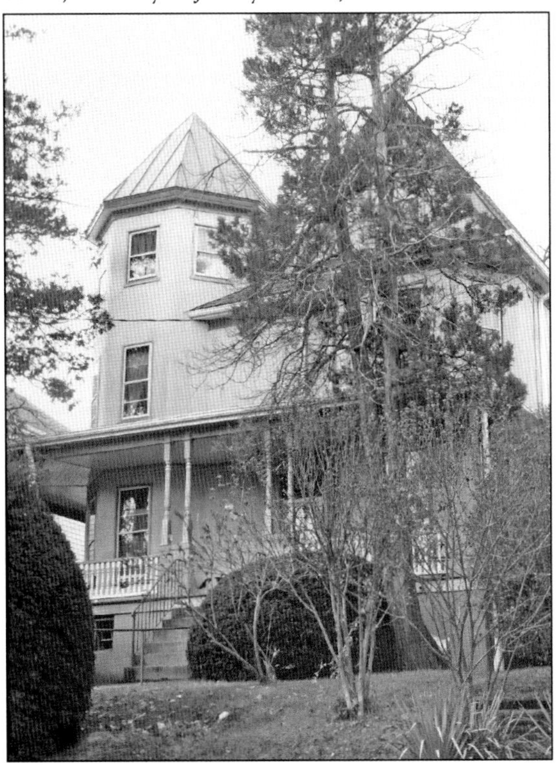

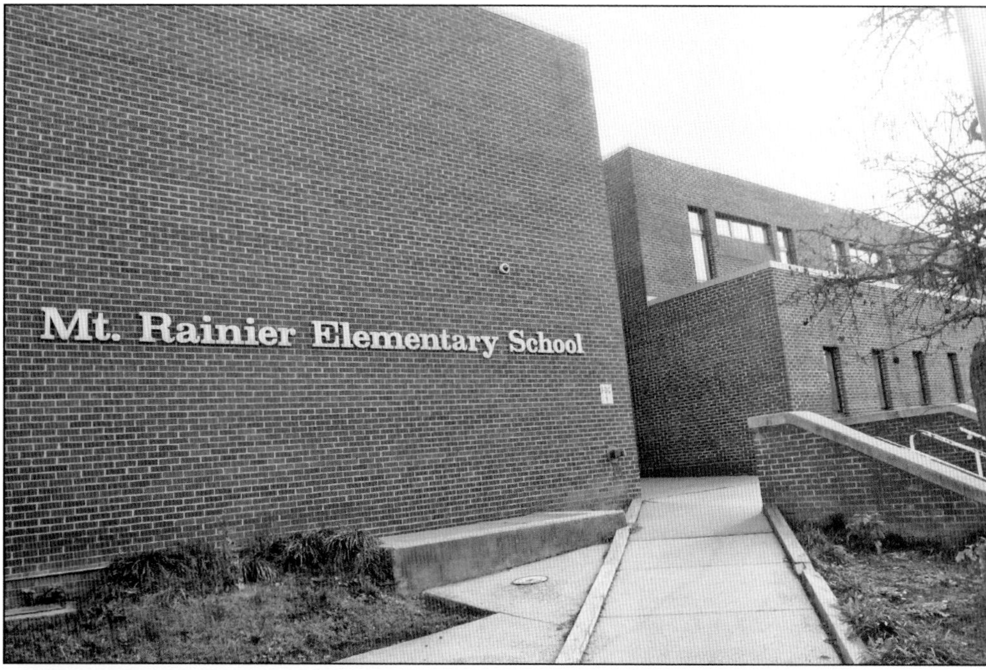

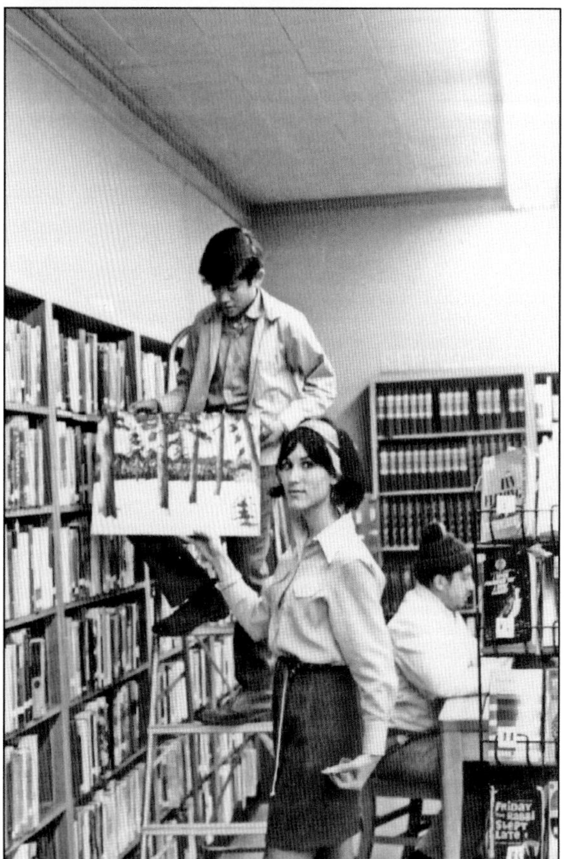

In the 1970s, the preeminence of the streetcar suburbs waned with the growth of outlying suburbs. In 1971, the city held a public hearing on the county school board's proposal to close Mount Rainier Elementary and move the children to an enlarged Thomas Stone Elementary. County executive William Gullett and County Council chair Winfield Kelly Jr. attended. The outpouring of support for the school convinced the county to rebuild it rather than consolidate at Thomas Stone. In 1977, Kelly, who became county executive, proposed budget cuts that would have closed the Mount Rainier Library. Again, community support kept it open. At left, Jesus Medrano, Mount Rainier Junior High School eighth grader, shows his work during a library art exhibit with art teacher Ann Springer looking on. Robert Parisi is seated at the table. (Above, courtesy of Jimmy Tarlau; left, courtesy of PGCMLS.)

From the beginning, the Mount Rainier Library was more than just about lending books. The library held art shows that promoted the works of residents. Local artist and longtime resident Minnie Barz (on the left in the photograph at right) shows her work to librarian Mary McCain. In a 1990s city newsletter, Barz advocated creation of neighborhood studio space where artists could work together and offer classes to the community. In the 21st century, the library became a place for those with limited means to utilize the Internet. The branch is unique in the county, with the city providing the space and the county providing the staff and books. Below, McCain reviews some pieces with Mount Rainier Elementary School art teacher Ronald Wilder. (Both, courtesy of PGCMLS.)

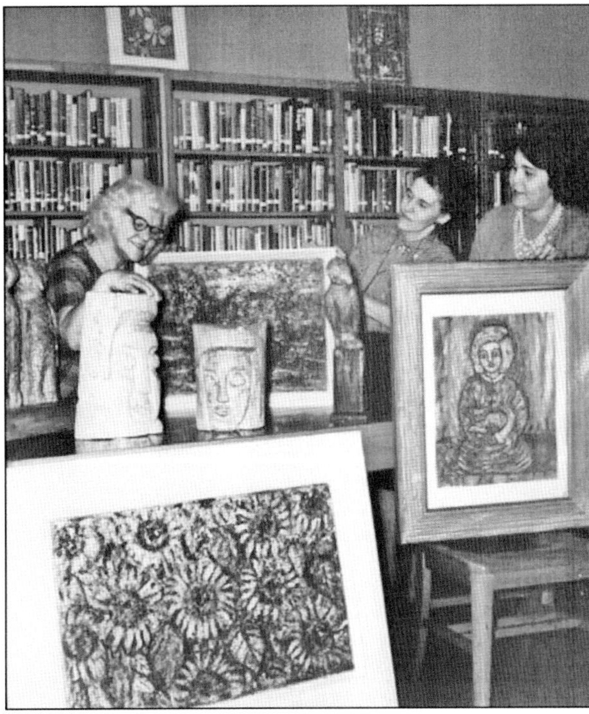

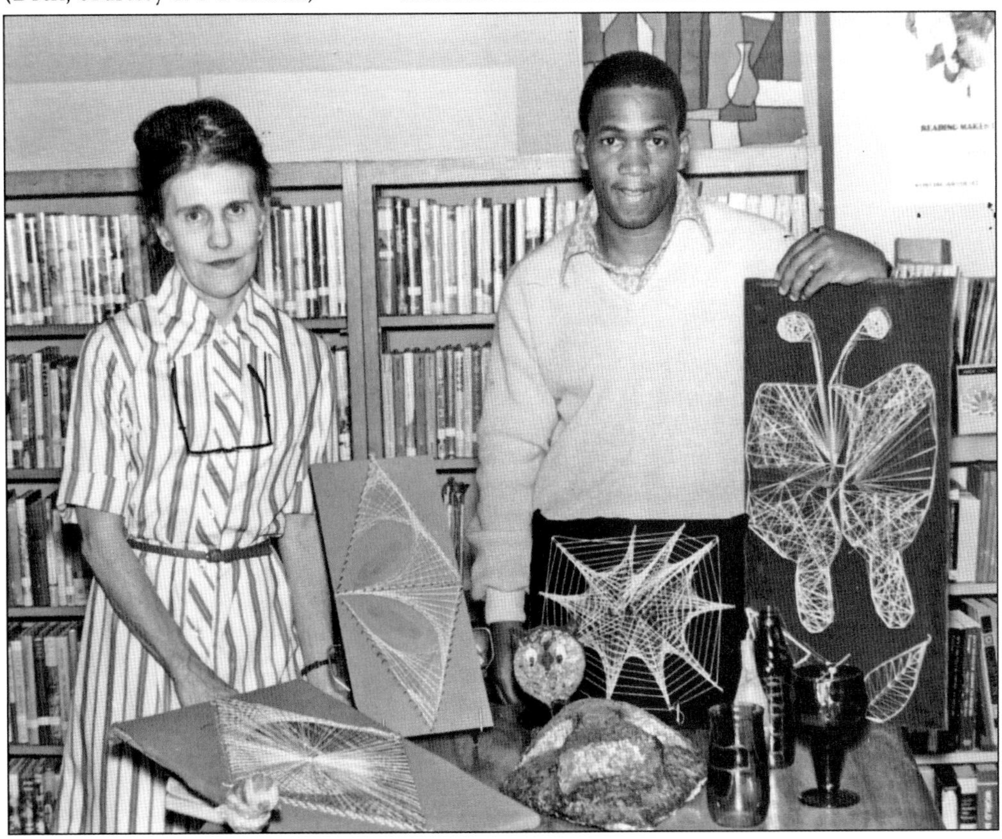

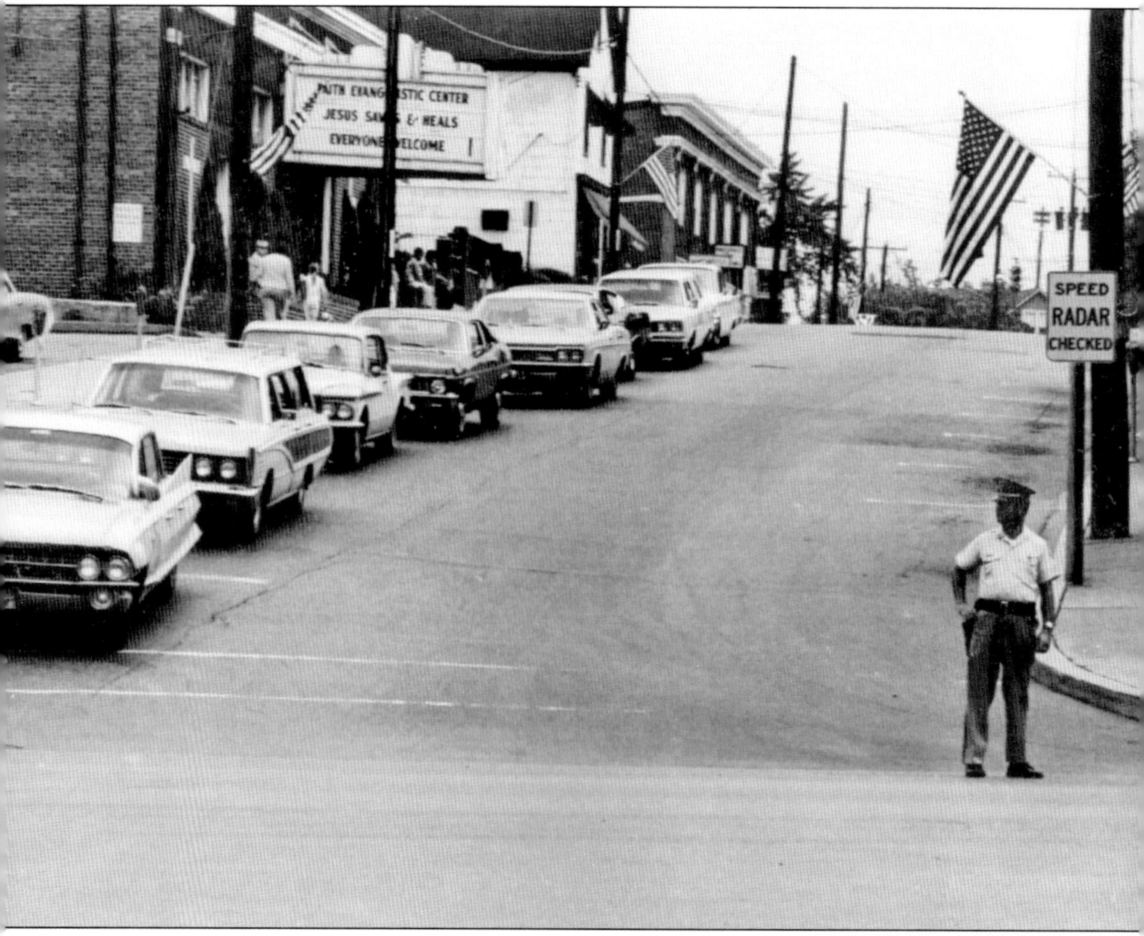

In 1970, Joseph Howell, a University of North Carolina graduate student, moved into 3501 Otis Street with his wife, Embry, and infant son. The urban studies department sent him to study a white working-class neighborhood. He made no secret of his research, yet was accepted into the neighborhood as a participant in the daily lives of his neighbors. His published field study, *Hard Living on Clay Street*, disguised the true location (revealed in later years). The book is an account of the blue-collar residents during the Vietnam War dealing not only with interpersonal conflicts but also with a changing society and a rapid shift in the neighborhood's racial composition. In conjunction with his study, an ethnographic survey was conducted (*Across the City Line: A White Community in Transition*), documenting the conditions and attitudes of 1970s Mount Rainier, Brentwood, Cottage City, and Colmar Manor. Howell's photographs documented 1970s streetscapes, including this Forth of July parade on Thirty-fourth Street. (Courtesy of Joseph Howell.)

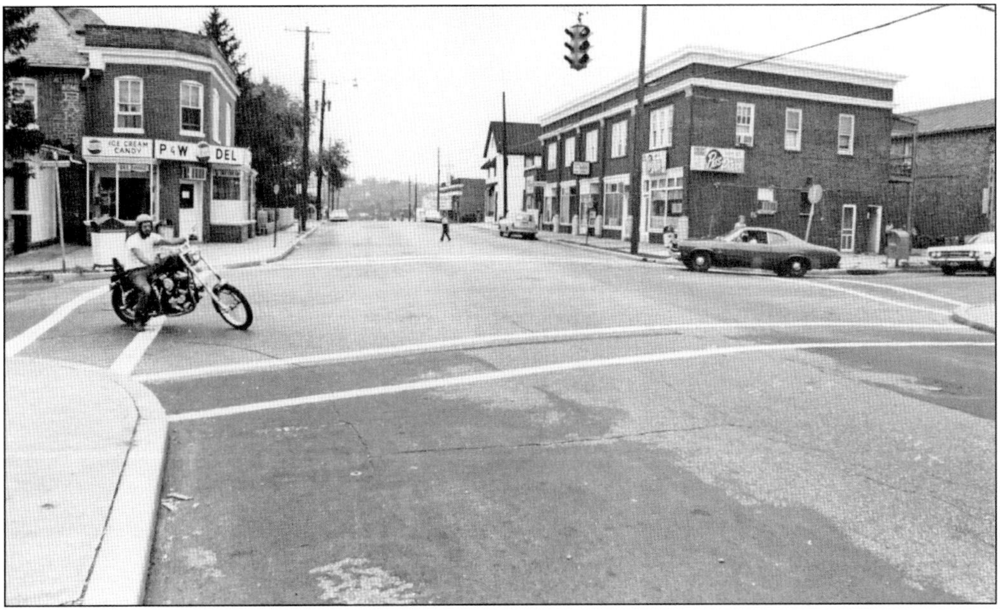

After the publication of *Hard Living on Clay Street*, one resident expressed the community's negative reaction by telling author Howell that it was the second worst thing to happen to the city in its history—the first being *The Exorcist* film (see page 75). Seen here are two views of the intersection of Thirty-fourth Street and Bunker Hill Road. The parade photograph is from the Washington Star collection, now held by the District of Columbia's Martin Luther King Memorial Library. (Above, courtesy of Joseph Howell; below, courtesy of DC Public Library.)

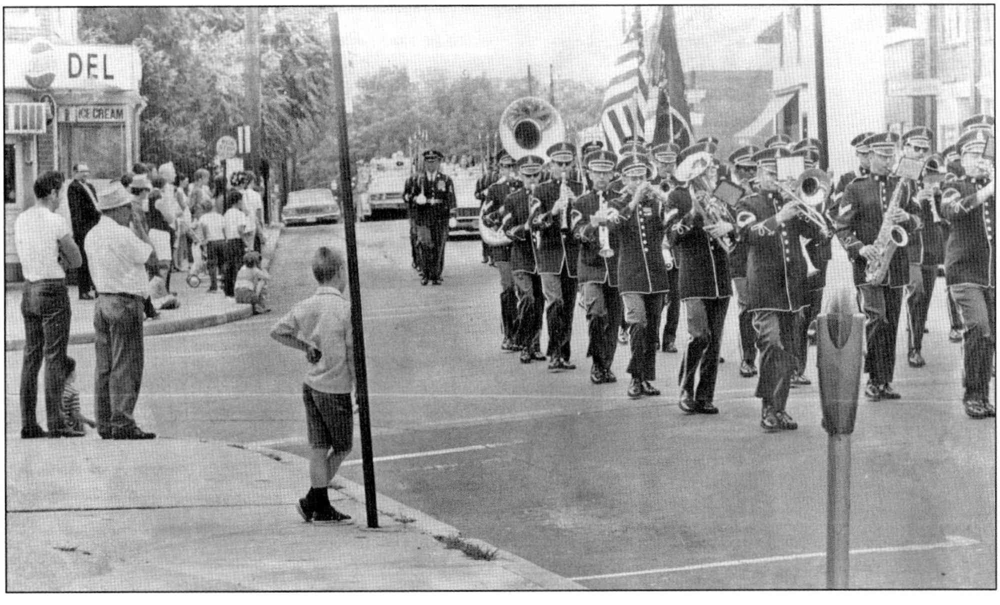

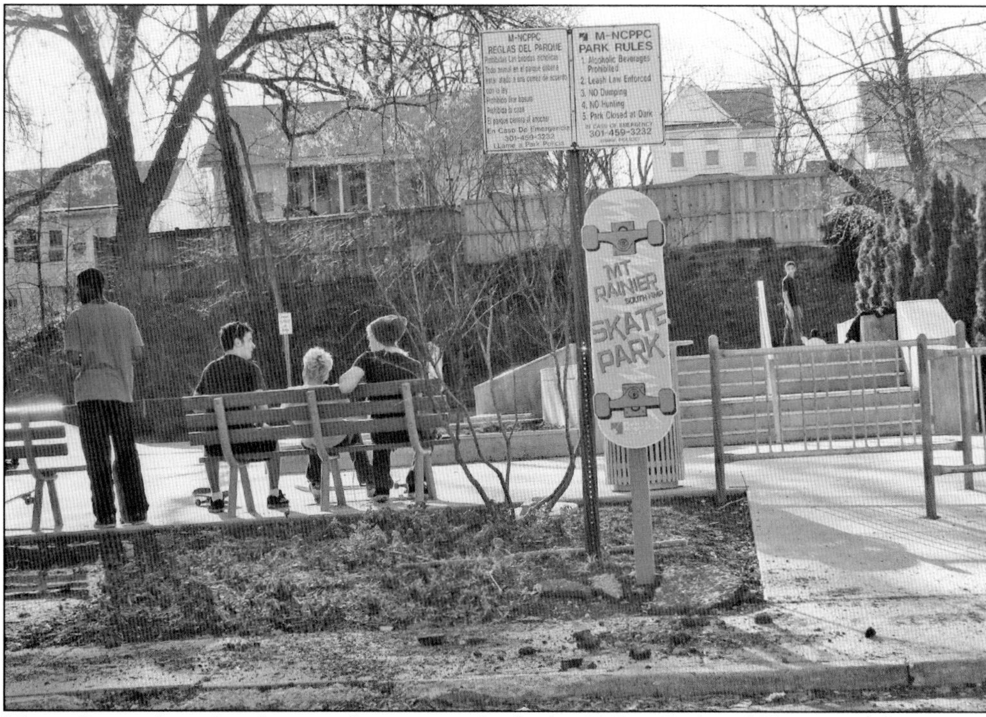

Mount Rainier has a long history of creating parks. In the 1940s, a Park and Playground Committee began creating playgrounds out of vacant lots. The old Huntemann field (location of Thomas Stone Elementary) became the first park; bulldozers furnished by Kaywood Gardens Construction Co. cleared the land for baseball diamonds. In the 1970s, the federal Parks in Cities program funded "pocket parks" built on small lots within residential areas. In 2009, the park at Wells Avenue and Otis Street (above) became the county's first skateboard park, following the evolution of activities young residents desired. In 2005, the park at Arundel Road and Thirtieth Street (below) was dedicated to the memory of former mayor Stanley Prusch and his wife, Pauline, who were instrumental in the creation of the park within view of their home at 4512 Thirtieth Street. (Both, courtesy of Jimmy Tarlau.)

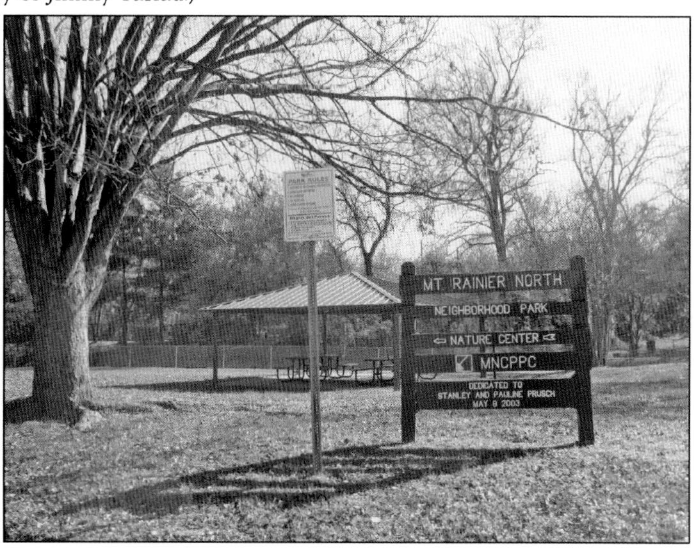

Five

Debates and Decisions, New Direction

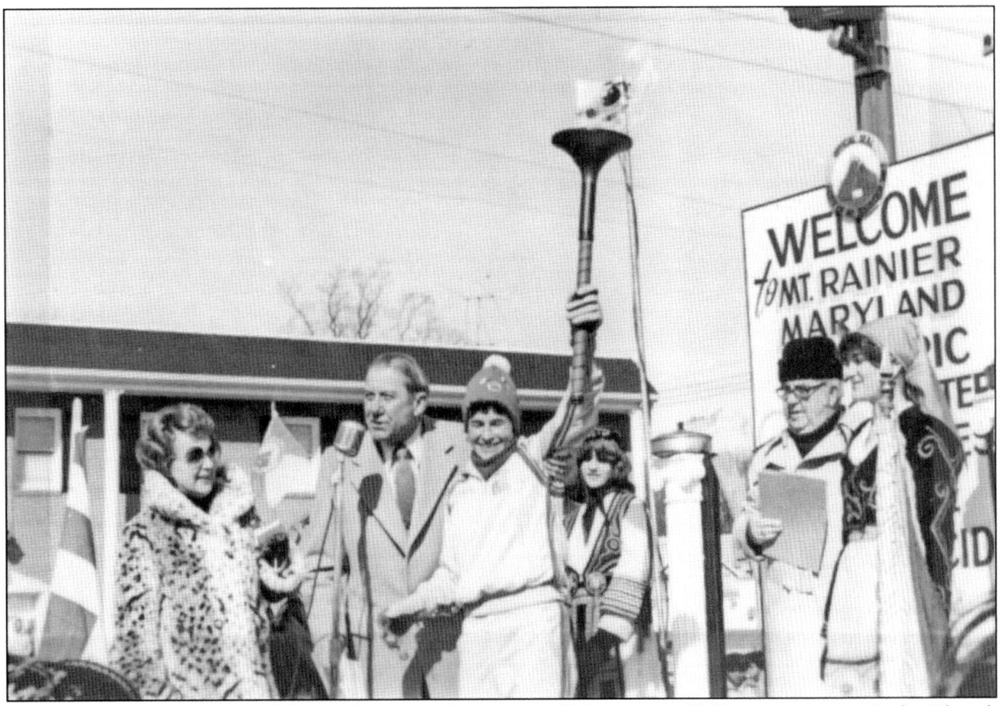

The Olympic torch passed through Mount Rainier on February 1, 1980, on its way to Lake Placid, New York. Mayor Linda Nalls (in fur coat) and former mayor Herbert Reichelt (at the microphone) encourage the relay runner who would carry it from the District of Columbia to Hyattsville. In the 1980s, a metaphorical torch passed to a new generation with a vision that revitalized an aging streetcar suburb. (Courtesy of City of Mount Rainier.)

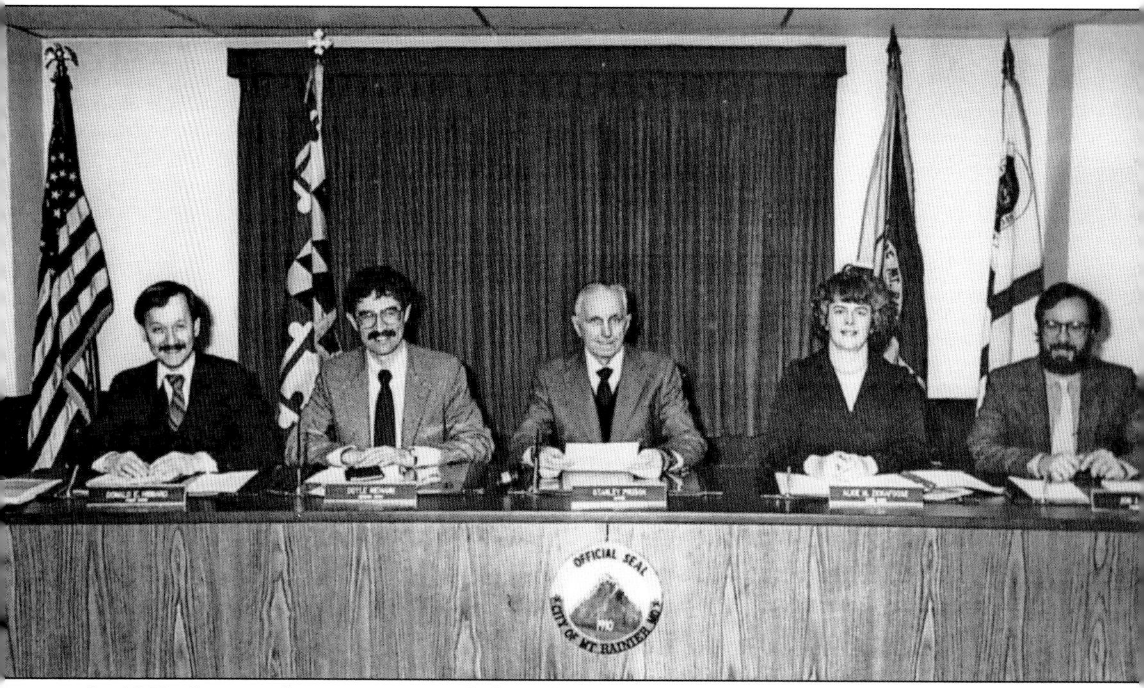

In 1981, the city charter was amended to eliminate the long-held practice of allowing voter registration for the city voter list on only two days each year. Increasing the eligible voters in part helped usher in a new generation of leaders. The *Washington Post* noted that the May 1983 election swept out the old guard: "The former councilmembers, all longtime residents ranging in age from 51 to 74, were replaced by a new generation of leaders, all younger than 37, who reflect the growing number of young families in the community." The new council then eliminated the separate voter list for city elections in favor of using the county's registration process. The eligible voters jumped from approximately 800 to more than 3,000. The new council members in 1983 were, from left to right, Don Hibbard, Doyle Niemann (who later became a county school board member and then state delegate), Mayor Stanley Prusch (who had defeated incumbent Linda Nalls), Alice Zickafoose, and Jon Moran. (Courtesy of City of Mount Rainier.)

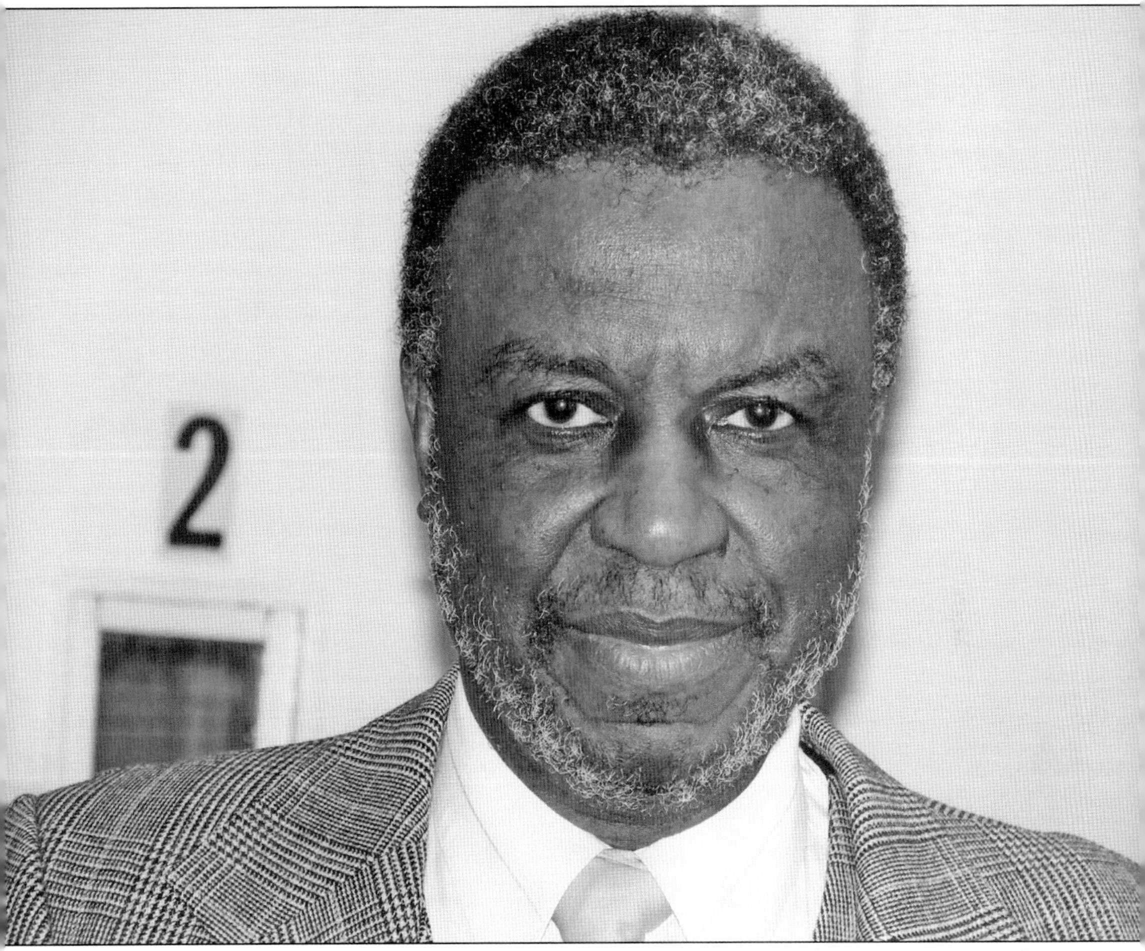

In 1980, the majority of black residents lived in the apartment complexes as renters, and no African Americans had served on the city council. The city had one black police officer, and all other black city employees were in public works. Change came in the 1985 election when two of five candidates running for the Ward 2 council seats—Sharon Ambrose and Otis Hayward—were African American. Hayward was elected the first black council member. In 1987, he was reelected, and Malinda Miles joined him on the council as the first black councilwoman. The first majority black council was seated in 2009 with Mayor Malinda Miles and Council members Ivy Thompson and Alta Morton. Among his accomplishments, Hayward, along with bike activists Steve McKindley-Ward and Bob Patten, succeeded in getting the county to create the Anacostia Tributaries Trail system. He was also active with the founding of the city's tree commission and anti-crime initiatives. During the 1990s, black homeownership greatly increased. In 1990, approximately 556 of owner-occupied housing units were white-owned, while 317 were owned by blacks; in 2000, these numbers were 385 and 422 respectively. (Courtesy of Robert Page.)

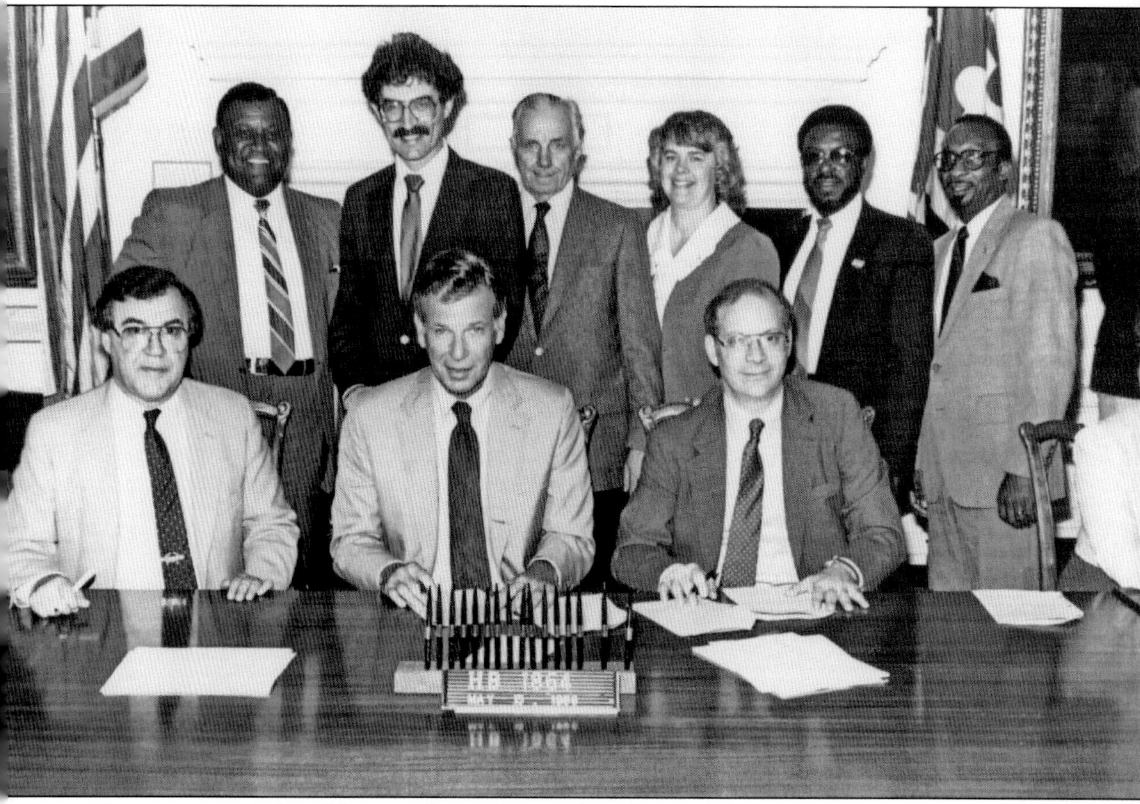

The outcome of a key debate in the 1980s greatly influenced future revitalization efforts: should city hall remain in the town center or move closer to the center of population in the apartment complexes near Queens Chapel Road? Election outcomes turned on that issue. The county offered the abandoned junior high school on Queens Chapel Road as a potential city hall site, but after studying the costs, Mayor Linda Nalls and the council decided it was too expensive. In 1983, Stanley Prusch defeated Nalls to become mayor with a new group of councilmembers who supported the school site. In 1986, Sen. Decatur Trotter secured $250,000 to purchase space in the school. Pictured at the bill signing are, from left to right, (first row) Senate president Melvin Steinberg, Gov. Harry Hughes, and House speaker Ben Cardin; (second row) Senator Trotter, City Councilman Doyle Niemann, Mayor Stanley Prusch, Councilwoman Alice Zickafoose, Councilman Otis Hayward, and delegate Nathaniel Exum. (Courtesy of City of Mount Rainier.)

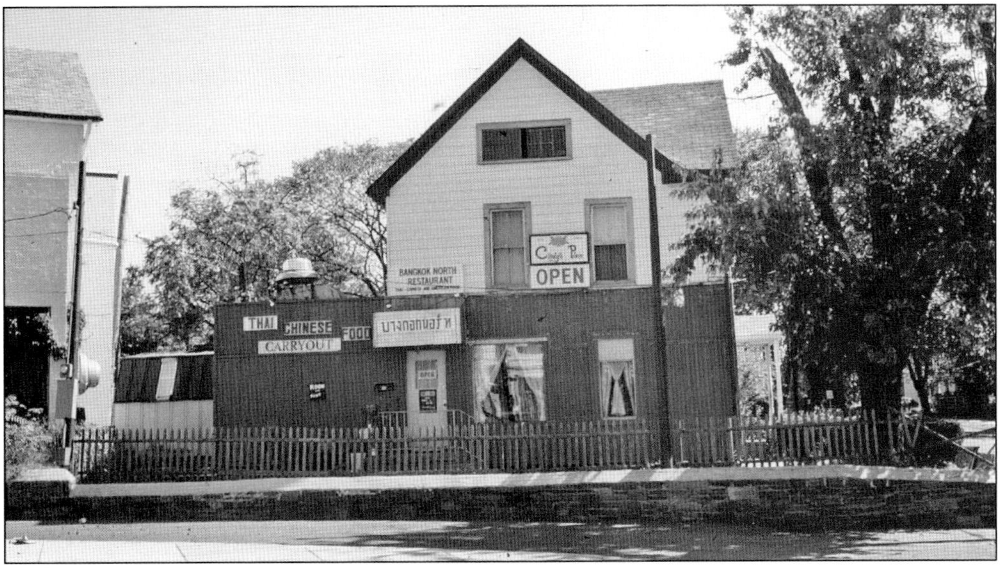

Technical requirements of Senator Trotter's bill kept the council from moving forward, and during the delay, Nalls defeated Prusch in 1989 with the backing of Citi-Pals, a group that believed city hall should stay in the town center to bolster revitalization. Trotter's revised legislation was approved in 1989, and the funding helped purchase the old house at 3500 Perry Street. The house can be seen as it appeared in 1912 on page 29. (Courtesy of M-NCPPC.)

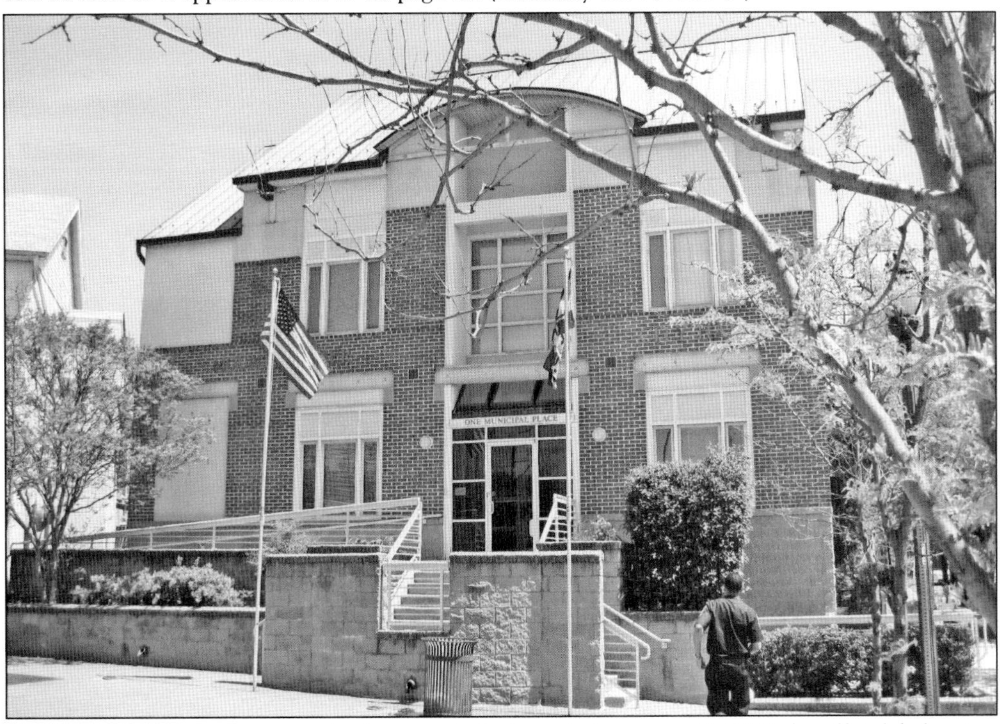

The ground-breaking ceremony for the new city hall was held August 13, 1992; the official dedication ceremony was October 22, 1994. Architect Norman Smith designed the building. With the end of the decade-long debate over keeping the city government in the city core, the council began a new effort to focus on town center redevelopment. (Courtesy of Robert Page.)

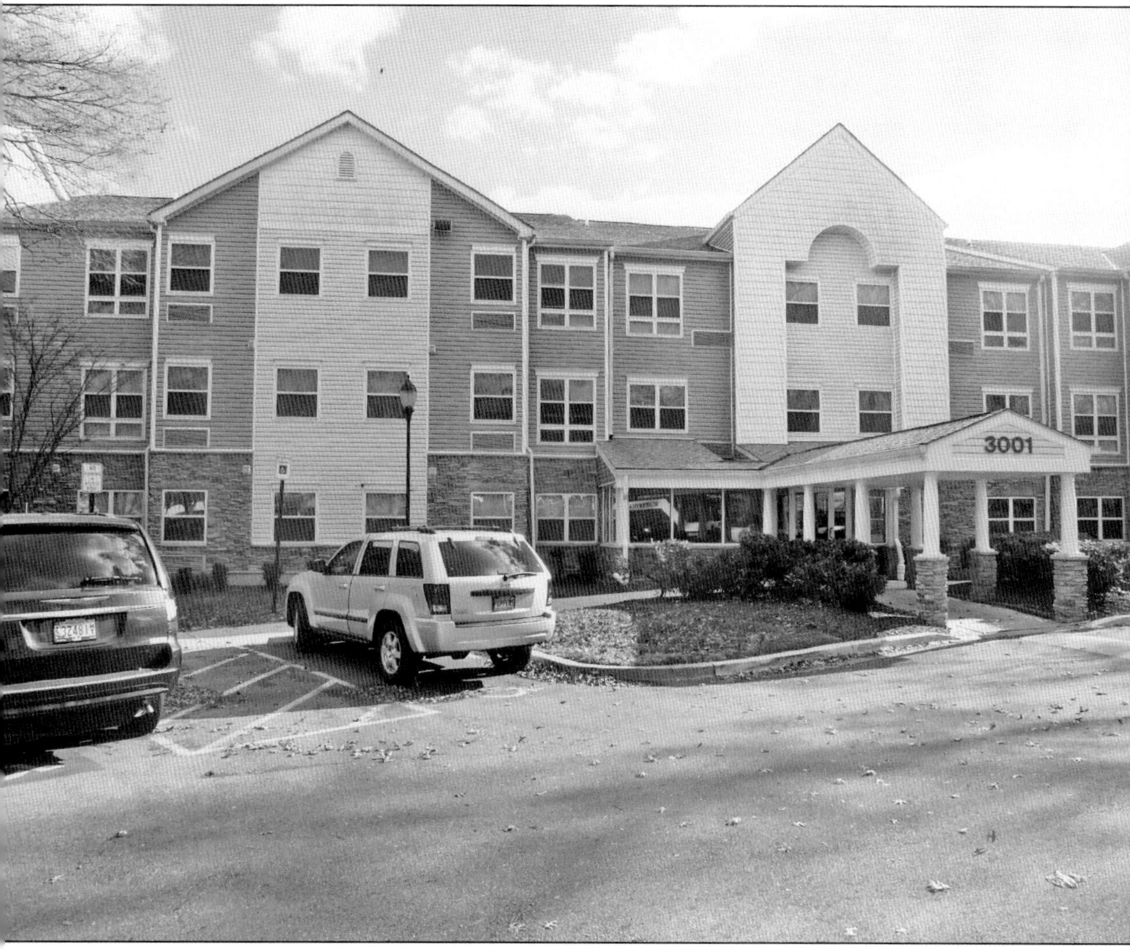

As the city worked on building a new city hall in the town center, the old junior high school continued to deteriorate and became not only an eyesore but the haunt of drug dealers. In 1988, the city council began asking the county to revoke the previously issued special zoning exception for the property, but the county continued to refuse the request. In 1990, the gymnasium roof collapsed and the building was condemned. Later in 1990, hearings were held for a new proposal—to build a senior citizens housing project—and soon after, Martin Miller Properties came to the city with a proposal for the senior housing project. Once the proposal was approved, events moved quickly. In early 1992, Mount Rainier Junior High School was razed; ground breaking occurred in June, and construction began. Rainier Manor Senior Housing opened in December 1992 on Queens Chapel Road. (Courtesy of Jimmy Tarlau.)

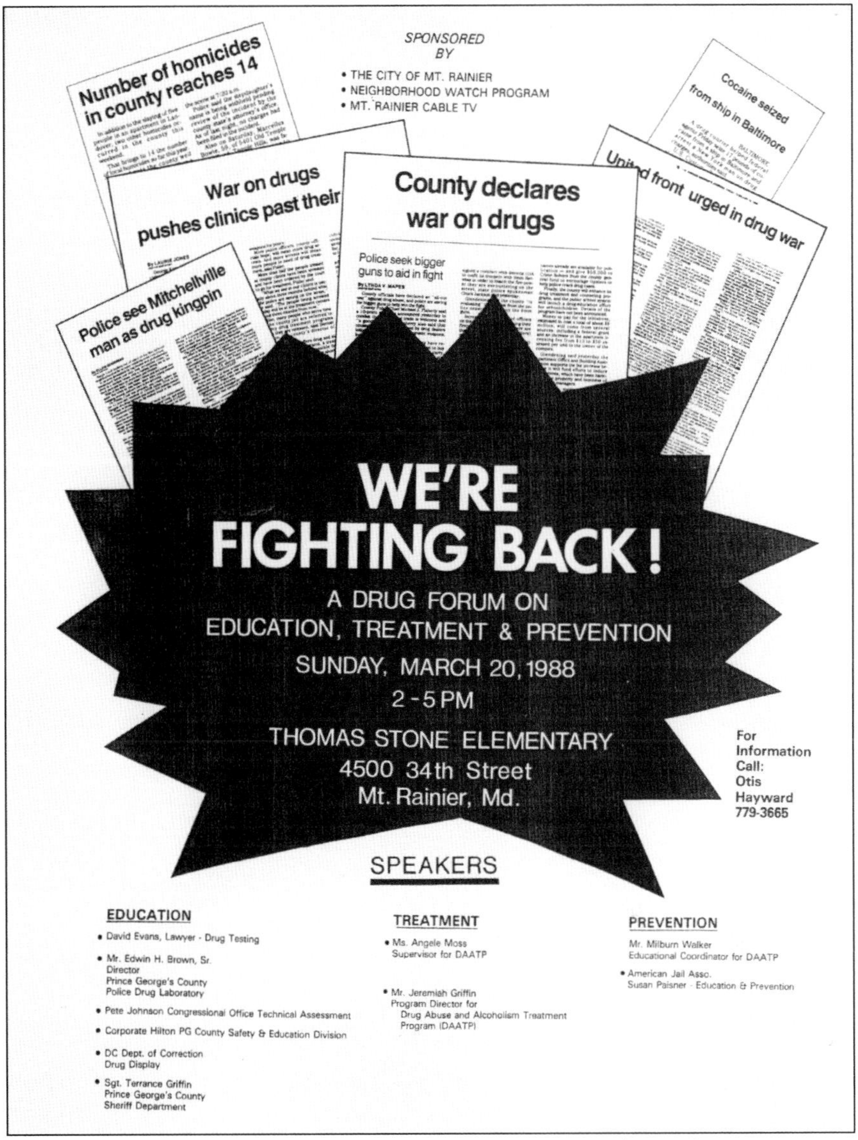

In the 1980s, illegal drugs joined the list of problems to overcome if revitalization was to succeed. Reminiscent of the fight against gambling in the 1950s, newspaper headlines again trumpeted the desire of residents to take back their neighborhood: "Mount Rainier Seeks to Shed Seedy Image" (*Prince George's Journal*, Sept. 1989) and "Working Class Mount Rainier to Repair Image" (*Washington Post*, March 1991). Crime-watch groups organized, and blighted properties were targeted for cleanup to deter crime. Residents recognized the connections between crime, aesthetics, and environmental issues. Many of the same people volunteered for the block watch, tree commission, and historic preservation committee. Grant money funded a drug-sniffing K-9 member of the police force, as well as efforts to improve the business district image, and plant 300 street trees. In 1988, the impact of illegal drugs resulted in a drug abuse prevention forum, as promoted in this flyer. Cross-border crime became a focus, so District of Columbia Ward 5 councilman Harry Thomas hosted a meeting of District, Prince George's County, and Mount Rainier officials to discuss the formation of joint police patrols along Eastern Avenue. (Courtesy of City of Mount Rainier.)

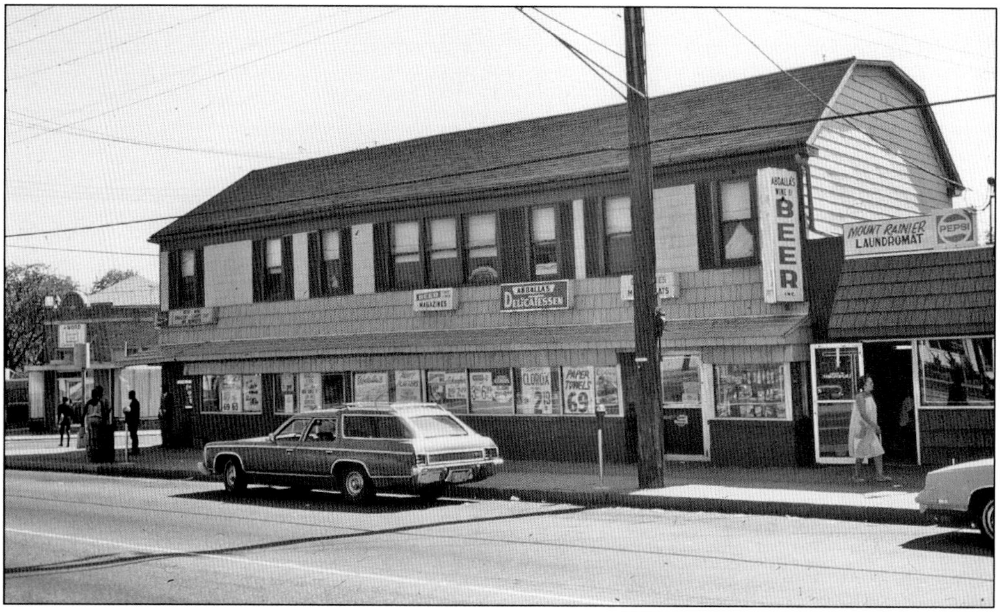

In the 1990s, as in past decades, the business district continued to represent the city to the thousands of commuters who passed through each day. Abdalla's Carryout (shown in the 1990s) was one of several liquor stores along the avenue. In 1989, a report faulted the city's businesses for presenting a "poor image of neglect and decay." Business district revitalization became a priority after city hall was completed in 1994. (Courtesy of M-NCPPC.)

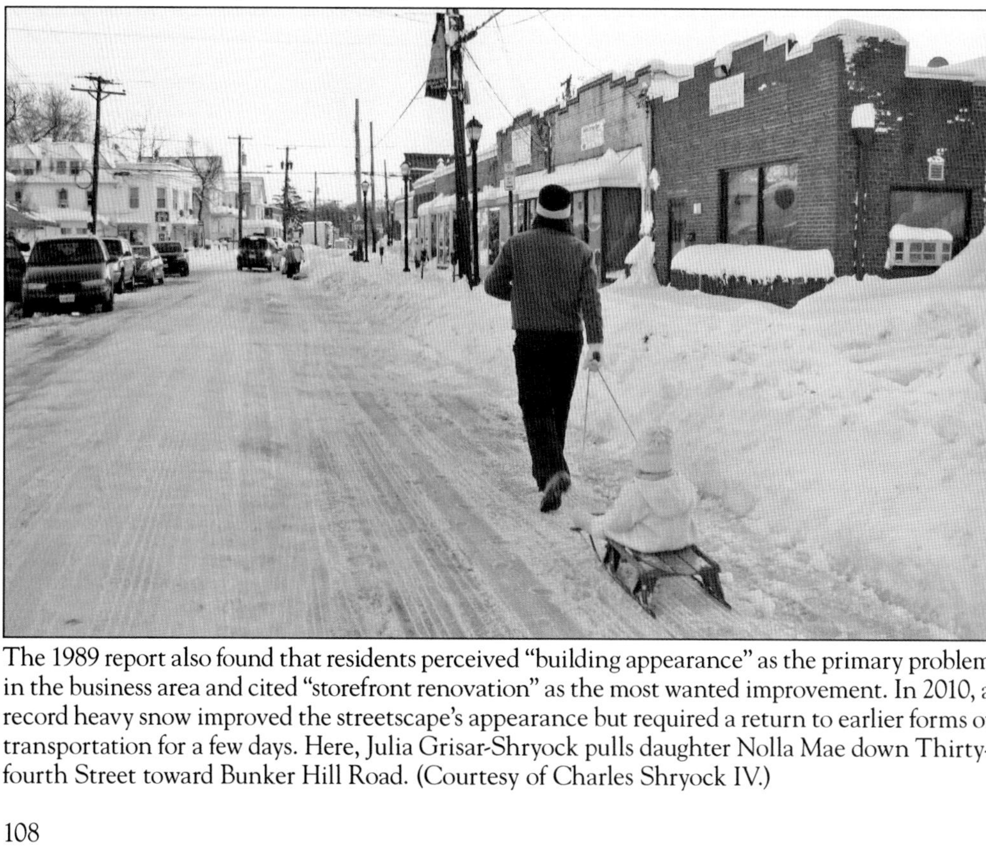

The 1989 report also found that residents perceived "building appearance" as the primary problem in the business area and cited "storefront renovation" as the most wanted improvement. In 2010, a record heavy snow improved the streetscape's appearance but required a return to earlier forms of transportation for a few days. Here, Julia Grisar-Shryock pulls daughter Nolla Mae down Thirty-fourth Street toward Bunker Hill Road. (Courtesy of Charles Shryock IV.)

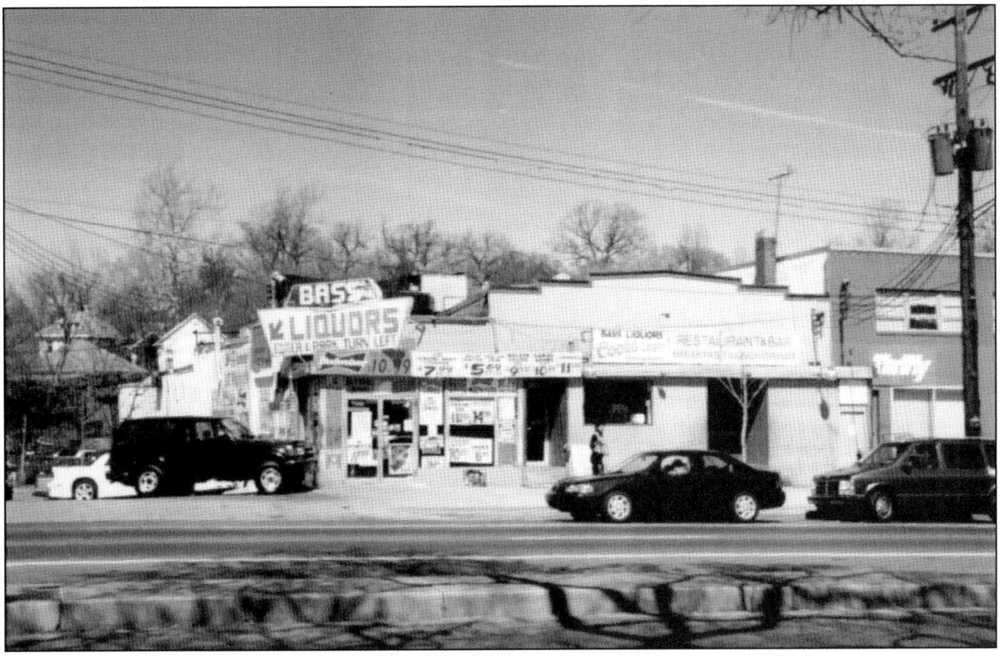

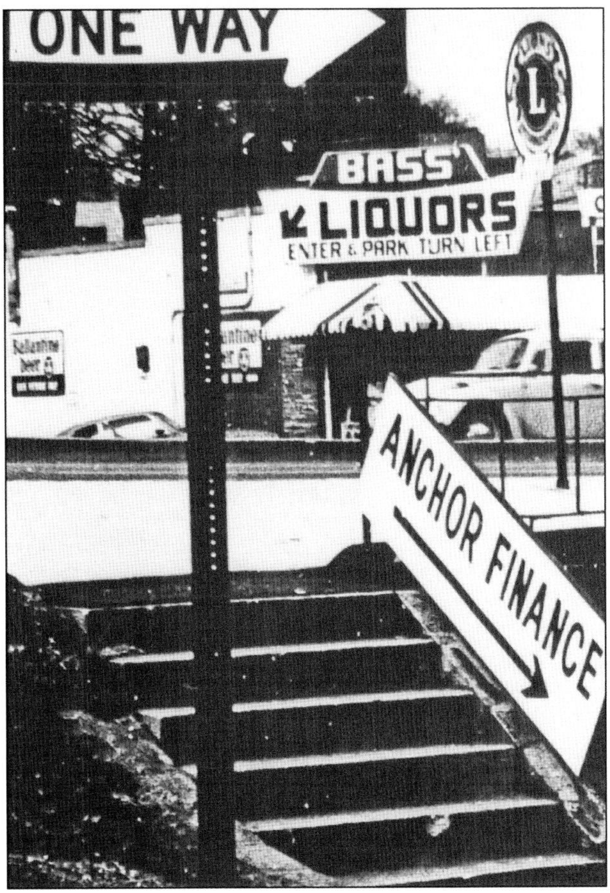

For decades after Prohibition, the Bass family operated its family-style restaurant on Rhode Island Avenue. Joseph Howell captured the scene in 1971 (right), which had not changed much in the 1990s (above). In the 1980s, the family sold to owners who focused on the more lucrative liquor sales rather than the restaurant. Many residents believed the business to be a focal point of crime that hurt revitalization efforts. The city challenged the license in 1984. The longtime business had supporters who argued that it was wrongly blamed. The city council became divided on the issue; new challenges to the license were led by civic activists, but the business fended off license revocation. In 1993, the carryout served approximately 500,000 customers and had gross revenues of $2.4 million. After many challenges, the city council rejoined the fight; the license was revoked in 2004. (Above, courtesy of City of Mount Rainier; right, courtesy of Joseph Howell.)

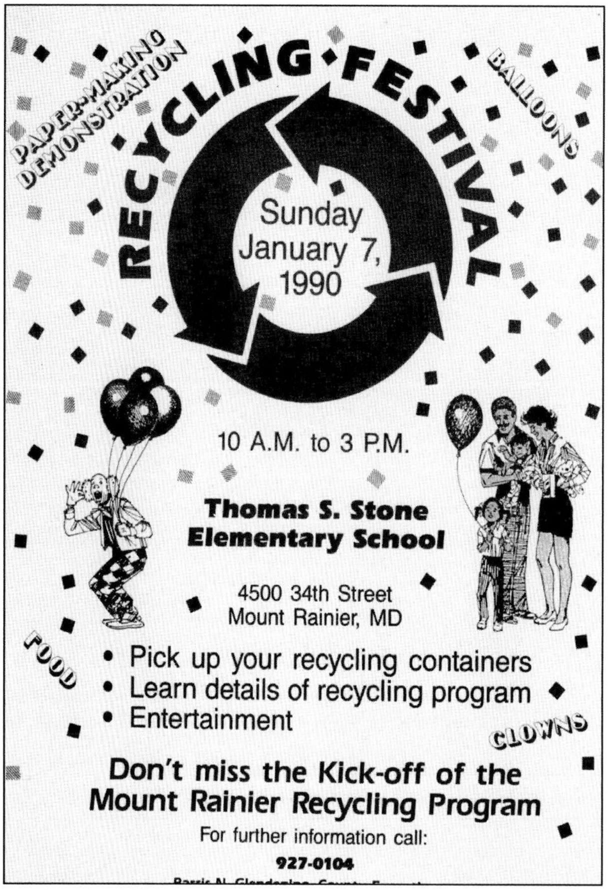

Simultaneously with the anticrime and historic preservation efforts, environmentalists in the community continued efforts begun in the 1980s for recycling and green buildings. Recycling of yard waste began in November 1991 when the city started utilizing the College Park composting facility. In 1995, the city took over collection of recycling from the county. Mount Rainier, with 87 percent household participation in recycling, led all other Prince George's County municipalities. The recycling program depended not only on the citizens, but also the public works staff, who pose below for the city's 75th anniversary history book in 1985. From left to right are Jesse Matthews, George Posey, Leonard Rose, Willie Smith, Frank Potts, Theodore Watson, Alfred Thompson, James Bright, and Tom Donnelly. (George Summers is missing from the photograph.) (Both, courtesy of City of Mount Rainier.)

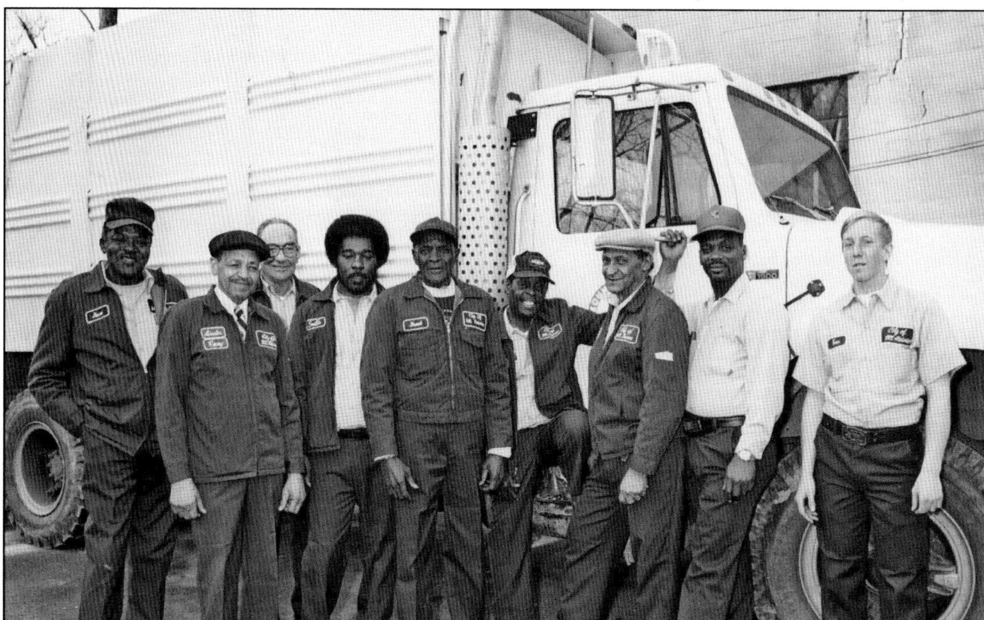

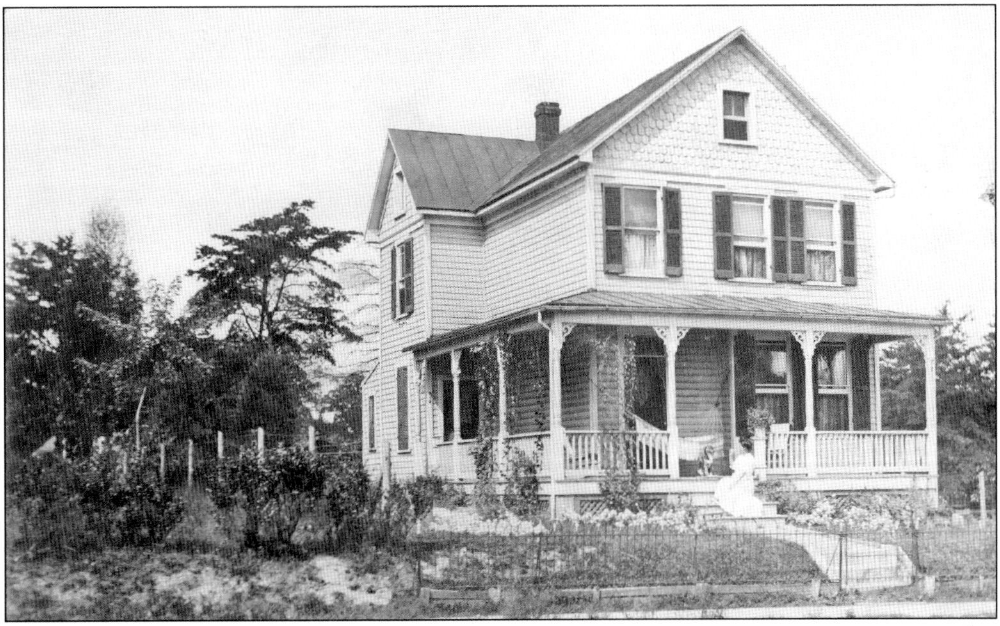

In 1990, the federal and state governments recognized the Mount Rainier Historic District after several years of research with the assistance of Maryland–National Capital Park and Planning Commission staff. The effort started in the late 1980s as a project of the Mount Rainier Community Preservation League. The project brought together many residents—longtime and new—to focus on preserving the city's historic architecture, generating pride of place, and energizing revitalization efforts. Shown are postcards from around 1910 made from photographs by W.R. Ross: the Harmon House (above), located at 4218 Thirty-fourth Street, and the 3700 block of Thirty-sixth Street (below). The continued existence of Mount Rainier's historic homes such as these fueled the desire to create the historic district. In 1993, the city's first Historic House Tour was held. (Both, courtesy of DC Public Library.)

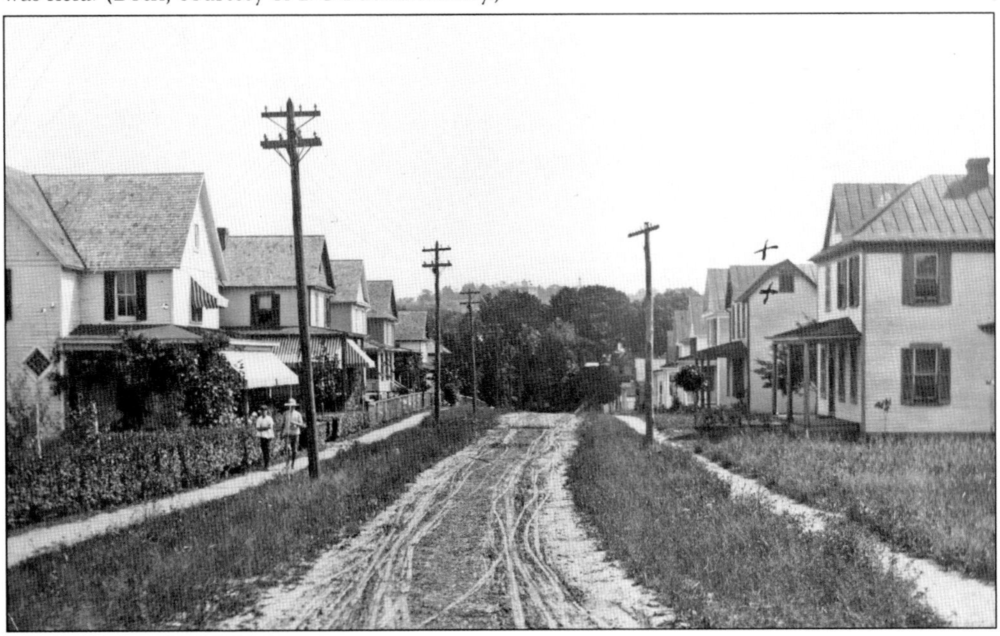

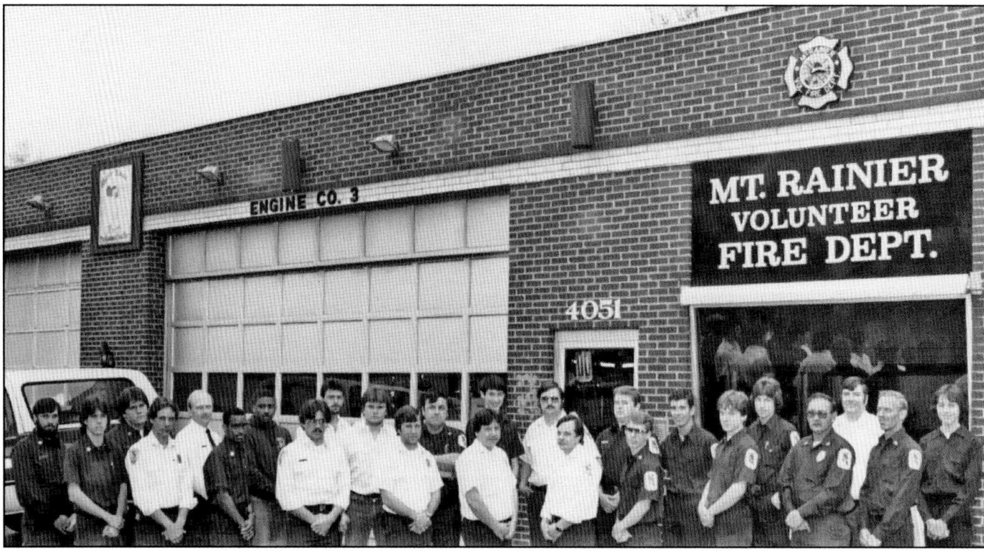

The Mount Rainier Volunteer Fire Department is pictured above at the firehouse during the city's 75th anniversary in 1985. In 1990, the MRVFD purchased the adjacent house, intending to raze it to create a parking lot. The city had subsidized the MRVFD since the 1920s to buy equipment, but the city council objected to the use of taxpayer funds for a real estate purchase. Tempers ran high on both sides. The council amended the City Charter, ending the direct subsidy. The MRVFD sued the city, claiming a flawed charter amendment process. In 1995, a settlement resulted in the house being sold back into private ownership. The MRVFD moved to the county-owned Bunker Hill Fire Station in 2000, leaving an empty building that in 2015 became a space for artists, Red Dirt Studio—an appropriate repurposing in the midst of the Gateway Arts District. (Above, courtesy of Bunker Hill Volunteer Fire and Rescue Co.; below, courtesy of Red Dirt Studio.)

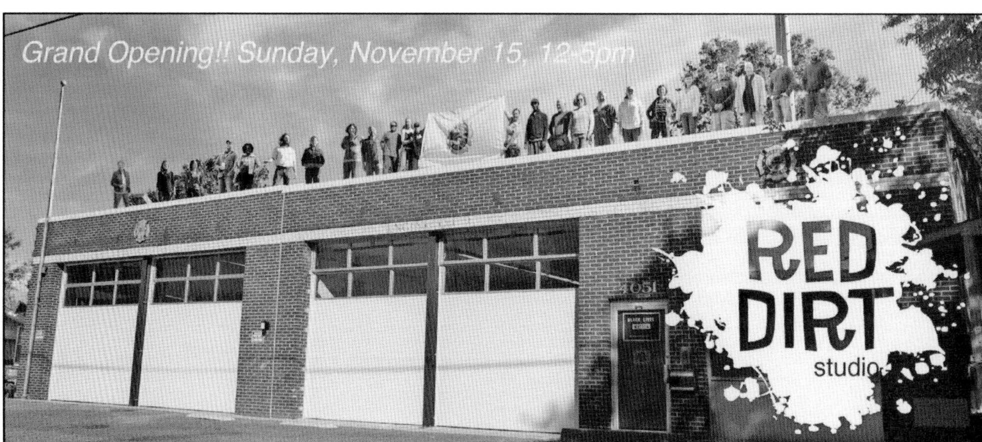

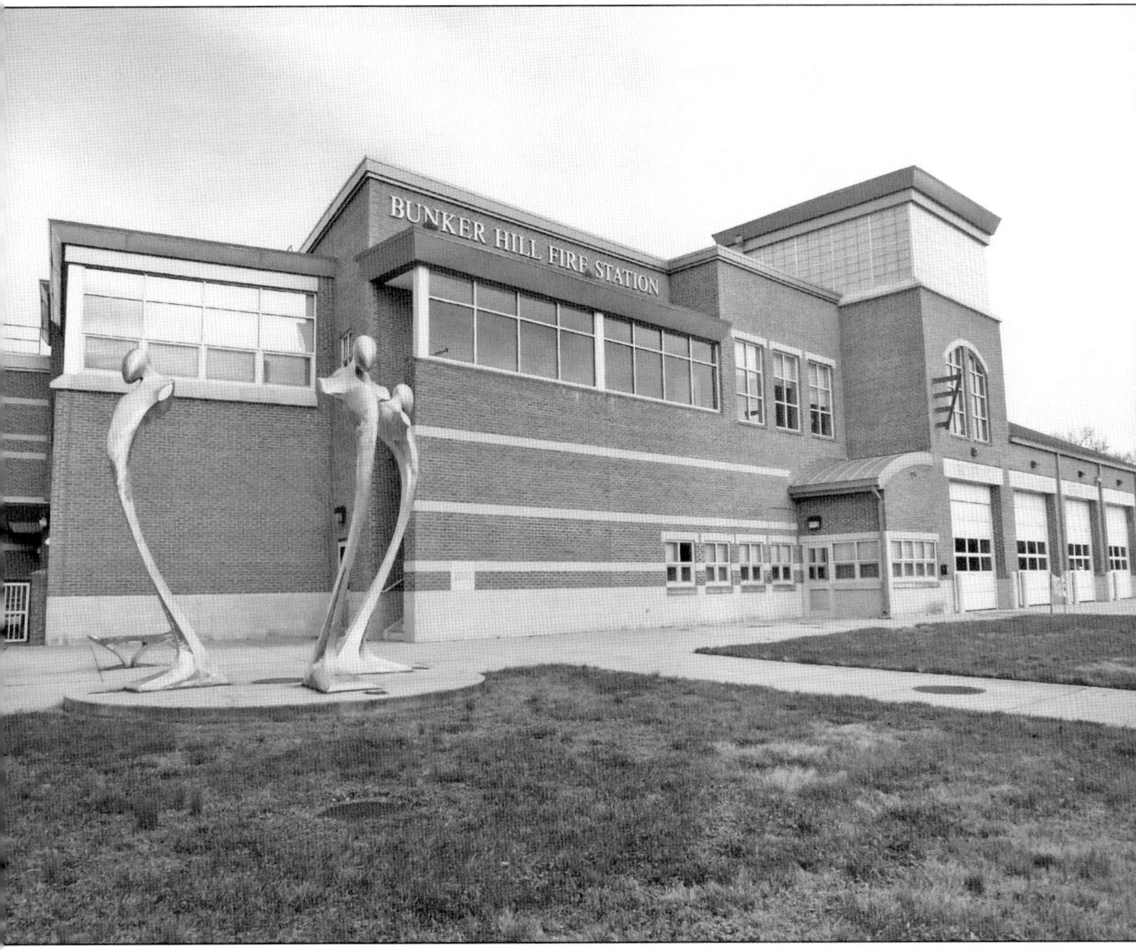

For many years, the county's volunteer fire departments were augmented with professional firefighters and paramedics supplied by Prince George's County. In the late 1990s, the county decided consolidation of several small volunteer fire departments into a new facility was necessary, and for that purpose purchased several properties in the 3700 block of Rhode Island Avenue. The location straddled the Mount Rainier–Brentwood border and was relatively close to Cottage City and Colmar Manor, location of the other volunteer fire departments. The long history of the MRVFD will come to an end; as part of the consolidation, the county mandated that the individual volunteer fire departments would no longer accept members, but that new volunteers would join the Bunker Hill Volunteer Fire & Rescue Association. *The Three Guardians*, a stainless-steel sculpture by Ayokunle Odeleye, in front of the new fire station represents the three volunteer companies that reside there. (Courtesy of Jimmy Tarlau.)

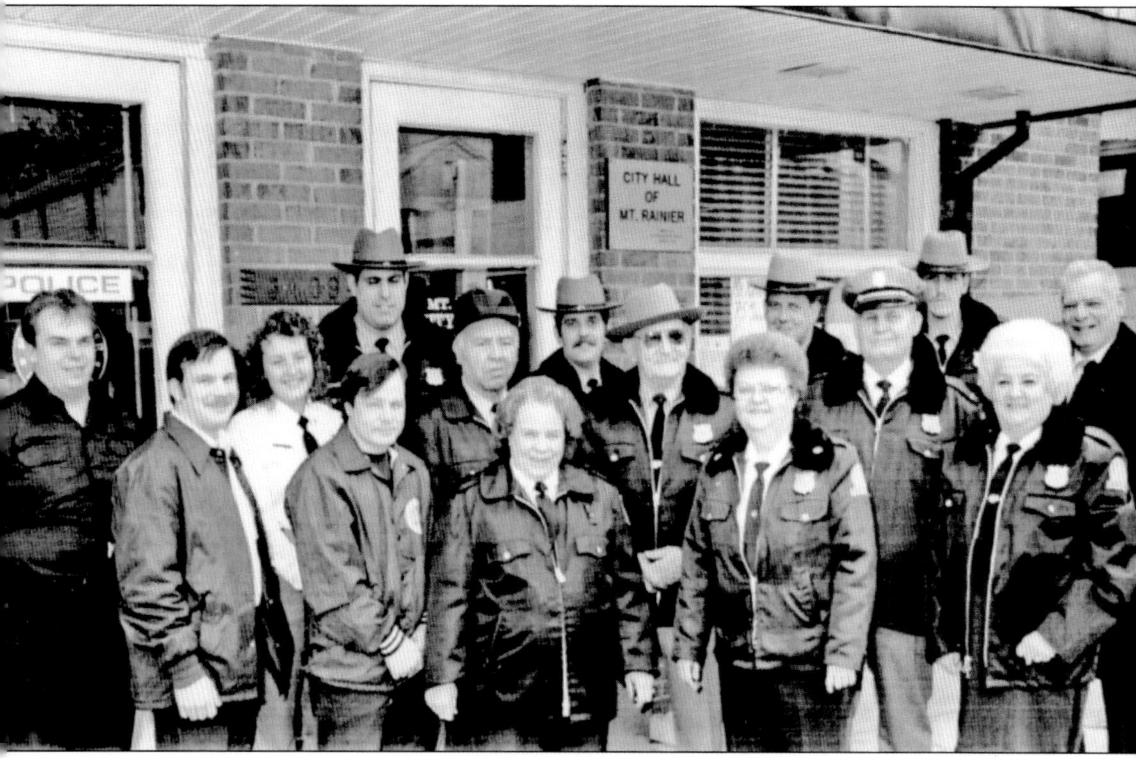

In 1992, the Mount Rainier police officers requested a collective bargaining agreement. For that to happen, the city council needed to adopt legislation to allow for collective bargaining. Civic leaders and activists were divided over the proposal; some feared it too expensive, while others saw it as a tool for recruitment and retention of officers. After lively public debates, on June 2, 1992, the council voted three to one (Mayor Nalls did not vote) to adopt the collective bargaining ordinance. Mount Rainier became one of the smallest municipalities in Maryland to allow collective bargaining. In 1985, the police department posed for the 75th anniversary history book. Pictured from left to right are dispatchers George Sullivan, Dennis Vermillion, Germaine Cloninger, and David Vermillion; officer Robert Szabo; Norman Hudley (Animal Control); dispatcher Joan Vermillion; officers Sheldon Hayes and James Suite; dispatcher Maxine Fuller; Sgt. Jack Clements; Lt. Charles Smith; officers Bruce Siler and Ann McCloskey; and Chief Denny Husk. (Not pictured are John Wojcik, Walter Smith, John Minick, Darlene Cullers, and Madeline Brown.) (Courtesy of City of Mount Rainier.)

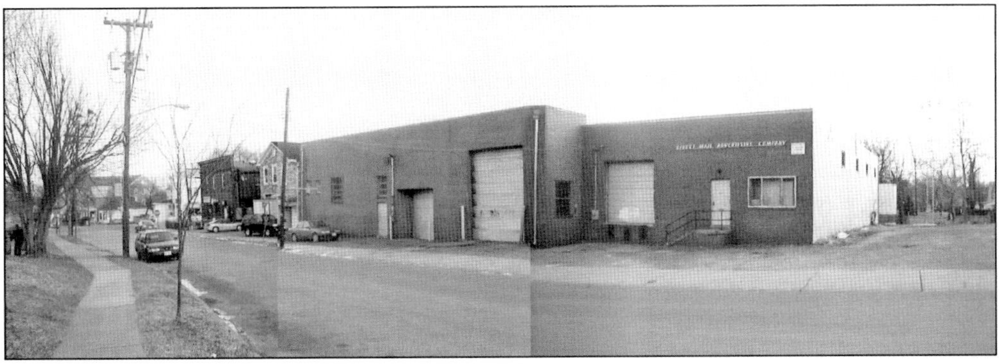

The concept of revitalization utilizing an arts district developed during the 1990s. The Mount Rainier Arts Guild formed in 1992. In 1999, an arts summit was held to explore establishing an arts district, and in January 2002, the Maryland Department of Business and Economic Development created an arts and entertainment district along Route 1 from Eastern Avenue to Hyattsville. The designation provided tax incentives for individual artists working and living in the District. In 2004, the county created the Gateway Arts District Overlay Zone. Joe's Movement Emporium opened in 1995 on Thirty-fourth Street and became a leader in establishing the arts district. A successful revitalization occurred when Joe's purchased a Bunker Hill Road warehouse (above), transforming it into a vital vibrant space. Joe's celebrates cultural diversity in the neighborhood through dance, music, and theater and leases space to other arts organizations. (Above, courtesy of Joe's Movement Emporium; below, courtesy of Robert Page.)

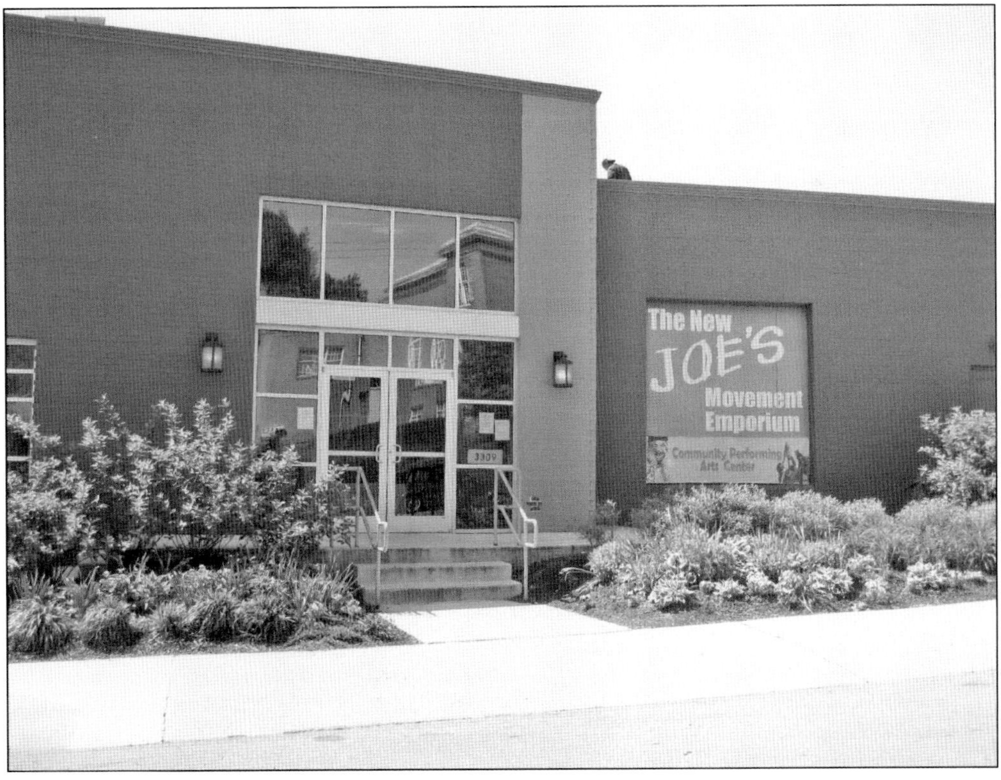

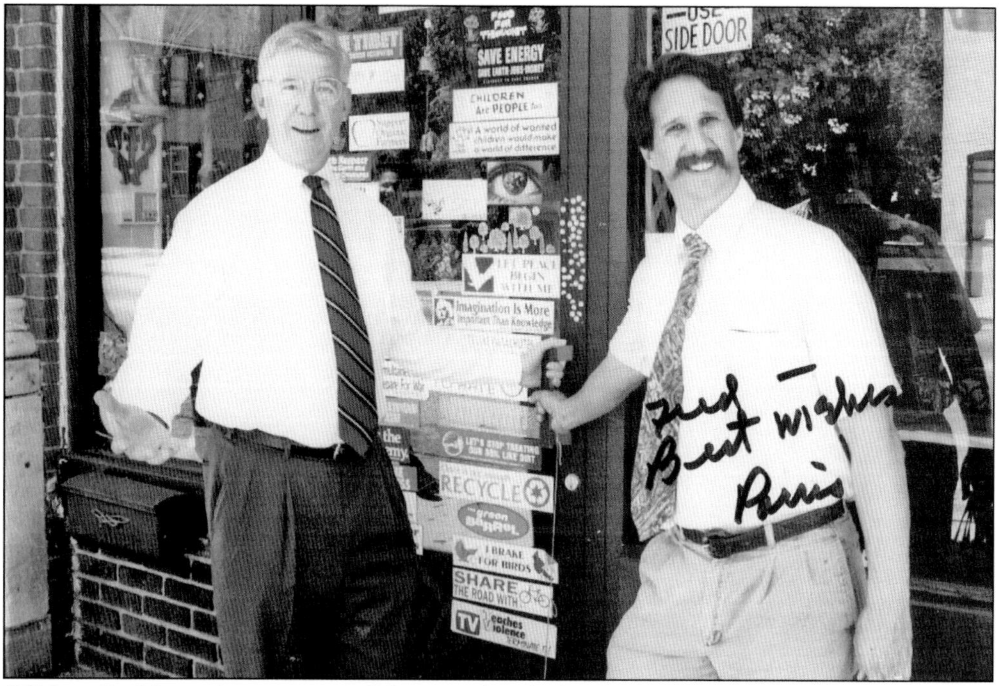

Of Mayor Fred Sissine's many accomplishments, the Rhode Island Avenue roundabout is undoubtedly the most tangible. Santana Miyazaki's painting (below) provides an aerial view of the circle. In 1999, the state began the project after intense lobbying from Sissine and the council. Sissine insisted on participation of residents in the project's planning. Commissioned artists created two monolithic mosaic sculptures and included the faces of local residents on the walls and bus shelters to represent the city's diversity. Gov. Parris Glendenning (above, left of Sissine), who began his political career on the Hyattsville City Council, was familiar with Mount Rainier. The circle promotes traffic safety for thousands of daily commuters, while also providing a visual and psychological sense of place for residents. Mount Rainier is no longer an amorphous stretch of US Route 1 between Hyattsville and Washington. (Above, courtesy of Fred Sissine; below, courtesy of Leslie Jenkins.)

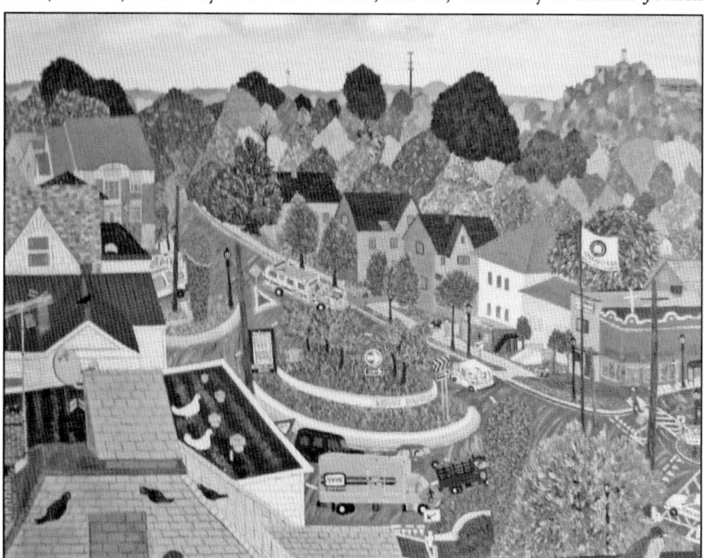

Six

CITY ON THE MOVE

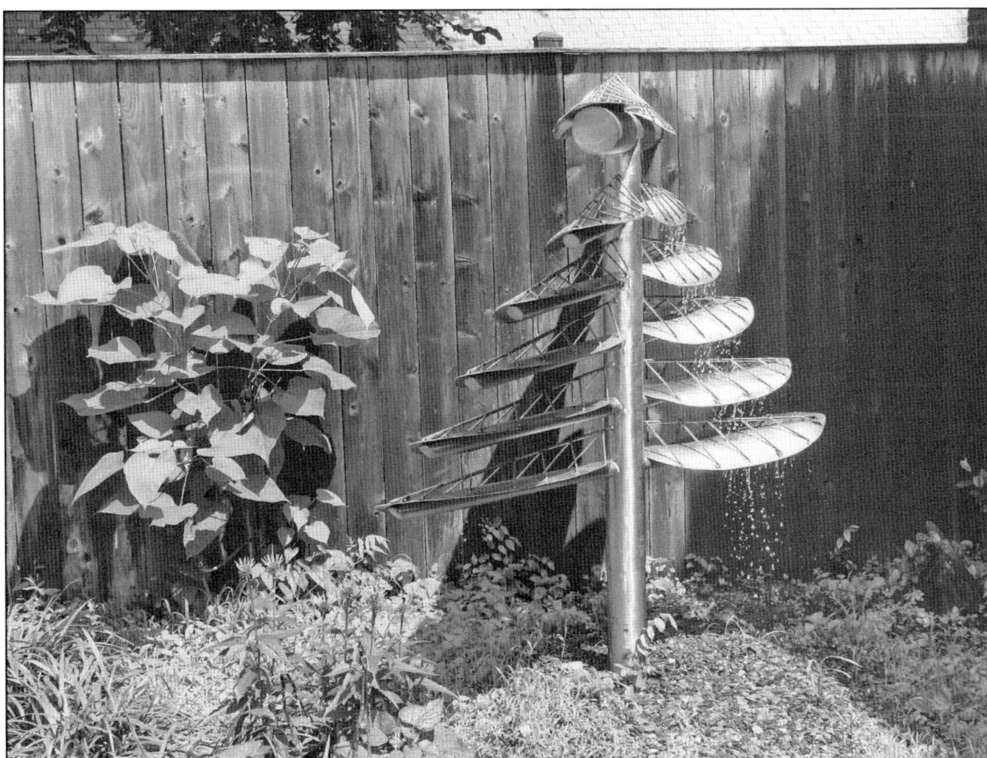

Rain Tree, by Mount Rainier artist Alan Binstock, could represent key elements of the "City on the Move" in the 21st century—the arts, concern for the environment, and movement. Rainwater from the Housing Initiative Partnership (HIP) Artists Apartments' roof cascades through the sculpture during storms, putting it into motion; water then flows into the surrounding rain garden to nourish the plants. (Courtesy of Robert Page.)

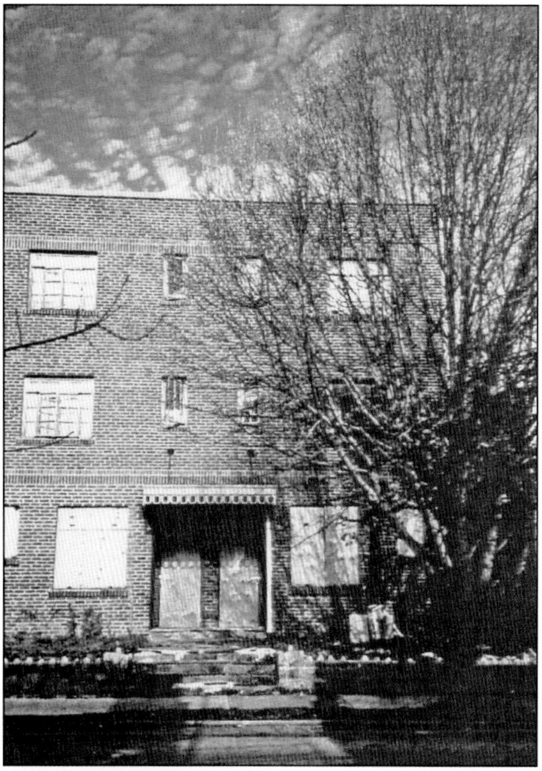

At the inception of the Gateway Arts District, there was recognition that the success of the arts district could result in making housing too expensive for artists. One of the first arts-related revitalization projects in the new district was purchase of the derelict Cole Apartment Building (left, located at 3801 Thirty-third Street) by Housing Initiative Partnership, a nonprofit dedicated to providing affordable housing, to create live/work space for artists. The city became a one percent limited partner in the project. The renovation included the addition of light-filled bays to the front of the building. The grand opening was held on July 23, 2003. The building included a green roof, a rain garden to collect runoff from the roof (see previous page), and many energy-efficient features. Below, local artist Alan Binstock's sculpture *Vines and Leaves* clings to the renovated building's corner. (Both, courtesy of City of Mount Rainier.)

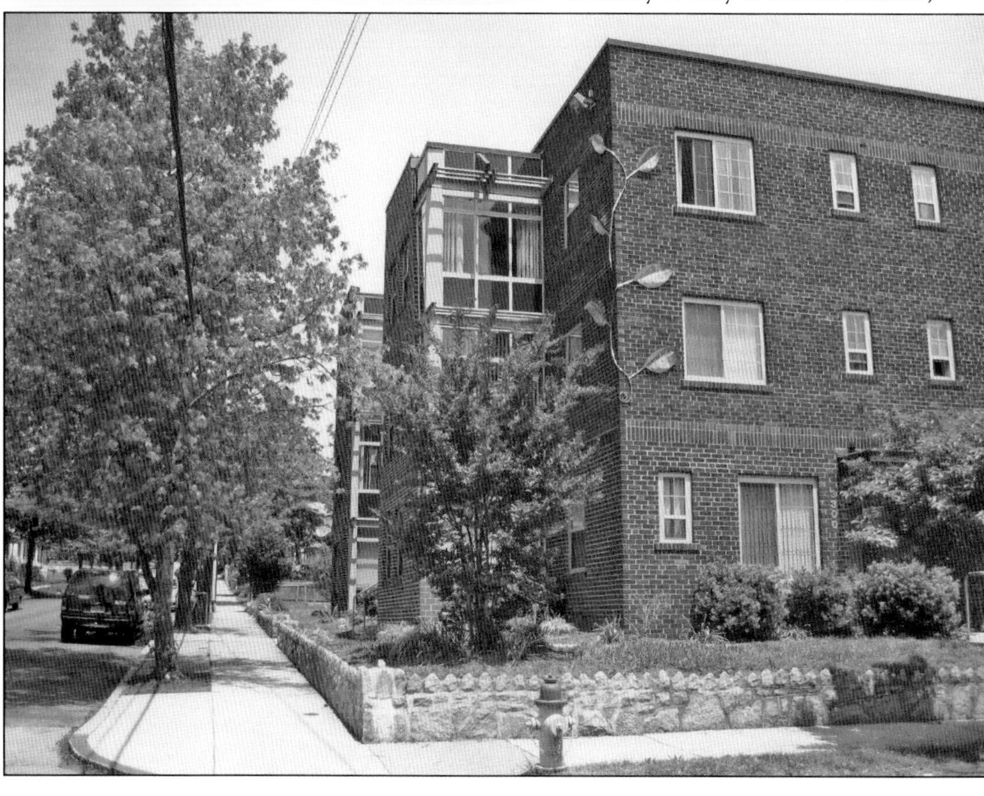

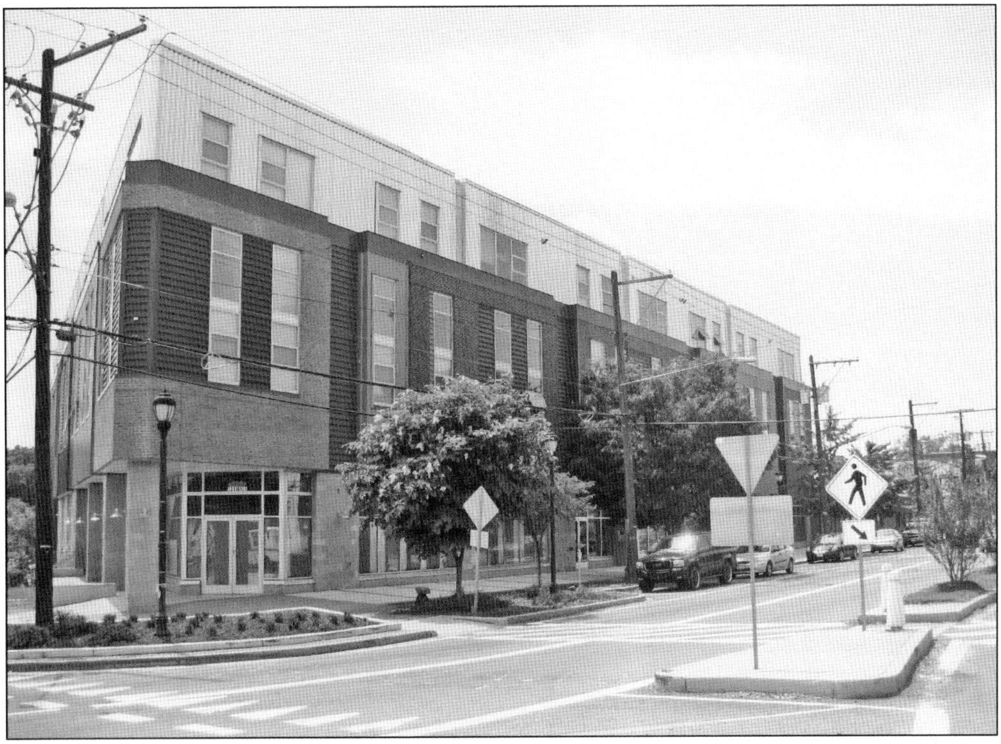

Artspace Projects Inc., with the backing of the Prince George's County Redevelopment Authority, built the Mount Rainier Artists' Lofts to replace a block of dilapidated commercial storefronts in Rhode Island Avenue's 3300 block (visible below behind the crowd gathered for the traffic circle's groundbreaking in 2000). The lofts provide affordable live/work units for lower-income artists. Since its completion in May 2005, the building has been a landmark for its distinctive architecture and prominent location. It also continued the mixed-use redevelopment focused around the Mount Rainier traffic circle. Future revitalization projects adopted the concept of providing street-level commercial space with residences above. The Mount Rainier Mixed-Use Town Center Zone—the first such zone in the county—was created in 1994 and provides guidelines for exterior changes to the facades in the downtown business district. (Both, courtesy of Robert Page.)

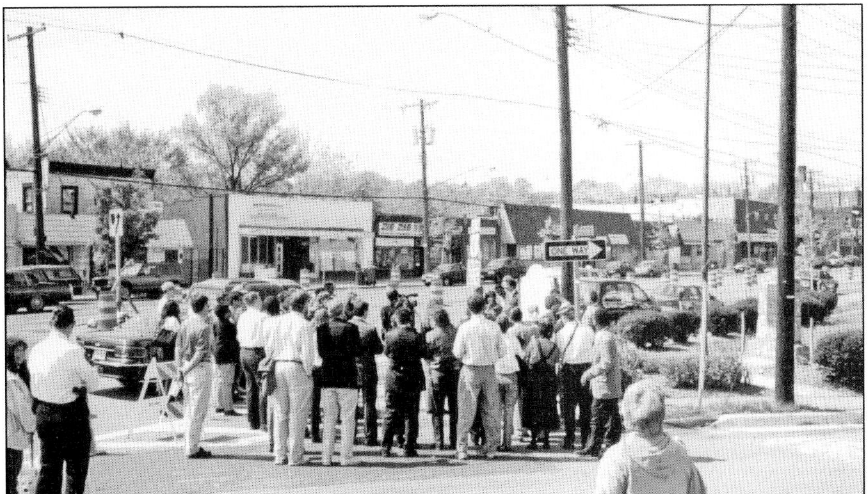

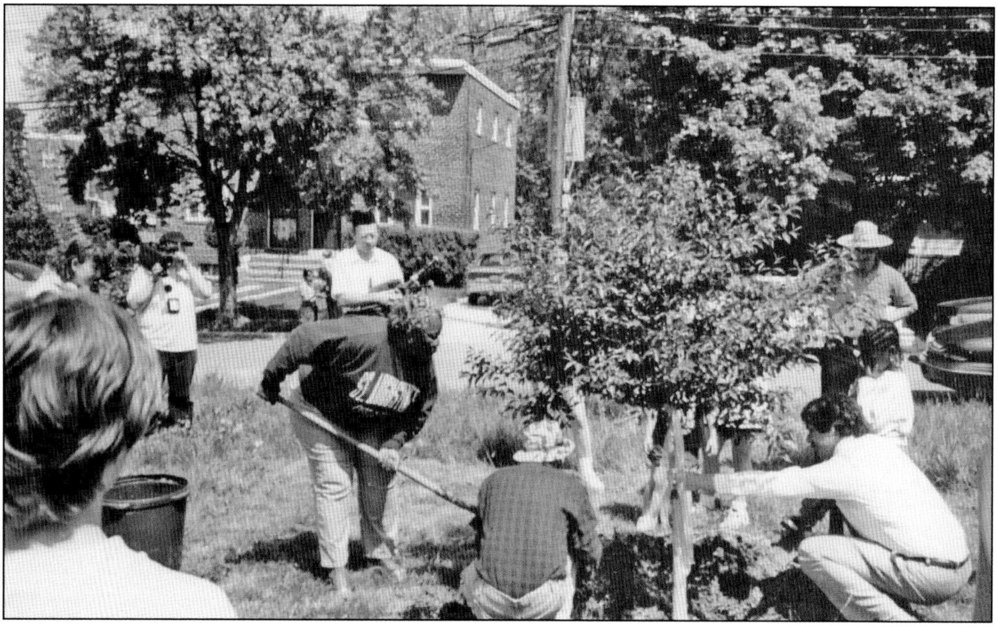

Mount Rainier's commitment to being green can be traced back to the 1930s with the mass planting of street trees (see pages 60 and 61). It continued with the creation of pocket parks, establishment of a tree commission, early adoption of a residential recycling program, and the building of a green police facility. During Arbor Day 2000 at Richardson Park, Mayor Fred Sissine holds a tree while Councilwoman Malinda Miles plants it. (Courtesy of Bryan Knedler.)

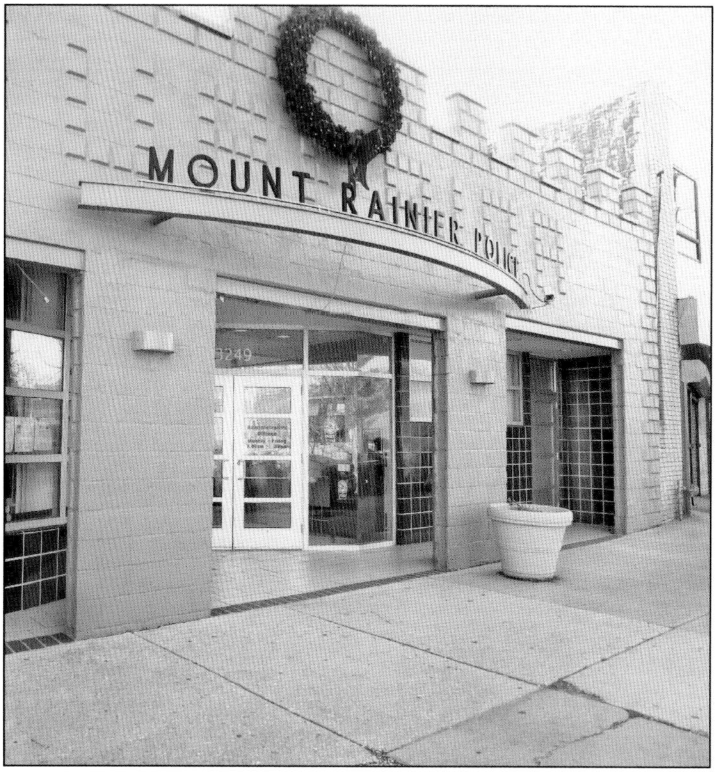

In 2002, the police department moved to 3249 Rhode Island Avenue, formerly an auto dealer and repair shop. The firm of Schick Goldstein teamed up with John Spears of the Sustainable Design Group to design the first green police station in the United States. The green features include recycling of 75 percent of construction debris, wood paneling made of sunflower seeds, a geothermal heating system, use of natural lighting, and floor tiles made of recycled automobile glass. (Courtesy of Jimmy Tarlau.)

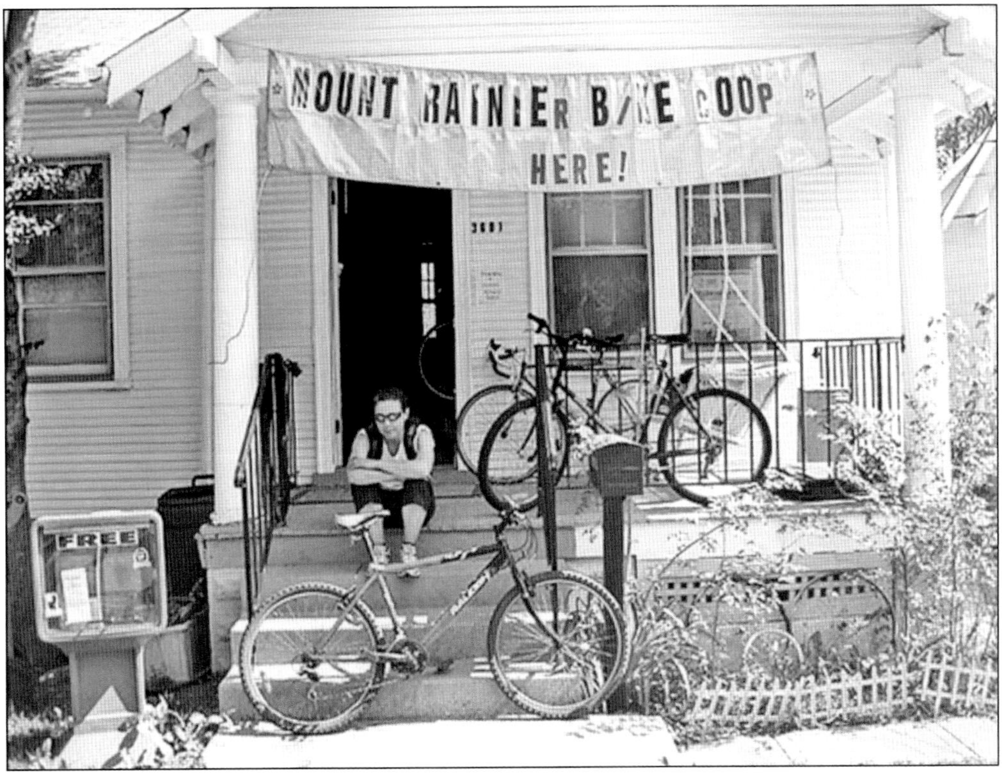

In connection with construction of the new firehouse in 1999, the county did not tear down 3601 Bunker Hill Road as planned, instead donating the bungalow to the city to be put to public use. The old house was in poor repair, but after renovations, it housed the community tool lending library, which was established with county grant funds, and the community bike cooperative, which had started out in the garage behind the old city hall. In 2009, a cooperative of area residents who heated their homes with stoves that burned dried corn were granted permission to build a storage bin behind the house. (Both, courtesy of Jimmy Tarlau.)

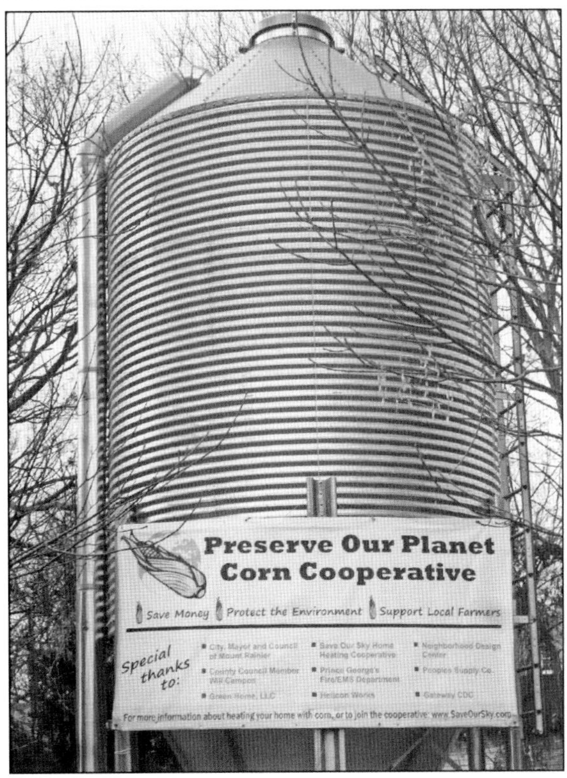

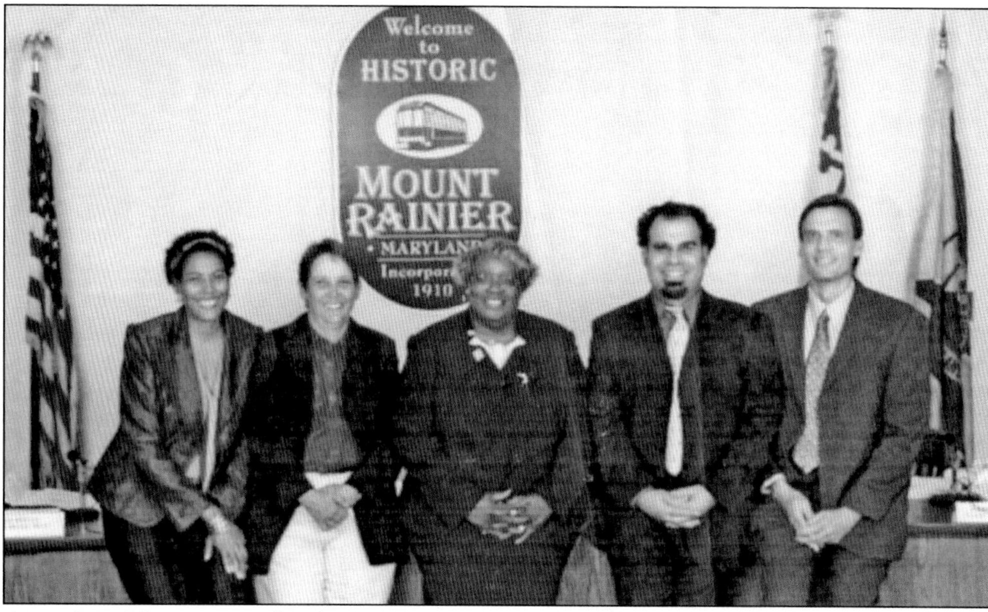

A number of firsts occurred at the century's beginning. Carol Gandee and Bryan Knedler became the first openly gay councilmembers in 1997, and Knedler became the state's first openly gay mayor in 2002. The 2003 election of Pedro Briones, the city's first Latino councilmember and the state's first openly gay Latino elected official, with Knedler and Gandee, made Mount Rainier one of four places in the United States with a majority gay council. In 2001, Michael Lawson, a renter rather than a property owner, became mayor. In 2003, Intisar Haamid, the first Muslim councilmember, along with Malinda Miles and Briones, created the first majority minority council. In 2005, Miles became the first black mayor. Pictured above from left to right are Alta Morton, Gandee, Miles, Briones, and Knedler. The 2009 council was the first majority black—and black female—council; pictured below from left to right are Ivy Thompson, Jimmy Tarlau, Miles, Morton, and Knedler. (Both, courtesy of City of Mount Rainier.)

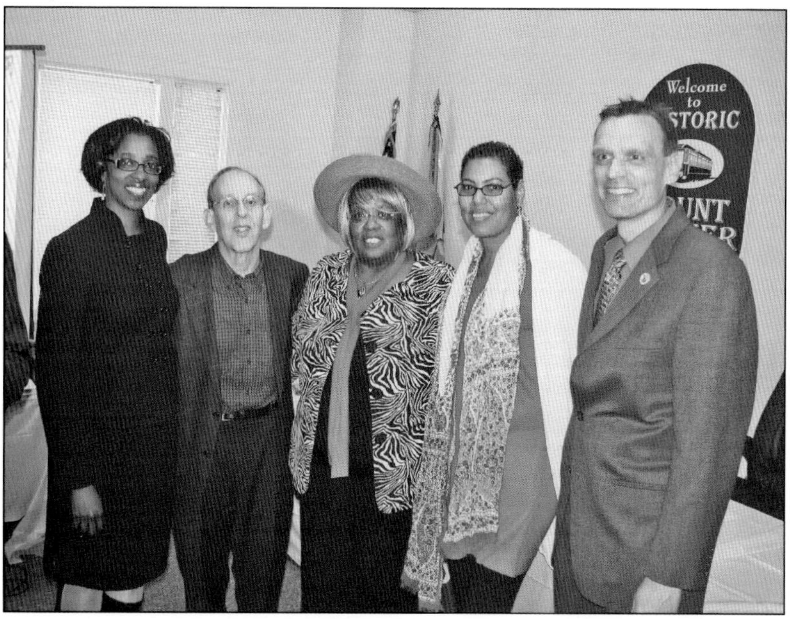

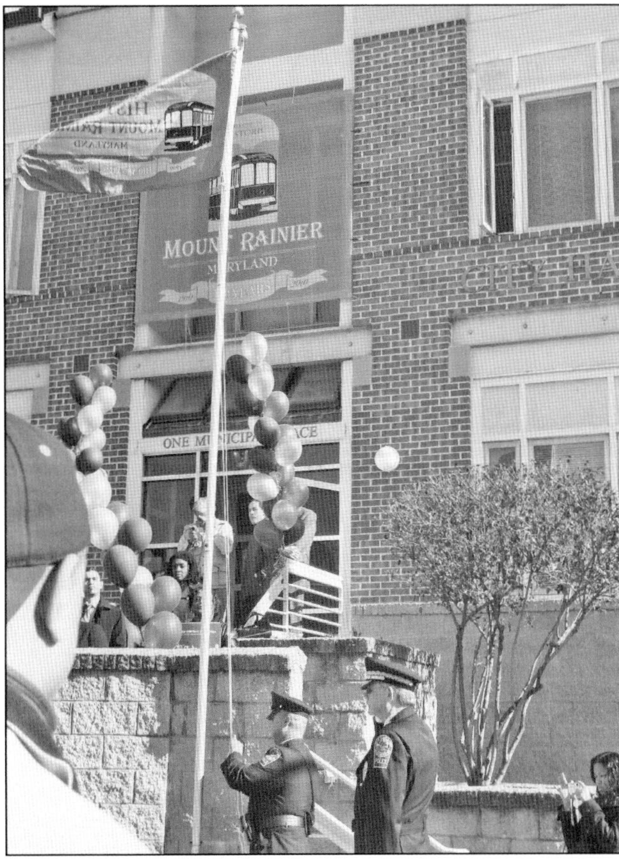

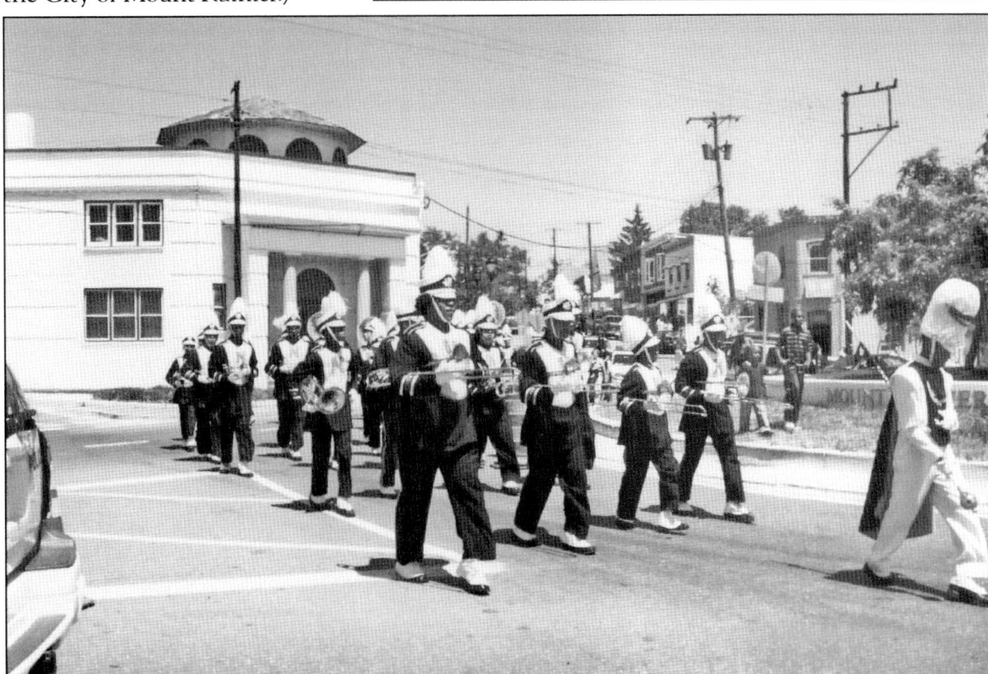

The City of Mount Rainier celebrated its centennial year with a series of celebrations including the raising of the centennial flag at city hall in January, a photograph exhibition, street banners, and a souvenir history booklet. On May 10, 2010, the Mount Rainier City Council held a special commemorative meeting in the same place where it first met on that day in 1910: Star-Potts Hall, which the city had recently purchased from the Order of the Eastern Star. The Northwestern High School Marching Band provided music in the Mount Rainier Day Parade, seen here rounding the traffic circle with the landmark Prince George's Bank building in the background. (Both, courtesy of the City of Mount Rainier.)

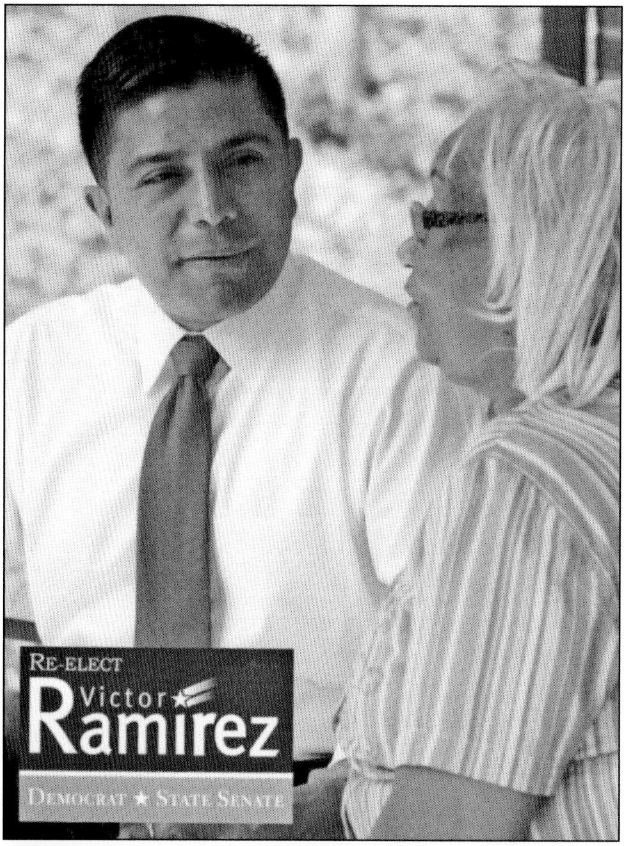

Progressive political stances continue to define Mount Rainier—opposing the War in Iraq, supporting a death penalty moratorium, and designating itself a nuclear-free zone. Demographic shifts continue as well, with African and Latino immigrants settling in Mount Rainier. The new arrivals revived local churches, including St. James and St. John's. Two immigrant families from El Salvador who settled in the city produced sons who entered politics. Victor Ramirez (left) was elected to the Maryland House of Delegates in 2003 and then to the Maryland Senate in 2010. Will Campos (below, speaking with a county police officer) became the first Latino elected to the county council (2004) and then was elected a state delegate in 2014. Latinos comprised 25 percent of the city's population in 2010. (Both, courtesy of Jimmy Tarlau.)

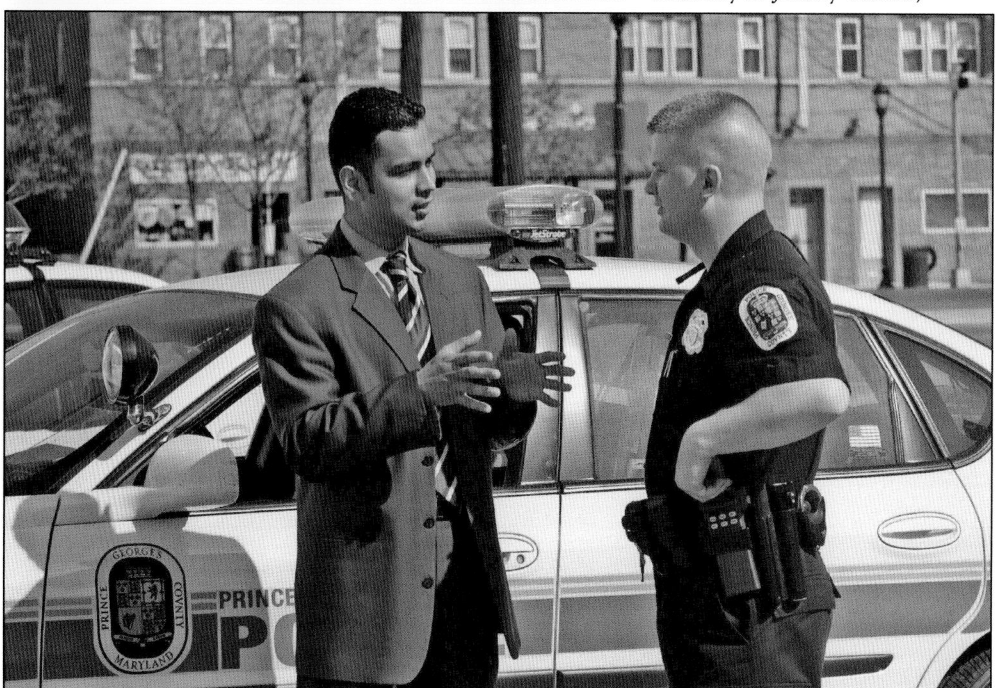

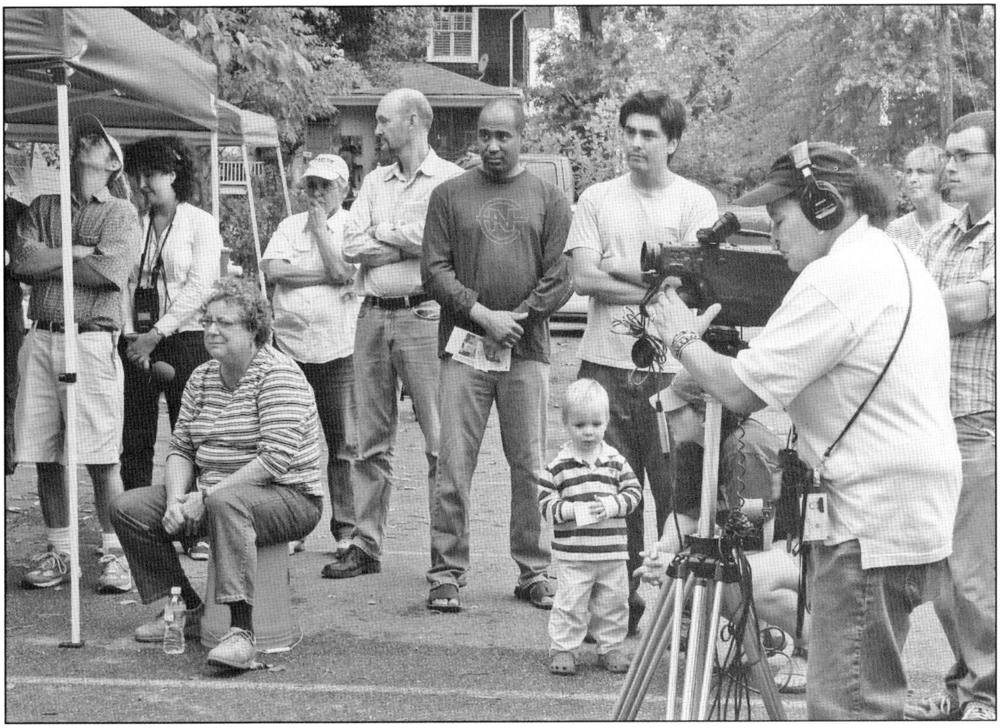

While the front porch once served as the place to get the local news, times have changed. In 1981, the city council embraced technology to connect residents with the first broadcasts of council meetings on the local cable channel. The city's cable television department, led by Graciela Carbonell (seen here filming a local event) and her husband, Bob Page, documented thousands of events over the next three decades. The city's first presence on the Internet came in 1996 when several municipalities set up a joint website for publicity and marketing purposes (the city created its own website in 2001). Green technology was embraced when the city built a green police facility and with the installation of solar panels on city hall in 2011. Also, historic homes—such as the one below one on Twenty-ninth Street—began to sport the panels in the first decade of the 21st century. (Above, courtesy of City of Mount Rainier; below, courtesy of Bryan Knedler.)

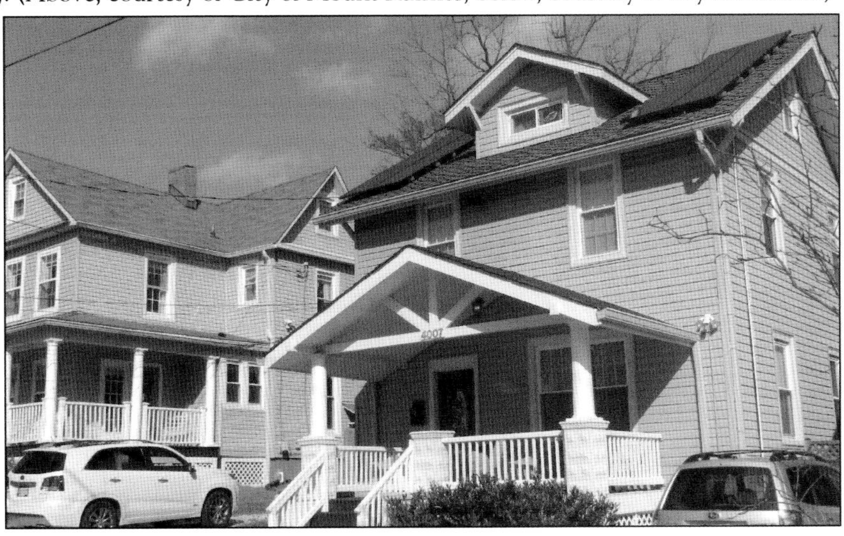

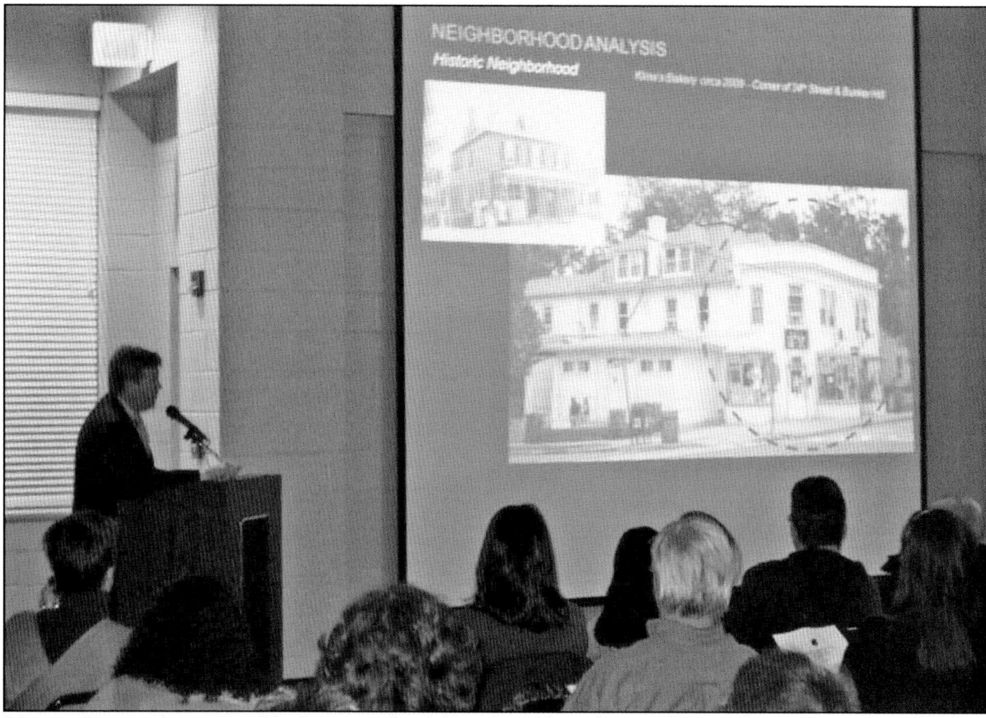

Mount Rainier's motto, "A City on the Move," evokes the evolution from streetcar suburb to progressive multicultural city during the 20th century. Its citizens dream of future improvement but cherish the past. Pictured here, architect and planner Lee Quill leads a citizen discussion in 2010 on proposed business district design standards using a slide that demonstrates how Klein's Bakery still stands but is hidden behind later alterations. (Courtesy of M-NCPPC.)

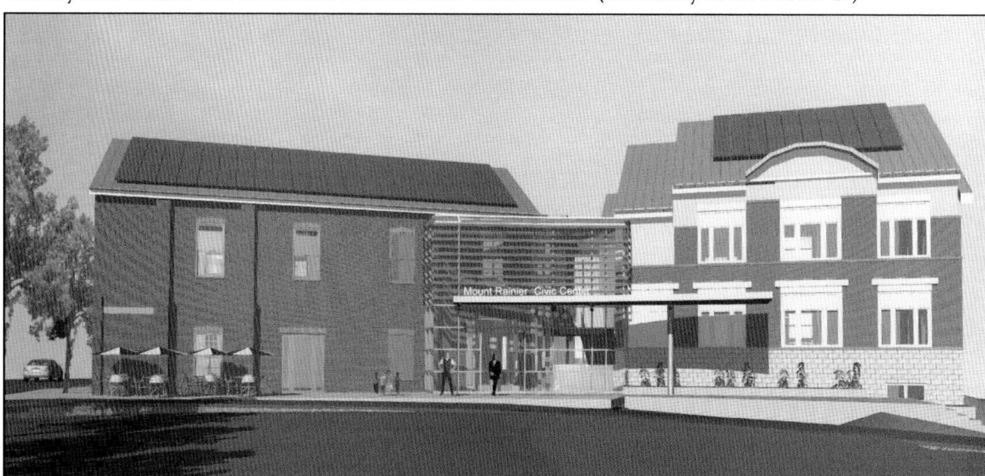

A 1988 Maryland–National Capital Park and Planning Commission report stated that Mount Rainier's "business area is one of the most 'overstudied' areas inside of the Beltway." More studies followed. If the city can move from planning to implementation, old and new will be melded to create a future civic center. Shown here is the proposed 2010 plan of Schick Goldstein Architects to bridge the divide between Star-Potts Hall (left) and city hall with a glass arcade. (Courtesy of City of Mount Rainier.)

INDEX